9/17

D1598184

Theologies of Liberation in Palestine-Israel

POSTMODERN ETHICS SERIES

Postmodernism and deconstruction are usually associated with a destruction of ethical values. The volumes in the Postmodern Ethics series demonstrate that such views are mistaken because they ignore the religious element that is at the heart of existential-postmodern philosophy. This series aims to provide a space for thinking about questions of ethics in our times. When many voices are speaking together from unlimited perspectives within the postmodern labyrinth, what sort of ethics can there be for those who believe there is a way through the dark night of technology and nihilism beyond exclusively humanistic offerings? The series invites any careful exploration of the postmodern and the ethical.

Series Editors:

Marko Zlomislić (Conestoga College)

David Goicoechea (Brock University)

Other Volumes in the Series:

Cross and Khôra: Deconstruction and Christianity in the Work of John D. Caputo edited by Neal DeRoo and Marko Zlomislić

Agape and Personhood with Kierkegaard, Mother, and Paul (A Logic of Reconciliation from the Shamans to Today) by David Goicoechea

The Poverty of Radical Orthodoxy edited by Lisa Isherwood and Marko Zlomislić

Agape and the Four Loves with Nietzsche, Father, and Q (A Physiology of Reconciliation from the Greeks to Today) by David Goicoechea

Fundamentalism and Gender: Scripture—Body—Community edited by Ulrike Auga, Christina von Braun, Claudia Bruns, and Jana Husmann

Theologies of Liberation in Palestine-Israel

Indigenous, Contextual, and Postcolonial Perspectives

Edited by

Nur Masalha and Lisa Isherwood

CONTRIBUTORS:
Samuel J. Kuruvilla, Naim Ateek, Marc H. Ellis,
Nur Masalha, Gareth Lloyd Jones,
Rosemary Radford Ruether, Lisa Isherwood,
Mark Braverman, Mary Grey, Nur Masalha

POSTMODERN ETHICS SERIES
4

PICKWICK *Publications* · Eugene, Oregon

THEOLOGIES OF LIBERATION IN PALESTINE-ISRAEL
Indigenous, Contextual, and Postcolonial Perspectives

Postmodern Ethics Series 4

Pickwick Publications
An Imprint of Wipf and Stock Publishers
199 W. 8th Ave., Suite 3
Eugene, OR 97401

www.wipfandstock.com

isbn 13: 978–1-61097–745-6

Cataloging-in-Publication data:

_____

Theologies of liberation in Palestine-Israel : indigenous, contextual, and postcolonial perspectives / edited by Nur Masalha and Lisa Isherwood.

246 p. ; 23 cm. —Includes bibliographical references and index(es).

Postmodern Ethics 4

isbn 13: 978–1-61097–745-6

1. Liberation theology. 2. Jewish-Arab relations. I. Title. II. Series.

DS119.7 T45 2014
_____

Manufactured in the U.S.A.

Contents

great homeletic stories

Contributors

Naim Ateek is a Palestinian Anglican priest and an Arab citizen of Israel. He is President and Director of Sabeel, an ecumenical theological centre in Jerusalem. He is the author of *Justice and Only Justice: A Palestinian Theology of Liberation*.

Mark Braverman is Program Director of Kairos USA. He focuses on the role of theology and the function of interfaith relations in the current search for a resolution of the conflict. He is the author of *Fatal Embrace: Christians, Jews and the Search for Peace in the Holy Land* and *A Wall in Jerusalem: Hope, Healing and the Struggle for Justice in Israel and Palestine*.

Marc H. Ellis is retired Professor of Jewish Studies at Baylor University and Director of the Centre for American and Jewish Studies. He has authored and edited more than twenty books, including *Beyond Innocence and Power: Confronting the Holocaust and Israeli Power*, and *Unholy Alliance: Religion and Atrocity in Our Time*. As a public intellectual, he has given testimony before the United Sates Congress, spoken at the United Nations in New York, in Vienna, and at the British House of Commons.

Mary Grey is Professor emeritus at the University of Wales, Lampeter, and until recently Professorial Research Fellow, St Mary's University, Twickenham and Hon Professor at the Institute for Theological Partnerships, University of Winchester. Her many books include, *Redeeming the Dream, The Outrageous Pursuit of Hope: Prophetic Dreams for the 21st Century, Sacred Longings: Ecofeminst Theology and Globalisation, To Rwanda and Back,* and *A Cry for Dignity: Religion, Violence and the Struggle of Dalit Women in India*.

Lisa Isherwood is Director of the Institute for Theological Partnerships, University of Winchester. She has written, co-authored or edited nineteen books including *The Power of Erotic Celibacy; The Fat Jesus: Feminist*

Explorations in Boundaries and Transgressions; Introducing Feminist Christologies; Liberating Christ; Patriarchs, Prophets and Other Villains (edited); and *Radical Otherness: A Theo/sociological Investigation* (co-authored with Dave Harris). She is an executive and founding editor of the international journal *Feminist Theology* and she sits on the international editorial board of *Feminist Studies in Religion*.

Samuel Kuruvilla is Assistant Professor, Department of Political Science, University of Kerala, Trivandrum, India. His most recent book is *Radical Christianity in Palestine-Israel: Liberation and Theology in the Middle East.*

Gareth Lloyd Jones, Professor Emeritus, University of Bangor, North Wales, studied in Cambridge, Jerusalem, and Yale University Divinity School. He taught at McCormick Seminary in Chicago and at Ripon College and Exeter College, Oxford. His PhD is from King's College, London. His main research interests have been the use of Hebrew among Christians during the early modern period, and latterly Judaism and Jewish-Christian dialogue. These interests are reflected in the Festschrift *Honouring the Past and Shaping the Future* edited by Robert Pope and presented to Prof Jones in September 2003. His publications include *The Bones of Joseph: From the Ancient Texts to the Modern Church: Studies in the Scriptures.*

Rosemary Radford Ruether is the Carpenter Professor of Feminist Theology at the Graduate Theological Union in Berkeley, California. For 28 years she was The Georgia Harkness Professor of Applied Theology at Garrett Theological Seminary and Northwestern University in Evanston, Illinois. She is author or editor of 28 books and 12 book collections in the areas of feminist and liberation theologies.

Nur Masalha is Professor of Religion and Politics at St. Mary's University, Twickenham and Director of the Centre for Religion and History and Holy Land Research Project. He edits an internationally refereed journal, *Holy Land Studies: A Multidisciplinary Journal.* His recent publications include *The Zionist Bible: Biblical Precedent, Colonialism and the Erasure of Memory, The Palestine Nakba: Decolonising History, Narrating the Subaltern, Reclaiming Memory; La Biblia leída con los ojos de los Cananeos;* and *The Bible and Zionism: Invented Traditions, Archaeology and Post-Colonialism in Palestine-Israel.*

Acknowledgments

THIS BOOK COULD NOT have been completed without the support and practical help of the Institute for Theological Partnerships, University of Winchester, which hosted (under the leadership of Professor Lisa Isherwood) a two-day conference on Palestinian Liberation Theology on 14–15 May 2011. Many colleagues and friends have also contributed to and shaped this volume, directly and indirectly, with ideas, criticism, conversations, material and editorial support. Several papers were received by Professor Nur Masalha prior to and independent of the Winchester conference and Professor Isherwood is very grateful to Professor Masalha for his generous invitation to be part of the wider project. The two editors are also very grateful for the good well and generosity shown by all contributors to the collection. Last but not least, the editors are particularly grateful to Khalid al-Ali and the Naji Al-Ali family for their kindness and help with and permission to use this beautiful Handhala cartoon by the late Naji Al-Ali as a cover for this volume.

Introduction

Nur Masalha *and* Lisa Isherwood

As WITH ALL ONGOING conflict situations opinions are deeply divided not simply over what are perceived to be the "rights and wrongs" of the situation but also of course over what the way ahead may be. Justice and truth as well as peace and reconciliation, terms often associated with deeply divided societies, oppression or conflict situations, themselves become flexible and negotiable terms, not always in a good sense. Some years ago Rosemary Radford Ruether mentioned to Lisa Isherwood that it seemed to her American peace and reconciliation hinged on, we make our peace you reconcile yourself to it! A statement akin to a popular "joke" circulating at the time about the Henry Kissinger peace zoo where the lion lies down with the lamb. When asked how this is achieved the man himself, American political scientist and diplomat Dr. Henry Kissinger, replied "It is easy, we get a new lamb every day." No flippancy is meant in either of these examples rather to highlight that even when we think we are talking about the same things some clarification is needed and a range of possibilities lie within even apparently transparent words and situations. And of course even peace is a highly politically motivated concept and does not guarantee justice.

What then can we do if even the terms and concepts we hope may bring resolution are themselves contested and open to further injustice? We have no answer except to say- keep talking, examining and investigating the very foundations of the conflict and give up on final answers and solutions rather work in the here and now to change where we can never believing that this is the end or that it contains "the right" but merely that it is different and in that difference there may just be more humanity, more peace and more justice- but probably never enough.

The issue of land is of course a basic one, we need a place to plant our feet if we are to build and identity and feel safe enough to be open to others. It is from my perspective a tragedy that anyone of us can feel e own what is after all a free gift to be nurtured rather than owned and dominated. However we am also aware that in that statement there may be a note of naiveté because even if we do not wish to own it we may wish to grow from it and be owned by it. It seems self evident [!]to Lisa as a Celt that we are grown by the land but also that with the arrival of those who think differently that foundational relationship is changed and the people who hold it often marginalised. This was that struck most forcibly struck Lisa in the testimonies of the older people in the documentary film *The Land Speaks Arabic* (2008). For many of them, Palestinian refugees driven out from their villages and land in 1948, the issue had not been about religious conflicts or even Jewish attachment to the land; as they explained there was no conflict between Jews and Muslims in the land prior to the arrival of modern European colonial-settlers in Palestine. The issue was European Jewish settlers, people who treated Palestine as "a land without people" (*terra nullius*) and sought exclusive control, ownership and domination of the land; colonial settlers who did not approach it with the same philosophy or way of life. This is we know just one of many of the complex issues involved but it was is point that speaks of clash of culture (colonial *versus* indigenous) and approach to land that we are perhaps not always aware of under the layers of religious and political rhetoric involved around this topic.

The collection concerns the development of contextualised theologies of liberation in Palestine and as part of the indigenous Palestinian people's struggle for justice and liberation. The work is innovative because of its inclusion of indigenous perspective within its remit and the introduction of new concepts such civil liberation theology. The collection offers other ways to look at biblical discourses and their impact on the ongoing conflict, ways to live peace, ways to be ethical when visiting these conflicted lands, understandings of resource ethics and even a new way to understand how we approach our understanding of liberation theology. No one claims they have found the answer and encouragingly none of the authors falls back on scapegoats and easy villains, the papers are more nuanced and creative than that. This is one small contribution to the ongoing conversation. This work goes beyond standard academic collections: it is aimed not only at the scholar experts/students but also at peace activists and policy makers. The editors hope the work will be of use not only in academic courses but also for practioners of conflict resolution , peace and reconciliation.

This collection is organised into three distinct parts:

- The first part, with chapters by Naim Ateek, Samuel Kuruvilla, and Marc Ellis, explores the evolution of theologies of liberation Palestine-Israel in contextual and comparative perspectives

- The second part, with chapters by Nur Masalha and Gareth Lloyd Jones, Rosemary Radford Ruether and Lisa Isherwood explores oppressive, fundamentalist, and power-driven imperialist approaches to the Bible and the Palestine-Israel conflict

- The third part, with chapters by Nur Masalha, Mary Grey and Mark Braverman, explores new paradigms and new approaches to liberation theology in Palestine

In chapter 1 Samuel Kuruvilla focuses the development of a theology of Christian liberation and contextual polity from its early origins in Latin America to one of its present manifestations as part of the Palestinian people's struggle for justice and freedom from the state of Israel. This chapter will be primarily dedicated to a historical and political analysis of the theological context, which includes three different strands. First, there was the development of theologies of liberation, as they are made manifest in Latin America and elsewhere. Next, there was the theology of other Palestinian Christians, and particularly that of the Al-Liqa group that contributed to the development of a contextual Palestinian theology of liberation within the 'occupied' context that is Palestine today. And finally there was the case of Palestinian Protestant Christian theologians such as the Rev. Dr. Naim Ateek and the Rev. Dr. Mitri Raheb who have raised definitional issues regarding liberation theology and Palestinian contextual Christianity.

In his contribution in chapter 2 Naim Ateek, a priest and pastor of the Arab Palestinian Congregation at St. George's Cathedral in Jerusalem, describes the eevolution of Palestinian lliberation ttheology and reflects on the economical of Sabeel from 1992 to the present. He locates the roots of Sabeel and its distinct brand of Palestinian Christian liberation in the first Palestinian Intifada (uprisings) which erupted in late 1987:

> Every Sunday, the sermon [at St. George's Cathedral] revolved around the injustice of the Israeli occupation, its oppressive expressions, and the human toll it was exacting on Palestinian lives. Every Sunday after

the church service, the Christian community of St. George's Cathedral together with some Christians from other churches gathered together to reflect, in light of the Gospel, on their life under the oppressive illegal Israeli occupation. People shared their stories and experiences. They struggled around the meaning of their faith. They were greatly inspired by Jesus Christ who lived all his life under the occupation of the Roman Empire. Jesus' life, teaching, and example became the standard and criterion for their own life. The most frequent questions were, how did Jesus respond to and resist the Roman occupation forces, and how can we respond today? How did Jesus help his followers maintain faithfulness to God living under the oppressive Roman occupation? The gospels provided guidance, invigorated discussion, and gave comfort, encouragement, hope, and strength to the local Christian community. The community of faith was doing theology on the ground in a deeply contextual, pragmatic, and meaningful way. The credit goes to the people themselves. The best critiques and ideas came from them. When reflecting on their faith and resistance, there was no doubt they were all sure that the way of Jesus is the way of nonviolence. Escapism and flight were not an option. It was clear to most of them that the armed resistance was not the way of Jesus, nonviolence was. This was the first established foundation for a Palestinian Liberation Theology. That is where it all began. If the Nakba of 1948 marked the destruction of the Palestinian community, the Intifada of 1987 marked the return to national consciousness, grassroots activism, and "liberation from below."

Marc Ellis's contribution in chapter 3 is a "encounter" kind of essay - especially his encounter with Naim Ateek and his work on Palestinian liberation theology. Marc Ellis asks: does the bbirth of a Jewish and Palestinian theologies of liberation have anything to Say about the future of Israel-Palestine? For many years Ellis has been writing on the question of theologies of liberation in Palestine-Israel. This began with an article in 1984 and a book, *Toward a Jewish Theology of Liberation* in 1987. Independent of his work, Naim Ateek's Palestinian theology of liberation was also being written during this same time period. Ellis argues that the link between a Jewish and Palestinian theology of liberation is much closer than assumed. Ellis shows how he and Ateek journeyed together and this journey combines an intellectual, spiritual and personal learning process which is relevant to time periods beyond their own. Ellis argues that, though the optimism of their theologies of liberation seems distant today, it may be time to once again broach the possibility of justice, reconciliation found in the pages of both works.

In Chapters 4 and 5 Nur Masalha and Gareth Lloyd Jones and explore the evolution of a fundamentalist theology of dispossession in Israel after 1967. Masalha argues that in modern times, a whole range of colonial enterprises have used the Bible. The book of Joshua and other biblical texts evoking the exploits of ancient Israelites have been deployed in support of secular Zionism and settler colonisation in Palestine. The mega narratives of the Bible, however, appeared to mandate the ethnic cleansing and even genocide of the indigenous population of Canaan. Masalha argues that, with the rise of messianic Zionism since 1967, a Jewish theology of zealotocracy, based on the land traditions of the Bible, has emerged in Israel–a political theology that demanded the destruction of the so-called modern Canaanites; since 1967 fundamentalist rabbis have routinely compared the Palestinian people to the ancient Canaanites, Philistines and Amalekites, whose annihilation or expulsion by the ancient Israelites was predestined by a divine design. This chapter focuses on the politics of reading the Bible by neo-Zionists and examines the theology of the messianic current which embraces the paradigm of Jews as a divinely 'chosen people' and sees the indigenous Palestinians as no more than illegitimate squatters, and a threat to the process of messianic redemption; their human and civil rights are no match for the biblically-ordained holy war of conquering and settling the "Promised Land."

Chapter 6 by Rosemary Radford Ruether discusses competing theologies in relation to the Israel-Palestine conflict between the Israeli state and the Palestinian people. The chapter focuses on competing theologies among Christians, both in the West and in Palestine, as these theologies interact with the Jewish community, both in Israel and in the West. Ruether outlines the major patterns of theology found in mainline churches which reinforce collaboration of these Christian churches with Zionism. These include an acceptance of the thesis that God has given the Jewish people the whole of the land of Israel/Palestine permanently and irrevocably in a way that ignores the rights the other peoples of the land, that the state of Israel is a fulfilment of prophecy and that the Christian churches owe uncritical support for the state of Israel as compensation for the Holocaust. Ruether illustrates such Christian Zionist theology in several major spokesmen for mainstream Churches, and show how such views arise in the context of manipulated Jewish-Christian Dialogue sessions.

Ruether (unlike Masalha or Lloyd Jones in chapters 4 and 5) does not focus on the more fundamentalist and millenarian forms of Christian Zionism, important as these are, but rather the often unnoticed and un-named themes of Christian Zionism which have shaped the behaviour and politics of the main bodies of Western Christianity. These expressions of Christian Zionism are deeply entwined with Western Christian imperialism toward the Middle East, represented by then British empire and now by American empire. Ruether also argues that the Jewish voice is also increasingly divided, in defense or in critique of the policies of the state of Israel. Christians interact with these divergent Jewish voices, as they seek to overcome the legacy of Christian anti-semitism and its horrific results in the Holocaust, but also in the debate in relation to the state of Israel. At the same time Palestinian Christians seek to unite their historically divided community to speak with one voice against their op-pression and the ethnic cleansing of their land by the state of Israel and to provide an alternative vision of a future Palestine for Israeli Jews and Palestinian Christians and Muslims. Ruether begins with an exploration of the theology of Christian Zionism, particularly as this has shaped mainstream Western Christianity.

Ruether's arguments are closely related to Palestinian liberation the-ology which has exemplified in the work of Naim Ateek and Sabeel above. Her works forms an important part of the systematic critic of Christian Zionist theology and its apologia for Zionism and the State of Israel and its representation of an authentically inclusive liberative theology of jus-tice for all people. Ruethers' approach helps put Palestinian liberation theology in context of the global liberation theology movement and ar-gue for its inclusion in international gatherings of liberation theology, such as the Ecumenical Association of Third World Theologians.

In Chapter 7 Lisa Isherwood considers the part monotheism plays in the-ologies of land and suggests a new approach to the concept of transcen-dence that neutralises the worst affects of monotheism which in her view leads to mono cultural and religious thinking that traps us in an unend-ing vertical theology that is self perpetuating. Isherwood does not feel the fluidity that is possible in this different approach is at odds with the God of the Hebrew scriptures and she suggest a new "horizontal wrestling" as a way out of the monotheistic trap.

Chapter 8 by Mark Braverman offers a new paradigm for a theology of land. He argues that Christian confrontation with the Nazi genocide produced a radical re-evaluation of theology with respect to Christianity's relationship to the Jewish people. Motivated by the urgent need to atone for the sin of Christian anti-Judaism, this revisionist movement focused on the repudiation of replacement theology. This revisionism has had profound implications for the current discourse on the political situation in historic Palestine. It directs and frames "interfaith" conversations in the West and promotes church policy designed to protect relationships with the Jewish community at the cost of the church's social justice mission with respect to human rights in historic Palestine. On a deeper level, this revisionist theology serves to support Christian triumphalist tendencies. Whereas the confrontation with the Nazi Holocaust presented an opportunity to confront this quality in Christianity, Christians instead chose to focus on anti-Semitism as the primary Christian sin. As a result, Christian triumphalism is actually reinforced, through an identification with a rehabilitated Judaism and an affirmation of the exclusivist nature of God's covenant with the Jewish people. In addition to this reversion to particularism, Christianity's spiritualization of the land has been disavowed, and a superior Jewish claim to the land is legitimized. In this chapter, Dr. Braverman discusses the implications of these issues for the development of a theology of land and the current quest for peace in historic Palestine and issues a call to the church to respond to this challenge.

Mary Grey, in chapter 9 reinforces Mark Braverman's perspective by focusing on new positive aspects to the situation now faced by the Palestinians and the new political context in the Middle East that is bringing much hope. She argues that despite what appeared to be political stalemate, despite the daily suffering and humiliation of people in the West Bank and Gaza, (and escalating harassment of the Israeli government) there are indications that the tide has turned. She also addresses challenges for spirituality, Church and theology.

In the final chapter Nur Masalha coins a new expression: "civil liberation theology" in Palestine. Masalha argues that while feminist, black and post-colonial theologies of liberation have flourished in the West, there is little discussion of indigenous and decolonising perspectives or civil and secular-humanist reflections on liberation theology. Inspired by the works of Palestinian visual artist Naji Al-Ali and public intellectual Edward Said, the chapter brings into the debate on theologies of liberation in Palestine-Israel a neglected subject: an egalitarian, nonedenominational theology rooted in decolonising methodologies. This civil liberation theology attempts to address the questions: how can exile be overcome? How can history be transcended and decolonised? And how can indigenous memory be reclaimed? The chapter brings into focus indigenous, humanist and non-religious ways of thinking on which Edward Said and Naji Al-Ali, in his famous figurative character Handhala, insisted. The character of Handhala, the eleven-year-old barefoot child, was inspired by real stories of barefoot Palestinian children in Lebanon's refugee camps. Handhala has become a powerful icon of Palestine and the symbol of Palestinian refugee struggle in the post-Nakba period for truth, justice return and liberation. The character of the witness/martyr Handhala, which epitomises contemporary civil liberation theology in Palestine, draws on contrapuntal approaches, decolonising indigenous methodologies and egalitarian non-denominational theologies derive from the cultural diversity and experiences of "historic Palestine." This civil liberation theology celebrates multiplicity of non-denominational voices and nurtures humanist, progressive, creative and liberative theologies which occupy multiple sites of liberation and can be made relevant not only to people of faith (Muslims, Jews, Christians) but also to secular-humanists.

1

Liberation Theology in Latin America and Palestine-Israel: Practical Similarities and Contextual Differences

Dr. Samuel J. Kuruvilla

The Origins of Liberation Theology

Liberation theology has complex origins which include the tradition of the church's thinking on politics and economics, going all the way back to the Church Fathers; more immediately Catholic Social Teaching and Catholic Action, which followed from that, with its motto of "See, Judge, Act;" Vatican II and the ferment which followed from it; European political theology; the educational philosophy of Paulo Freire; and the "Christian-Marxist dialogue" of the 1960s (Dawson 1998).

Catholic Social Teaching and the long tradition on which it draws such as Leo XIII's *Rerum Novarum*, promulgated in 1891, condemned the bad living conditions of the urban poor of Europe. Since then, successive Popes have taken it upon themselves to condemn European liberal capitalism while taking a stand in favor of the poor and the down-trodden. Pius XI in 1931 issued *Quadragesimo Anno* which affirmed certain Christian attributes in socialism such as the sharing of property for the common good, something long advocated by Christian reformers over the ages. All Popes since Leo XIII, while staunchly conservative and fiercely anti-Communist, were still sympathetic to moderate versions of socialist endeavor.

Vatican II, called by Pope John XXIII in 1962, took the concern with peace and justice further. Paul VI's Encyclical *Populorum Progressio* was concerned with the question of worldwide poverty and development, particularly in the two-thirds world. It traced "Third World" poverty to the impact and continuing end-results of colonialism, neo-colonialism, unfair trade practices and the great inequality in power among the nations. It was critical of *laissez-faire* capitalism that was responsible for ensuring the wealth and prosperity of Western elite societies at the expense of deprivation and poverty in much of the rest of the world. However, it spoke of "development," which still entailed capitalism, as a "new name for peace" (Dawson 1998, 126).

When the Vatican II Conference was over, two conferences in Latin America, one in Medellin in Colombia and the other in Puebla, Mexico, took these ideas further and first came up with the phrase, "theology of liberation" (Boff 1987, 9). For theologians like Gustavo Gutiérrez, the term "development" could not fully embrace the needs of the people and especially the poor of Latin America, who were being sidelined in the lop-sided development that takes place in most third world countries. On the Protestant side, an organization known as "Church and Society in Latin America" (popularly known by its Spanish acronym of ISAL-*Iglesia y Sociedad en America Latina*-Church and Society in Latin America), had been founded by Richard Shaull and supported by the World Council of Churches-WCC (Smith 1991, 17). This organization was involved in developing what they termed a theology of revolution, as opposed to a theology of development. As a Protestant theological cum social action movement, ISAL, in its early days, was convinced that a gradualist approach to social transformation in Latin America was quite inadequate, given the entrenched and exploitative nature of the rule of dominant groups in these countries.

Shaull and his organization were interested in trying to develop a Christian basis for revolutionary socio-political transformation, one that would not necessarily involve the need for violence (Rider 1998, 61). The theology of revolution certainly made its mark on Latin American Catholic theologians who were already becoming more and more ecumenically-oriented as a result of the post-World War II changes and the Second Vatican council. In the late 1960s, ISAL itself began to feel that the terminology of a so-called theology of revolution was not particularly appropriate to the Latin American situation and then the term liberation began to be spoken of.

The works of European political theologians, in particular Jürgen Moltmann and Johann Baptist Metz, were also important. They regarded Christianity as a "critical witness in society" (Gutierrez 2001, 208). European political theology was very evident in the writings of all the main liberation theologians, especially those trained in Europe in the 1950s and 1960s. Both Moltmann and Metz sought to make theology responsive to its socio-political situation.

The Main Emphases of Liberation Theology

Liberation theologians have always insisted that their interpretation of theology was not just a "re-interpretation of what is generally known as Western theology," but an "irruption" of God active and living among the poor (Chopp and Regan 2005, 469). Liberation theology, at least in the way it was practiced in Latin America, claimed to be a new method of developing a theology that would seek to address the "seemingly hopeless" situation of the poor people of Latin America.

I shall seek to highlight four key themes of liberation theology in this essay. The first was the priority of praxis. For Gutiérrez, theology was a "second step," reflection on action. However for Gutierrez, this "reflection on action" should also be based on the "indisputable" Word of God, the Holy Scriptures of the Christian faith. In this context, the Brazilian Catholic theologian Hugo Assman argued that, " . . . the Bible, tradition, the magisterium or teaching authority of the Church, history of dogma, and so on . . . even though they need to be worked out in contemporary practice, do not constitute a primary source of 'truth-in-itself'" (Assman 1975, 104–5).

Assman has also been critical of the hermeneutical approach of many so-called liberation theologians, critiquing the relevance and necessity of a biblical hermeneutics, which did not take into consideration the masses of new techniques and data offered by secular and social sciences as well as the need to think practically about the situation at hand. He was equally critical of the "biblicists" as well as those Marxist historians and analysts who sought in his view to impose a "fundamentalism of the Left" by attempting to transplant biblical paradigms and situations into this world without understanding their historical context and situation. He saw the theology of liberation as a critical reflection on the present historical situation "in all its intensity and complexity." Instead of the Bible, the "text" of current reality should be the situational précis point that requires analysis and theologizing. As a result, the main issue for Assman was one of hermeneutical criteria. He had little use for those who claim that the best sets of hermeneutics available to Christians are located in the "sacred text," arguing instead for an analysis of reality based on the circumstances of "today" (Assman 1975, 104–5).

Rather, it was liberative action which was the indispensable basis for reflection. Early on, the Exodus paradigm was normative: the poor were seen as engaged on a journey from slavery to freedom, escaping the bondage of class and debt. The theme of the kingdom of God was also prominent. All liberation theologians make a link between liberation and God's justice as the primal theme in Christian theology. Gutiérrez denied wanting to fashion a theology from which political action was "deduced" (Gutierrez 1974, intro-ix). What he wanted, rather, was to let ourselves be judged by the word of the Lord, to think through our faith, to strengthen our love, and to give reason for our hope from within a commitment which seeks to become more radical, total, and efficacious. It is to reconsider the great themes of the Christian life within this radically changed perspective and with regard to the new questions posed by this commitment. This is the goal of the so-called theology of liberation (Gutierrez 1974, ix).

The insistence on beginning with praxis led to a new hermeneutic. Juan Luis Segundo defined the hermeneutical circle as "the continuing change in our interpretation of the Bible which is dictated by the continuing changes in our present-day reality, both individual and societal" (Hennelly 1979, 109). Segundo's method was made up of four steps that correspond to a kind of theological circle. The first step requires recognition of reality on our part that automatically leads to ideological suspicion of that reality. Secondly, the application of "ideological suspicion" entails its application to the whole theological superstructure in general. Thirdly Segundo calls for a new way of experiencing and living theological reality, which would in turn lead us to a kind of exegetical suspicion (that would mean a suspicion that current biblical interpretation did not take into account important data). Fourthly he recommended the development of a new hermeneutic that would provide a new way of interpreting "our faith," based on Scripture, with many of the new academic as well as critical-analytic techniques at our disposal (Hennelly 1979, 109). Bible reading began with the experience of oppression, which led to suspicion of current Biblical interpretation, which led to new readings of Scripture, which led to new views of society.

Second, liberation theology sought to establish itself not in relation to the institutional church or the academy, but in relation to the *communidades di base* (in Spanish, the base communities) of peasants and workers who constituted the church. These communities form the root from which pastoral workers, priests and theologians sought to develop their theologies of liberation (Witvliet 1985, 138–39).

Base communities have been described as "grassroots communities" where Christians seek to form and live out their Christian witness in their historical situation (Chopp and Regan 2005, 471). While present in all Latin American states, base communities became most popular in Brazil, where they at one time numbered in the hundreds of thousands. It was in recognition of this fact that the EATWOT Congress in Sao Paulo, Brazil in 1980 was focused on the ecclesiology of Basic Christian Communities (BCC's). BCC provide the basis for a historical praxis of liberation that comes before theological manifestation. They also act as a source of ecclesiology as well as a place where the "poor and the oppressed" manage to get a place of their own in the historical process. The BCC were always firmly located within the entrenched feudal and semi-feudal forces of bourgeois control in the Latin American nations.

The BCC owe their origin to a wide nature of factors, including the great shortage of priests in Latin America, the desire of the laity to be an active part of the church in the region and the natural desire on the part of the masses for a Latin American church that was responsive to their wishes and aspirations. In short, BCC were a manifestation of the contextualization of Latin America's hitherto heavily Euro-centric church and religio-cultural sphere. As stated earlier, the necessity for social resistance could also give rise to a group of people meeting to coordinate various policies of community action in the light of Gospel teachings. There have been frequent periods and places in the modern history of Latin American states when and where it was extremely dangerous for anybody to be part of a BCC, inviting almost certain incarceration and death, if detected (Witvliet 1985, 138–39).

Thirdly, Liberation theology espoused the "option for the poor." Liberation theologians took as their starting point, the reality of social oppression and misery around them and as their end-goal, the elimination of this kind of misery and "the liberation of the oppressed" (Smith 1991, 27). Christian Smith (1991) summarized liberation theology as an attempt to "reconceptualize the Christian faith from the perspective of the poor and the oppressed." For Jon Sobrino (Chopp and Regan 2005, 475), the poor were a privileged channel of God's grace (Chopp and Regan 2005, 475). According to Phillip Berryman, liberation theology was, "an interpretation of Christian faith through the poor's suffering, their struggle and hope, and a critique of society and the Catholic faith and Christianity through the eyes of the poor" (Berryman 1987, 4).

Fourth, awareness of the failure of development programs led to the use of Marxist analysis to try to understand what was going on in society. Chopp and Regan (2005) described this process thus:

> Liberation theology is a critique of the structures and institutions that create the poor, including the primary identification of modern Christianity with the rich. In order to do this, liberation theology engages in dialogue not only with philosophy but also with the social sciences. As a theological discourse of critique and transformation in solidarity with the poor, liberation theology offers a theological anthropology that is political, an interpretation of Christianity that may be characterized through the term "liberation," and a vision of Christianity as praxis of love and solidarity with the oppressed (Chopp and Regan 2005, 471).

Again it has been postulated that it might be best to think of liberation theology as an entirely new genre of theology based on a specific faith-praxis. Liberation theology was specifically focused on Christian praxis amidst the poor, the oppressed and the deprived of this world (Chopp and Regan 2005, 473). In its emphasis on analysis, liberation theology was a "contextual" theology, albeit mainly in relation to the social, political and economic context. Eventually, the option for the poor led to an awareness of the importance of native forms of spirituality in liberation theology (Hawley 1995).

This kind of analysis meant a different understanding of sin. No longer primarily moralistic, it looked first at sinful structures, the ways in which society was organized, which more or less forced individuals into sinful action. What was called for, therefore, was not just personal change, but a change in social, political and economic structures.

Liberation theology was often criticized for being overly political, but for Gutiérrez, liberation in its full form denoted salvation in Jesus Christ. In Gutiérrez's view, liberation in Jesus can be denoted as a single salvation process, which concerns the very identity of Christianity and the mission of the church (Gutierrez 1974, 11). Gutiérrez constantly reminded First World Christians that the subject and ultimate goal of liberation theology was not "theology," but "liberation." The ultimate call of every "servant of Christ" was to the task of liberation, and not to the task of theology, "unless that theology is a servant of liberation" (Ruether 1992, 27). This was a point frequently emphasized by Gustavo Gutierrez in the discussions leading up to the Third Latin American Bishops Conference (CELAM-III), as well as in his talk during the press conference after the Conference at Puebla, Mexico, February 1979 (Gutierrez 1974, 11).

The American Feminist Catholic theologian Rosemary R. Ruether meanwhile emphasized that there could be no neutral theology, anymore than there could be neutral sociology or psychology. "Theology" could be used either as a good and positive tool on the side of all of humanity, by being on the side of the oppressed, or else it could be used "as a tool of alienation and oppression," by being on the side of the oppressors (Ruether 1992, 27).

Christian Liberation Theology in Palestine

Most Palestinian theologians own their debt to the Latin American liberation theologians (Lende 2003, 51). The Palestinian Anglican theologian Naim Ateek (1989) always used the term "Palestinian Liberation Theology" to refer to his work (Ateek 1989, 51). The Sabeel (river or stream of life in Arabic) Centre that he helped to found in East Jerusalem has modeled itself in its activities as an interdenominational ecumenical centre/institute for the development of a Palestinian Christian theology of liberation in the "Holy Land." At the same time, there are crucial differences between the Latin American and the Palestinian context. In the first place, Latin America was a continent where the vast majority of the poor are Christian. In Palestine, Christians are only a tiny minority. This means liberation theology cannot simply be transposed from one situation to another.

Secondly, the option for the poor in Latin America was about class. In Palestine, all Palestinians are oppressed. Class in Palestine was largely focused on the difference between town and village dwellers in the Palestinian Territories and socio-religious differences between Arab Muslims, Muslim Bedouins, Druze, Arab Christians and other non-Arab Muslim groups dwelling in the territory of Palestine-Israel. What was being dealt with here was a perverse form of racism where Semites are discriminating against Semites.

Thirdly, it could be argued that the Exodus paradigm does not play out in Palestine. Palestinians find themselves in the role of the dispossessed people. This has raised acute difficulties for biblical study. Palestinian theologians have been much exercised by how to read the Hebrew bible.

Finally, Palestinian theologians do not have the background in Marxism which many Latin American theologians had. To them, it was an alien form of analysis and they sought to turn elsewhere for understanding society. All Palestinian liberation/contextual theology practitioners tend to interact and relate (intellectually, culturally, and politically) more with the (formerly colonial) West, than with their fellow (formerly colonized and oppressed) global Easterners or Southerners (Christians of South Asia, the Far East, and Western or sub-Saharan Africa, for instance). This is partly about where wealth, power and global political control was centered in today's world, but it may also reflect a kind of "elitist" or "superior" Arab understanding of the so-called "two-thirds" world. The Arab psyche, and in this context, the Arab Christian psyche, demands recognition from Western Christians as one of the most western-oriented of Christian minority groups in the Eastern Mediterranean region. They see this as a reflection of the historic ties that Arab Christians have had with Christians in the European West during the long centuries of Islamic rule in this region. Ties between Western and Eastern Christians were particularly cemented during the period of the Crusades, which saw a sustained Western intrusion into the region, both from a military, colonial and religio-cultural point of view.

The Ottoman territories of the "Near East" or "Middle East" were also one of the first regions outside Europe penetrated and influenced by Western Christian missionaries and administrators, thereby having a considerable cultural impact on the life and prospects of Arabic-speaking Christians in the area. Many Arab Christians migrated and settled in parts of Latin America, North America, parts of Europe and Australasia, thereby fuelling ties between these largely "developed" regions of the world and the Arab Christian homeland of Syria, Palestine, Lebanon and Egypt-Jordan.

Early Influences in Contextualization of Theology in Palestine: The Al-Liqa Centre in Bethlehem

The Bethlehem-based organization known as Al-Liqa (in Arabic, Encounter) was set up in 1982 with the aim of creating dialogue and understanding between Christians and Muslims. Initially, the organization formed part of the Tantur Ecumenical Institute for Theological Studies, Jerusalem, and was actually part of one of their ecumenical outreach programs. Tantur was set up in 1971 after the Vatican bought and then subsequently leased the hill-top land between Bethlehem and Jerusalem on the old Jerusalem-Hebron road to the University of Notre Dame (USA) for 50 years to build and operate an ecumenical research institute in an internationalist, albeit Catholic ambience. The inspiration to form Tantur evolved from the Second Vatican Council where some of the Catholic, Orthodox and Protestant participants from the Holy Land asked Pope Paul VI to start an ecumenical research institute in Jerusalem.

Tantur's mainly international focus, in keeping with its use as an overseas research institute of the University of Notre Dame in the United States, meant that local Palestinians felt increasingly ill-at-ease there. Tantur's programs were mainly focused on Jewish-Christian dialogue, emphasizing the priorities of the American sponsors of this organization. Palestinians were looking for a centre that would address specifically the issue of Muslim-Christian dialogue and Al-Liqa separated from Tantur and established itself as a separate centre in 1987. Al-Liqa was first set up in the mid-1980s in Beit Sahour, a suburban town close to Jerusalem and one of the Christian triangles in the West Bank comprising Beit Lahem-Bethlehem, Beit Sahour and Beit Jala.

Al-Liqa's success at that time (a tradition that it continues even now), was that it was able to bring together Christian and Muslim leaders and theologians in the land to explore issues of contention as well as agreement between them. This itself was crucial as it occurred during a period when there was a general tendency among people of all faiths in Palestine-Israel to look abroad for help towards other foreigners of similar faith, rather than spend time dialoguing with their own brothers and sisters of different religions at home. It was not to expected that major issues (political and theological) of difference between the two faiths' approaches could be solved easily, but the dialogue set up helped to ease built-up misunderstandings as well as even certain theological misapprehensions and tensions, thereby creating channels for further communication and vital personal networks of communication that could always be activated at will and when there was a crisis in inter-faith and inter-communal relations. Al-Liqa, in this sense, had an important niche in the Palestinian faith landscape (Dumper 2002, 132–33).

Al-Liqa was not only dedicated to theological studies, but to research into all aspects of life, religious, cultural and secular, of the indigenous people of the Holy Land region. It sought to develop a contextualized theology that took into consideration the existence, needs and cultural aspirations of the Muslim and Christian communities of Israel-Palestine-Jordan. While Sabeel's main focus was on advocacy work in the West, seeking to make Western Christians understand the situation of Palestinian Christians, Al-Liqa focused on developing a sense of unity and purpose among Palestinians of all religious persuasions and inculcating in them a sense of purpose about their shared culture and socio-religious heritage. The document "Theology and the Local Church in the Holy Land: Palestinian Contextualized Theology," published by the Al-Liqa centre stated that:

> Our contextualized Palestinian theology does not mean isolating ourselves, withdrawing within ourselves or writing a new theology developed outside the general trend of Christian thought or in contradiction to it. What we mean is a theology which can live and interact with events so as to interpret them and assist the Palestinian church in discovering her identity and real mission at this stage of her earthly life. (*Al-Liqa Journal* 1987)

Dr. Geries Sa'id Khoury was the founding director of the Al-Liqa Centre for Religious and Heritage Studies in the Holy Land. For him, Palestinian contextual theology should inculcate a spirit of national awareness among Palestinian Christians. It should be a means by which the Palestinian national struggle becomes a common struggle of all Palestinian people for a free, secular and democratic homeland. A common understanding and request of Palestinian Contextual Theology in this context has been the demand for achieving a secularized and nationally responsible education system in the Palestinian territories that reflects the sensitivities and aspirations of the Christian community within Palestine. In short, Palestinian Contextual Theology, as propagated by the Al-Liqa centre in Bethlehem, has sought to develop a sense of awareness about the Christian Arab heritage of the Holy Land and its myriad facets, including theological, philosophical, historical and political factors that have contributed to the development of the unique identity and psyche of the Christian Arabs since the early Middle Ages of the European era.

The Al-Liqa centre sought to temper the overtly Islamic attitude of the Palestinian educational system, so as to create an awareness of the contributions made by Christian Arabs to the development of Arab civilization. Geries Khoury himself has stated how there were literally hundreds of thousands of Arabic language Christian manuscripts stored in the libraries of various museums and patriarchates (various monastic as well as patriarchate libraries), awaiting detailed study and translation as well as an adequate importing of this concealed knowledge into various publications, books, journals and otherwise, so that the scholarly world might be aware of the great contributions made by the Christian Arab sphere to the development of interreligious and other dialogue in the greater Middle Eastern region. He lamented the fact that this knowledge has been so far, over the last thousand years or more, concealed from the popular eyes of both the East as well as understandably the West.

Medieval Christian theologians in the Arab world generally wrote their theology in the vernacular Arabic language, though other Semitic and Greek languages were used in church and seminary services. Indeed, the Arabic language was a major factor fostering the unity of various theologians belonging to various competing Middle Eastern churches of different shades and variations of theological leanings. Khoury himself, in the course of his extensive research into medieval Arabic Christian literature (he has two PhD degrees, both from Italian universities in medieval Arabic philology), has discovered that the Arabic church theologians often acknowledged that the divisions among them were more due to linguistic differences, perpetuated among Christians from different "national" church and sectarian traditions within the Middle Eastern region, than due to theology as is usually thought. Palestinian Contextual Theology sought to highlight the contributions made by the Arab Christians to the development of an Arab Christian-Muslim dialogue during the time of the Islamic Caliphate in the Middle East and its potential lessons for the present period in the field of Islamic-Christian dialogue.

After the arrival of Islam, it was a necessity for Levantine Christians to enunciate a theology that would be contextual, indigenous, and would appeal to the new Muslim rulers in the language of their choice, namely Arabic. Non-Greek, non-Byzantine Christians of the territories conquered by the Muslim armies saw their arrival as a form of salvation against the totalitarian theocracy of the Byzantine Greeks. It could be argued that the Oriental church survived because it bothered to enter into a dialogue with the Arabs. Arabic was not the first language of choice for Christians when the Muslims arrived in the Levant in the 7th century AD. However, it rapidly became the lingua franca as communication between the conquerors and the conquered was a must for both mutual as well as national survival. The Oriental church found better cause for survival under the Arabs that under the Byzantines, who tended to be contemptuous of those Christians unwilling to accept the Greek language and Orthodoxy in all its totality.

In contrast, today, after centuries of living under Islamic and proto-Islamic rule, Levantine Christians are largely united among themselves and with other fellow non-Christians by virtue of their common culture and the Arabic language. The centre sought to make dialogue between Christians and Muslims in Palestine the centre-piece of their efforts in favor of developing an all-encompassing national consensus on the Palestine problem (Khoury 2006, 95). Palestinian Christian theology must be concerned with a dialogue with Islam as well as with Judaism. Khoury related how Palestinians were a victim of an "ideologized" reading of scripture that is used to argue that the land of Palestine is actually the "Promised Land" of the Jewish people. He referred to Leviticus 25:47 with its theology of the "resident aliens," and stated that it would be impossible from a theological as well as political perspective, for the Palestinian people to accept such a claim to their land. Khoury makes the specific claim that the Palestinian Christian claim to interpreting the Old Testament and the whole question of the "holy" land must be done in a way that goes much deeper than contemporary Zionist Jewish political interpretations and definitions (Khoury 2006, 99).

A Palestinian contextualized theology was "a meeting place for East and West, for Christian and Muslim, for Christian and Jew, for Palestinian and non-Palestinian. It was the promise of a nation in the Holy Land. It was a theology of communication between peoples, cultures and religion." Geries Khoury's preferred term for any nascent endeavor to develop a Palestinian theology of liberation was simply just "Palestinian theology." He was not against the term "liberation theology" but would prefer to call any theology that sought to root the local Palestinian church within its own local context and setting, by the seemingly nationalist term of a Palestinian theology. For Khoury, liberation theology or Palestinian theology did not start yesterday or today. Christianity was born in Palestine and Jesus Christ himself, born under the Roman occupation of the region, was in many respects the first preacher to speak and teach a Palestinian theology of liberation.

This again was a point repeatedly made by Naim Ateek and other Palestinian theologians and clerics interested in contextualizing theological practice in Palestine-Israel. Geries Khoury emphasized that Palestinian Contextual Theology was not a theology in any way against or in opposition to Islam. He quoted the historic experience of the Orthodox Patriarch of Jerusalem, Sophronius, who sought the middle path of co-existence and collaboration between the historic Christian community of Jerusalem and the Holy Land and the new Islamic conquerors of the region. The contextualization of the Christian faith in the new Islamic settings in the Holy Land involved a theology of dialogue with Islam, through which Sophronius managed to save the mother church of Jerusalem by a mixture of compromise, collaboration and astute diplomacy (Khoury 2006, 102).

For Khoury, the indigenous Christian church in Palestine would not be able to survive unless it could consider itself an integral part of the Palestinian people in the Israel-Palestine region in general. Khoury, as a member of the old Palestinian community within the state of Israel that was born within the British Mandate of Palestine (similar to Naim Ateek, Michel Sabbah, and others, with the possible exception of Mitri Raheb), gave a call in the context of the Israeli-Palestinian conflict for the Israelis to leave the occupied territories. He exhorted Palestinian Christians to consider the Israeli occupation of their territory as a real "sin," the only solution to which would be for the Israelis to vacate the "occupation" (Khoury 1992, 75).

A difference from Latin America was the emphasis on ecumenism. Geries Khoury emphasizes the necessity of developing an ecumenical community theology that would reflect the richness and historical diversity of the different Christian faith traditions in the Holy Land. As he put it:

> There is not a separate Orthodox, Catholic, Lutheran, or Anglican need for justice, or work, or land or identity. Different traditions should bring their riches not their arguments or anything which undermines the strength of our unity. For the contextualized theology is in the message of all the church together . . . It is in an ecumenical theology through which we seek to encourage church unity of word and action (Khoury 2006, 96).

Khoury was insistent that Palestinian Contextual Theology should seriously consider more cooperation between the nations of the south, especially in the field of ecumenical exchange. He was certain that Palestinian Contextual Theology was and has to be a theology of the Third World. In this context, he saw many similarities between the situation of the Palestinian people and that of the black South Africans under the Apartheid regime. For Khoury, the need of the hour was for the Palestinian Christians, whatever their denominational affiliation, to develop an "ecclesiology of the local church" that would serve to overcome the historic fragmentation and divisions that the church had been exposed to over the ages, thereby enabling the Christian inhabitants of Palestine to speak with one voice. He felt that only in this context could the survival of the Palestinian Christian community as a coherent, sustainable and self-reliant Arab group in the region be ensured.

Fr. Rafiq Khoury, who also wrote frequently in the Al-Liqa journal, argued that Middle Eastern Christians have a special vocation for Islam and the Islamic world. Their relation with Islam and the Islamic world was what makes Middle Eastern Christians "unique" in the Christian world. Middle Eastern Christians have a long history under Islam, for approximately three centuries as a majority in the region and later as a minority, though a relatively large one for centuries, until the turn of the twentieth century. The Constantinian "acceptance" of Christianity as the official faith of the Roman Empire meant that Palestine became a "Christian" land for roughly three centuries until the arrival of, first, the Sassanid Persians and then shortly after that, the forces of the Islamic Caliphate. There were however two Christian Empires, one in East and the other in the West and as a result two "versions" of the "one and only" Catholic Christian faith developed.

One point made repeatedly by Khoury in his analysis of the role and history of Middle Eastern Christian churches was the fact that these churches and the groups represented by them have never known the "privilege" of having an ethno-political entity that corresponds to their wishes ruling over them. Native Arab as well as Palestinian historians and theologians, whether Christian or Muslim have never viewed the Byzantine Empire, while solidly Greek and Christian, as a "localized" entity, preferring to see it as a foreign group. This was despite the fact that the predominant language of the Levant till well into the Arab Era was either Greek or Aramaic, the language spoken by Jesus Christ Himself (Khoury 2007A, 108).

Khoury warned that Christians in the Middle East should not seek to create an ethnically homogeneous and politically independent entity of their own in the region, as any attempt in the past to do so has only resulted in catastrophe. He referred to the Christian political experience in Iraq under the immediate post-Mandate phase in the 1920s and Lebanese Christians' fateful dalliance with a controlling stake in political sovereignty in Lebanon.

The Christian condition as a minority in the Middle East has seriously affected the social and psychological condition of Levantine Christians. Khoury quoted from various pastoral letters of the Council of Catholic Patriarchs in the Middle East to show how the status of a minority in the Middle East has negatively affected Christians to the extent that they are being increasingly forced to migrate in large numbers, due to a crisis of confidence in their continued residence in the region (Khoury 2007A, 108). The Islamic experience remained "a decisive and rich experience" in the eyes of Middle Eastern Christians (Ruether 1992, 9).

As Rafiq Khoury put it:

> This (Islamic) history left an indelible imprint on the Christian Churches which makes of them not only Churches within Islam but also Churches for Islam. When we want to determine our vocation and mission, Islam is an obligatory path (Khoury 2007A, 109).

At the same time the millet system under the Ottoman Empire served to solidify the differences between the people. In Rafiq Khoury's opinion, only the establishment of a truly ecumenical framework in the Middle East would ensure Christian survival (Khoury 2007B, 17). He quotes from the statement of the Catholic Patriarchs of the East in their first common message in 1991, which maintained, "In the East, we will be Christians together or we will not exist" (www.opuslibani.org).

Rafiq Khoury maintained that the process of "inculturation" in the Middle East was always an unfinished process. The Middle East today was characterized by the tendency towards Westernization and globalization on the part of an elite as well as a largely secularized middle class, while at the same time, there was a deep appreciation and understanding of indigenous culture and religious identity on the part of a large mass of the population. Because Christians are identified with the West, their Muslim neighbors sometimes distrust them. Rafiq Khoury wished to address this suspicion.

Contextual Theology: A Definition

Naim Ateek used the term "liberation theology" to describe what he is doing. The Lutheran Mitri Raheb as well as the Latin Patriarchate's Fr. Rafiq Khoury preferred the term "contextual theology." What lies behind this difference in terminology was essentially the need to engage with both Judaism and Islam.

"Contextual theology" can be said to have three meanings. In the first place it can simply be a synonym for liberation theology. Thus the Indian theologian K. C. Abraham wrote: "The aim of contextual theology is not only to understand and interpret God's act, or to give reason for their faith, but to help suffering people in their struggle to change their situation in accordance with the vision of the gospel. Liberative praxis is the methodology for contextual theologies" (Abraham 1992, 8). Occasionally, Raheb used the phrase like this. Secondly, the term was used to signify the recognition, originating in the sociology of knowledge, that all discourse is placed. There was "no view from nowhere." As Abraham, again, put it:

> Creative moments in theology have arisen out of the church's response to new challenges in a given historical context. They bear the cultural and social imprints of the time . . . Theologians of every age are committed to interpreting the Gospel of Jesus in a way (that is) relevant and meaningful to the realities around them (Abraham 1992, 5).

Thirdly, it originated in the attempt first of missionary theologians, and then of indigenous theologians, to express theology in terms of the symbols and values of a particular culture. Stephen B. Bevans spoke of contextual theology as,

> a way of doing theology in which one takes into account the spirit and message of the gospel; the tradition of the church; the culture in which one is theologizing; and social change within that culture, whether brought about by western technological process or the grass-roots struggle for equality, justice and liberation (Bevans 1992, 1).

The Christian faith can be understood and interpreted, according to Bevans, not only on the basis of "scripture and tradition," but also on the basis of "concrete culturally conditioned human experience" (Bevans 1992, 1–2). Contextual theology reflects on the "raw experience" of the people. It represents an amalgamation of Christian concepts, stories and symbols on the one hand, with the particular indigenous culture of the people on the other (Bevans 1992, 1–2).

There has been a growing realization worldwide that contextualized or local theologies are the key to the future appeal of the Christian faith. As Jose M. de Mesa (2003) puts it:

> Contextuality in the field of theology denotes attentiveness, the determination to listen to the voice of the poor; and conscious and intentional rootedness in the culture, in religion, in the historical currents, in the social locations and situations of people as well as in gender. It aims to alter conditions in the Church and in society that are counter to the deep intent of the Gospel and seeks to include voices which have been excluded in the participative process of theologizing (Mesa 2003).K. C. Abraham likewise argues that "Theologians of every age are committed to interpreting the Gospel of Jesus in a way (that is) relevant and meaningful to the realities around them" (Abraham 1992, 5). Mitri Raheb (1995) seeks to make the Christian faith relevant or contextual to the Palestinian faithful as part and parcel of their own culture. He has written of the necessity for the Palestinian church to be totally "Arabised," starting from the top of the ecclesiastical hierarchy, through the clergy and right down to the base-laity. This "Arabisation" of the leadership of the church should spread to include theology as well as education. In his view, only this kind of essential "Arabisation" would bind the native Arab Christian people of Palestine to "their church, their society, and their country" (Raheb 1995, 25). Naim Ateek (1989) too has written of the need for the (very Europeanized and Euro-centric) church in Palestine-Israel to "contextualize its faith and theology," thereby seeking to address and answer the important issues facing native Arab Christians and society in the region (Ateek 1989, 71). He writes:

> . . . the contextual concerns of the Church, although predominantly political in appearance, are deeply and ultimately theological in nature. These needs are perpetually frustrated by the increasing complexity of the political conflict . . . The duty of the Church in Israel-Palestine today is to take its own concrete and local context seriously. It (the Church) needs to incarnate itself in its context so that it can be the voice of the oppressed and the dehumanized (Ateek 1989, 72).Writing in 1989, Ateek acknowledged that the church in Palestine-Israel had hardly begun to contextualize. He has since sought to do this, with an

emphasis on the political context. Palestinian Christianity has long roots dating right back to the time of Christ. Even during the Byzantine era, Palestinian Christians did not have any experience of being part of the ruling group as the Byzantine church in Palestine was ruled and controlled by Greeks and Cypriots (Ruether in Raheb 1995, 7). During the Islamic era, the majority of the Palestinian people slowly converted over to the ruling faith and by the eve of the Turkish conquest of Palestine in 1519, the land had become majority Muslim (Ruether in Raheb 1995, 8). Coupled with this was the almost continually disturbed nature of Palestinian society that has resulted in large-scale emigration over the last 100 years or more (Raheb 1995, 15–16). Today, native Christians in Palestine worry more about whether they can ensure adequate quorum in their churches to make them practically viable as part of the "living stones" of the Holy Land (Raheb 1995, 8, 24–25). Palestinian Christians are small in number, but their contributions to society vastly outnumber their actual population. Their institutions, schools and hospitals dot the Holy Land and they are actively involved in rendering valuable social services to the Palestinian population at large.

This brief look at some of the main practitioners of theology in Palestine reveals the overlaps, but even more the differences with liberation theology in Latin America. These theologians begin from the same place, oppression, but the different situation means they develop in a quite different way. In Palestine, Christians and Muslims are both part of an oppressed people. Palestinian theologians must understand Islam not as a precondition for mission, but for survival. All of these theologians take the gospel seriously and, in this situation of conflict, their emphasis is on peace and reconciliation, although they recognize the importance of the struggle to be free. For them, non-violence and dialogue are the way to liberation.

References

Abraham, K. C. 1992. "Third World Theologies." *CTC Bulletin (May-December)* 8. In "Towards a Contextual Theology," edited by Lourdino A Yuzon, *CTC Bulletin, Chapter 1, XII (2)–XIII (1 and 2) (July 1994-September 1995)*. The reference is to the internet version available at http://www.cca.org.hk/resources/ctc/ctc94–02/1. Yuzon.htm.

————. 1996 *Liberative Solidarity: Contemporary Perspectives on Mission*. Tiruvalla, India: Christava Sahitya Samithi.

―――. 2004. *Third World Theologies: Commonalities and Divergences*. Eugene, Oregon: Wipf & Stock.

Al-Liqa Journal, 1987. "Theology and the Local Church in the Holy Land: Palestinian Contextualized Theology." Bethlehem: Al Liqa Centre. The reference is to the internet version at http://www.al-liqacenter.org.ps/eng/p_materials/eng/theology.php.

Assman, Hugo. 1975. *Practical Theology of Liberation* London: Search.

Ateek, Naim. 1989. *Justice and Only Justice: A Palestinian Theology of Liberation*. Maryknoll, New York: Orbis.

Berryman, Philip. 1987. *Liberation Theology: Essential Facts about the Revolutionary Movement in Latin America and Beyond*. Philadelphia: Temple University Press.

Boff, Leonardo, and Clodovis Boff. 1987. *Introducing Liberation Theology*. Maryknoll, New York: Orbis.

Bevans, Stephen B. 1992. *Models of Contextual Theology*. Maryknoll, New York: Orbis.

Chopp, Rebecca S., and Ethna Regan. 2005. "Latin American Liberation Theology." In *The Modern Theologians: An Introduction to Christian Theology since 1918*, edited by David Ford and Rachel Muers, 469–84. Oxford: Blackwell.

Dawson, Andrew. 1998. *The Birth and Impact of the Base Ecclesial Community and Liberative Theological Discourse in Brazil*. Lanham: Rowman and Littlefield.

Dumper, Michael. 2002. *The Politics of Sacred Space: The Old City of Jerusalem in the Middle East Conflict*. London: Lynne Rienner.

Gutierrez, Gustavo. 1974. *A Theology of Liberation*. London: SCM.

―――. 2001. *A Theology of Liberation: History, Politics and Salvation*. London: SCM.

Hawley, S. 1995. "Does God Speak Misquito." PhD dissertation, Oxford University.

Hennelly, Alfred T. 1979. *Theologies in Conflict: The Challenge of Juan Luis Segundo*. Maryknoll, New York: Orbis.

Khoury, Geries. 1992. "Palestinian Christian Identity." In *Faith and the Intifada: Palestinian Christian Voices*, edited by N. S. Ateek, R. R. Ruether, and M. H. Ellis, 71–76. Maryknoll, New York: Orbis.

―――. 2006. "Olive Tree Theology-Rooted in the Palestinian Soil." *Al-Liqa Journal* 26 (June) 58–108.

Khoury, Rafiq. 2007A. "Earthly and Heavenly Kingdom: An Eastern Christian Perspective." *Al-Liqa Journal* 28 (August) 106–16.

―――. 2007B. Christian Communities in the Middle East: Current Realities and Challenges in the Islamic Context." *Al-Liqa Journal* 28 (August) 6–19.

Lende, Gina. 2003. *A Quest for Justice: Palestinian Christians and their Contextual Theology*. M.Phil diss., University of Oslo.

Mesa, José M. de. 2003. "Contextual Theologizing: Future Perspectives, East Asian Pastoral Review 40,no.3." In *Theses on the Local Church: A Theological Reflection in the Asian Context* , FABC Papers 60, 54. The reference is to the internet version available at: http://eapi.admu.edu.ph/eapr003/mesa.htm.

Moltmann, Jürgen. 1998. "Political Theology and Theology of Liberation." In *Liberation the Future: God, Mammon and Theology*, edited by Joerg Rieder, 60–80. Minneapolis: Fortress.

Opus Libani. 1991. "The Future of the Churches in the Middle East." In *First Statement of the Catholic Patriarchs of the East*. Bifkaya-Lebanon: Opus Libani, 24 August 1991. The reference is to the internet version available at: http://www.opuslibani.org.lb/cpco-english/img00591.htm.

Raheb, Mitri. 1995. *I Am a Palestinian Christian*. Minneapolis: Fortress.

Ruether, Rosemary Radford. 1992. *To Change the World: Christology and Cultural Criticism*. London: SCM.

———. 1995. "Foreword." In *I Am a Palestinian Christian*, Mitri Raheb, vii–x. Minneapolis: Fortress.

Smith, Christian. 1991. *The Emergence of Liberation Theology: Radical Religion and Social Movement Theory*. Chicago: University of Chicago Press.

Witvliet, Theo. 1985. *A Place in the Sun: An Introduction to Liberation Theology in the Third World*. London: SCM.

2

Reflections on Sabeel's Liberation Theology and Ecumenical Work (1992–2013)

Dr. Naim Ateek

Evolution of Palestinian Liberation Theology: Historical Background

Palestinian theology of liberation is one of the latest expressions of liberation theologies that has emerged since the 1960s in Palestine. Five important factors and events make up the background to the emergence of this theology.

THE PALESTINIAN CHRISTIAN COMMUNITY

On the eve of the Nakba (catastrophe) that befell the Palestinian people, the picture of the Palestinian Christian community can be described as a community divided into many denominations belonging to both eastern and western rites, a variety of Orthodox, Catholic, and Protestant churches. Most of the churches lacked indigenous leadership. Most of the indigenous clergy were trained as pastors, many of them with very little theological training. The Bible was not accessible to most Christians. Even for the small Protestant Churches, the availability of the Bible, in light of the establishment of the state of Israel, proved at times a liability rather than an asset because of the misuse. After the catastrophe hit, the immediate need for the churches, was to address the humanitarian crisis of the thousands of Palestinian refugees who became homeless. In short, the Palestinian Christian faith was built on simple trust in God. It was not resilient enough or deep enough to withstand the political storm of the loss of their homeland, Palestine. The prophetic response was weak and individualized. As a result of the Nakba, the Christian community like its larger counterpart, the Muslim community was thrown into total disarray.

THE NAKBA

The 1948 Nakba and its aftermath was a devastating shock to the whole Palestinian people. Approximately three quarter of a million Palestinians fled in fright or driven out by force from their towns and villages, both Christians and Muslims. In those days very few people around the world were aware of the tragedy that befell the Palestinians. Yet the Nakba was the basic catastrophic event that shattered Palestinian life for years to come and condemned most of our people to a life in refugee camps on the West Bank, the Gaza Strip and in scattered camps in the surrounding Arab countries; and eventually to the formation of diaspora communities throughout the world. It is the Nakba, its consequences, repercussions, and ramifications that Palestinian Liberation theology eventually had to address. Most of the indigenous clergy of the land fled with their families, or were forced out. Those that remained within what became the state of Israel had to endure, together with their congregations, the agony of the imposition of martial law and a system of control that deprived them of their basic human rights (Ateek 1989, 32–38).

THE HOLOCAUST

What stood out in the West was the tragedy of the holocaust which preceded the Nakba by a few years. Western Christians, by and large, were glad to see European Jews find a home after their unbelievable loss, by the establishment of a state of their own on the land of Palestine.

It is important to remember, however, that the Zionist Movement had been in existence for over 100 years (1897) and the Balfour Declaration had been issued by the British Government 20 years earlier (1917) promising Jews a home in Palestine, During all those years, the Zionists were pressuring the British mandatory power to accelerate the fulfillment of the promise. Indeed the increasing legal and illegal Jewish immigration to Palestine contributed to the escalation of violence between the indigenous Palestinian Arab population and the Zionists whose goals aimed at devouring the whole country.

Were it not for the Holocaust, it would be difficult to believe that the western leaders would have shown sufficient sympathy to the Zionist project as to grant them such a big share of Palestine. One cannot over exaggerate the psychological influence which the holocaust played in the creation of the state of Israel.

Paradoxically, in spite of all their cruelty against Jews, Hitler and his Nazi party have posthumously contributed to the creation of the state and/or certainly helped speed up the process of its creation. The tragedy of the holocaust, undoubtedly, must have affected the WWII victors and caused them to give the Zionist Jews over 50 percent of Palestine in the Partition Plan of 1947. If the Nakba eventually became the basis for the emergence of Palestinian Liberation Theology, the holocaust was an essential part of its background.

THE 1967 WAR

the war of 1967 was a watershed. The Israeli Army occupied the West Bank including East Jerusalem and the Gaza Strip, as well as large areas of the surrounding Arab countries. At the same time, it caused major internal shifts in the Israeli political parties moving the whole country farther to the right. By the second half of the 1970s the Zionist Movement started shifting from a secular to a religious form of Zionism; and from an emphasis on the holocaust to an emphasis on the Torah. This shift proved to be of great significance. It inspired and stimulated the confiscation of Palestinian land, the building of the settlements, and the whole settler movement. The use of the Bible proved to be a more potent tool to attract support for Israel than even the use of the holocaust.

THE FIRST INTIFADA OF 1987

Up until the first intifada, the Palestinians waited for justice to come from the outside, especially the UN, but the UN was unable to implement its own resolutions on Palestine due to the position of the western powers and especially the United States and its power of veto. The first intifada showed the world that the grassroots of the Palestinian community could themselves take a nonviolent stand for justice.

The Beginnings

St. George's Cathedral

When the first intifada erupted, I was the priest and pastor of the Arab Palestinian Congregation at St. George's Cathedral in Jerusalem. Every Sunday, the sermon revolved around the injustice of the Israeli occupation, its oppressive expressions, and the human toll it was exacting on Palestinian lives. Every Sunday after the church service, the Christian community of St. George's Cathedral together with some Christians from other churches gathered together to reflect, in light of the Gospel, on their life under the oppressive illegal Israeli occupation. People shared their stories and experiences. They struggled around the meaning of their faith. They were greatly inspired by Jesus Christ who lived all his life under the occupation of the Roman Empire. Jesus' life, teaching, and example became the standard and criterion for their own life. The most frequent questions were, how did Jesus respond to and resist the Roman occupation forces, and how can we respond today? How did Jesus help his followers maintain faithfulness to God living under the oppressive Roman occupation? The gospels provided guidance, invigorated discussion, and gave comfort, encouragement, hope, and strength to the local Christian community. The community of faith was doing theology on the ground in a deeply contextual, pragmatic, and meaningful way. The credit goes to the people themselves. The best critiques and ideas came from them. When reflecting on their faith and resistance, there was no doubt they were all sure that the way of Jesus is the way of nonviolence. Escapism and flight were not an option. It was clear to most of them that the armed resistance was not the way of Jesus, nonviolence was. This was the first established foundation for a Palestinian Liberation Theology. That is where it all began. If the Nakba of 1948 marked the destruction of the Palestinian community, the Intifada of 1987 marked the return to national consciousness; and for the Christian community in particular the return to a more authentic faith and hope in God.

JUSTICE AND ONLY JUSTICE

As this was going on, the manuscript of *Justice and Only justice, A Palestinian theology of Liberation* was being published by Orbis. As soon as the book came out in 1989, it was launched at St. George's Cathedral. This was followed by the first international Conference with ten international theologians present and the participation of a good number of local Christians. It was held in 1990 at the Tantur Institute for Ecumenical Studies in Jerusalem (Ateek, Ellis, and Ruether 1992). The Palestinian Liberation Theology movement was modestly launched inside as well as outside the country.

Sabeel Ecumenical Liberation Theology Centre

Sabeel was not established formally except a few years later. By then, a group of concerned Christians, clergy and lay, men and women became the founders and later the first board of directors. There was a period of discernment during which lectures and workshops were held sporadically in the Jerusalem and Bethlehem areas. At the end of 1992, the name Sabeel was adopted. Sabeel is Arabic for the path or the way and also a spring of water. We were determined to walk the way of justice and peace. Sabeel was established in two geographic locations, namely, Jerusalem and Nazareth and with three important agendas: an ecumenical agenda for the Christian community of the land (Ateek, Duaybis, and Tobin 2007); an interfaith agenda especially between Christians and Muslims; and a justice and peace agenda that involved people locally and internationally including the participation of Jewish peace activists (Ateek 1989, 151–59; 2008, 3–14).

Important Goals of Palestinian Liberation Theology

It is important to remember that Palestinian Liberation Theology was being addressed to a small Palestinian Christian community living in the midst of a larger Palestinian Muslim community all—Christian and Muslim—in urgent need for liberation.

Be that as it may, in order for it to be a theology of liberation, it was important:

- to analyze the context of injustice and oppression as realistically and faithfully as possible (Ateek 1989, 18–49; 2008, 15–48).

- to be anchored in both the Bible and in the reality on the ground (Ateek 1989, 74–150; 2008, 51–150).

- to empower Christians and encourage them to strengthen their faith in the God of justice and love so that they do not lose faith in God in spite of the oppressive occupation (Ateek 1989, 163–88).

- to give the people hope for the future and inspire them to resist the evil through tools that are authentically true to their faith, i.e. through nonviolence (Ateek 2008, 15–34; 95–96; 178–87).

- to emphasize that faithfulness to God and to Jesus Christ meant critiquing and condemning violence from whichever source. (Sabeel Documents 2005; Kairos Palestine 2009)

Essential Themes

The Concept of God

By and large, the people of the Middle East whether Muslims or Christians are people of faith. Ours is not a secular society. With the exception of relatively few, our people possess a monotheistic faith. This is proclaimed by Muslims five times a day from the minarets "There is no god but God. . ." and acclaimed daily at the beginning of Christian liturgy in the various churches: "In the name of the Father, Son, and Holy Spirit"—One God. What the conflict over Palestine had shaken and questioned was the nature and character of God. Is God the God of love and justice? Does God love all people equally? It was, therefore, essential to remind, restore, establish, and affirm the basic nature of God in the midst of the injustice and oppression against the Palestinians. Moreover, it was important to remind Christians that our clear concept of God has come to us experientially through the coming of Jesus Christ. This experience of God through Jesus Christ was handed down through the living Christian community since Apostolic times. It was the living witness of the life, teaching, crucifixion, death, and resurrection of Jesus Christ. If Christians wanted to know what God is like they needed to look at Jesus Christ; and if they wanted to have a glimpse of the nature of God, they needed to see what Jesus Christ taught us about God and showed us in his life and relationships with others.

In this way, Jesus Christ becomes the hermeneutic or criterion by which we can measure the authentic word of God for us. Christians need to differentiate between the written word of God, i.e., the Bible, and the living or incarnate Word of God, i.e., Jesus Christ. The living Word helps us discern and interpret the written word.

This means that through the life, death, and resurrection of Christ we have discovered that God is the God of love and mercy, the God of peace and forgiveness, the God of truth and justice. We discovered that

God's love is all inclusive and unconditional regardless of race, ethnicity, or gender. Once we are able to grasp and affirm the nature of the God we believe in, as we have experienced it in the coming of Jesus Christ, we are better able to judge whether what is written in the Bible or what we say or do is authentically of God and in accordance with God's nature, character and will or in accordance with human prejudices and self interest.

Due to the abuse of the interpretation of the Bible by Zionist Jews and western Christians, it seemed mandatory to establish this foundational truth about God's nature. In other words, the confiscation of the land and the expulsion of the Palestinians cannot be justified by biblical text as originating with God because they are contrary to the nature and character of God. Similarly, the violence of the occupation cannot be sanctioned by the God of love and justice. A Palestinian theology of liberation had to begin by an understanding of God. What kind of a God do we believe in? Everything else seemed to hinge on this basic tenet of faith.

Indeed, the Bible and especially the Old Testament contains texts that reflect a violent God. These texts cannot and must not be used as reflecting an authentic concept of God. They reflect a primitive human understanding of God that was discarded, challenged, and overcome even within the Old Testament itself. By using Jesus Christ's life and teachings as a hermeneutic, it is possible to a great extent, to judge whether God is involved or uninvolved in what is happening. It is wrong to transfer, assign, and allocate the crimes and injustices that are committed by the cruelty and evil deeds of human beings to the loving and merciful God. Once this is realized, it is possible to turn to the Bible and look carefully at the use, misuse, and abuse that were happening on a daily basis (Ateek 1989, 77–92; 2008, 72–77).

THE BIBLE

The Bible has been the object of much misuse and abuse; and the need to correctly understand and interpret it is a daunting task that is difficult to attain. We know from the history of the Christian church in various parts of the world, how the Bible has been used to justify many things. In fact, since the Bible is a large book and its writing spans hundreds and probably thousands of years, it is possible to prove anything if one selects random texts. Christians have justified war, slavery, polygamy, discrimination against women and many other evils by appealing to certain biblical texts. When it comes to the conflict over Palestine, the examples are plentiful. What follows are a few examples that are relevant to our topic:

The Tribal vs. the Universal and the Exclusive vs. the Inclusive

In the conflict over Palestine, the Bible has been at the center of the conflict. If rightly used, it is capable of inspiring people for the work of justice and peace. However, when wrongly interpreted, it can drive people to violence and war. Unfortunately, the Bible, especially the Old Testament has been used to support Israeli injustice, the confiscation of Palestinian land, and their ethnic cleansing. It was clear to me from the beginning of my journey for a theology of liberation that the movement in the content of the biblical books as arranged, moves largely from a tribal and exclusive understanding of God to a gradual inclusive and more universal understanding. Although one can find the universal breaking through the tribal in some of the material, it took hundreds of years and the impact of political events to induce the emergence of the more inclusive concepts (Ateek 1989, 92–102; 2008, 53–56, 67–77).

In such a movement, and due to the propensity of human nature, it is easy for people of every century to mistake the tribal and exclusive as the authentic message of the Bible. This tension between the tribal and universal continues to affect us today. I have tried to show that in my understanding of the Bible, God has always been the loving and inclusive God, but people's understanding of God had to develop and mature over many centuries. This is due to the basic fact that people expressed their faith in God in accordance with their limited knowledge of God and the world around them. Therefore, the movement from exclusiveness to inclusiveness has been very slow.

As an example, I have used the story of the fall of Jericho (Joshua 6). According to the text, it is God who gives the injunction to Joshua to "utterly destroy all in the city, both men and women, young and old, oxen, sheep, and asses, with the edge of the sword" (6:21).

"Is such a passage, which is attributed to God, consistent with how God is revealed in Jesus Christ? If not, we must say that it only reveals a human understanding of God's nature and purpose that was superseded or corrected by the revelation in Christ. In other words, such passages are revelatory of a stage of development of the human understanding of God that we must regard, in light of Christ's revelation, as inadequate and incomplete." (Ateek 1989, 83) Such passages have been used by Jewish militants to call for the annihilation of the Palestinians. Rabbi Israel Hess of Bar Ilan University stated bluntly in an article that the extermination of the Palestinians is mandated by the Torah (Ateek 1989, 85).

The Nationalist Strands vs. the Prophetic Strands

Similarly, it has been clear to me that after the Exile, one can detect the emergence of three strands that can generally be described as nationalist, law oriented, and prophetic. By the time of Christ, these strands become more pronounced in society. The nationalist strand reflected the human tendency to use the armed struggle and even go to war to defend one's own. While this strand continued to develop and expand until it led to the disaster of AD 70 and the destruction of Jerusalem by the Romans, there was another strand which emphasized faithfulness to God through observance of the law. At the same time, there was a prophetic strand that was developing emphasizing God's concern for justice and truth as well as concern for the poor and the marginalized in society.

Although the Jewish community decided to abandon the nationalist strand after the second Jewish revolt, I have interpreted the rise of the Zionist movement at the end of the 19th century as a return to the military and nationalist option. The Zionists were ready to use military force to displace the indigenous people of Palestine. The descendants of the Pharisees that emphasized loyalty to Torah developed what later became known as Rabbinic Judaism. Some of those have remained staunch anti-Zionists while others walked the way of Zionism and became strong supporters of the state of Israel (Ateek 1989, 92–100).

I believe that the prophetic tradition was picked up by Jesus who tried repeatedly to draw attention to the essence of the prophetic tradition, "Woe to you, scribes and Pharisees, hypocrites! For you tithe mint and dill and cumin, and have neglected the weightier matters of the law, justice and mercy and faith; these you ought to have done, without neglecting the others" (Matthew 23:23) (Ateek 1989, 97). This prophetic tradition was picked up by the Church, although at times it strayed from Jesus' message; and many Christian leaders are unwilling today to lift up their prophetic voice against the injustice and oppression of Israel's illegal occupation of the Palestinian territories.

Today, the prophetic ministry of the church should still be one of its greatest priorities (Ateek 1989, 71–73).

Bible and Land

One of the most important aspects of the conflict over Palestine has to do with the theology of land. In fact, if one is looking at the conflict from its religious perspective, the theology of land constitutes the heart of the conflict. Land theology stands at the center of a Palestinian liberation theology. Although I have written much about this topic, I feel I am still barely scratching the surface.

One of the basic biblical and theological texts comes from the Torah itself, the most authoritative part of the Bible for religious, especially Orthodox Jews. The land belongs to God and the people are only strangers entrusted with the land by God: "The land shall not be sold in perpetuity, for the land is mine; for you are strangers and sojourners with me" (Leviticus 25:23) (Ateek 1989, 103–9; 2008, 51–66). Although this theological principle is foundational and carries with it the principle of stewardship and responsibility before God, it has been interpreted by Jewish religious Zionists as well as Christian Zionists (Ateek, Duaybis, and Tobin 2005) in a very narrow, exclusive, and particular way to mean the Jewish people alone. This is a good example of how a broad theological principle can be abused through arrogance and ignorance. In primitive times and in various parts of the world, people believed that the land belonged to the god/gods who in turn entrusted it to the king or the tribe/people. This same view is expressed when God commands the ancient Israelites not to encroach on the land of Edom, Moab, and Ammon because God had already allotted it to their distant relatives (Deuteronomy 2:1–23).

In today's world, Leviticus 25:23 can have a deeper and broader theological implication. The land of Palestine/Israel can be seen as a symbol or a paradigm for the whole world. The whole world belongs to God and every nation is entrusted by God to care for the land given to it. The land must not be defiled or polluted by injustice otherwise it will thrust its inhabitants out (Ateek 1989, 105–9; Ateek and Prior 1999, xi–xv).

The book of Jonah offers us another important example. Written towards the end of the Old Testament period, the writer critiques three exclusive popular theologies of his day, namely, the theology of God, people of God, and land. Jonah makes clear that God is the God of the whole world and has never restricted God's activities to the people of Israel alone. Moreover, God is the God of love who loves all people and cares for all, even the Assyrians who were perceived as the worst enemies. The prophet Amos, several hundred years before the book of Jonah was written, had said, "Are you not like the Ethiopians to me, O people of Israel? says the Lord. Did I not bring Israel up from the land of Egypt, and the Philistines from Caphtor and the Arameans from Kir?" (Amos 9:7). Furthermore, God is not concerned only about the "land of Israel" but all lands including the land of the Assyrians that historically destroyed the northern kingdom of Israel in 722 BC.

The gifted author, not the prophet Jonah, uses Jonah, an Israelite prophet known for his bigotry and narrow nationalism to drive home to the reader through this allegory, God's inclusive love and care for all people and lands regardless of their race or ethnicity. "God shows no partiality to any culture or nation or race or ethnic group. God's love encompasses all of humanity, not just the people of Jonah" (Ateek 2008, 67–77).

In many ways, the New Testament theology of land follows from that of the book of Jonah. The New Testament moves beyond an exclusive theology of God, people, and land. God is the God who loves all people (John 3:16) and Jesus' ministry is not limited to Jews but is extended equally to Romans, Greeks, Samaritans, Canaanites, and others. The people of God are not limited to the offspring of Abraham, Isaac, and Jacob but extended to all those who believe (John 1:12–13). In Jesus Christ, the whole world is sanctified and God's love and mercy encompass the world.

The Way of Nonviolence

As mentioned earlier, although there are biblical texts that reflect primitive concepts of god and the violence of god, I believe that the central message of the Bible is about nonviolence and peace. I have made this point clear in all my writings because it is crucial for peace (Ateek 1989, 134–38).

It is important to point out that the early Christian community combined two messianic strands, son of David and suffering servant. The son of David strand was important for the early Christians in order to emphasize Jesus' lineage from King David in fulfillment of Old Testament prophecies; and the suffering servant strand as expressed by the prophet Isaiah. It is clear to me that although the early Christian community believed that Jesus Christ came from the lineage of David, he did not adopt David's way nor was he inspired by David's actions. Instead, Jesus walked the way of the Suffering Servant through his suffering and death on the cross. The way of King David is the way of violence and war while the way of the Suffering Servant is the way of nonviolence and peace where the person is willing to submit to suffering rather than to inflict it on others. Jesus was aware of the ideologies and theologies of the various religious and political groups of his day but he chose a different way. What then was the way of Jesus, "1) to stand for justice and truth without picking up the sword—that is, to resist evil without using evil methods; 2) to rise above the ways of the world without abandoning involvement and commitment to the poor and oppressed; 3) to seek the humanity of the oppressor without losing integrity by appeasement or collaboration; and 4) to love and worship God without adhering to a strict and closed religion" (Ateek 2008, 92–103).

Palestinian Liberation Theology rejects violence and critiques the way Christians, after the 4th century, militarized Jesus and moved into Christendom waging wars under the banner of the cross and killing people in the name of Christ. Since the establishment of the state of Israel, the Israeli government has chosen to walk the way of Christendom in their own "Jewishdom." This is the way of violence and war and can never lead to a permanent peace with security (Ateek 2008, 100–103).

Jerusalem

Although it is possible to address the question of Jerusalem from its political side, I have chosen to lift a vision for its future by the use of several biblical texts. The first two texts come from the OT. Nehemiah 2:19–20 reflects the most exclusive vision for Jerusalem, ". . .but you have no share or claim or historic right in Jerusalem." It is narrow and racist. Psalm 87 on the other hand, represents one of the most inclusive texts in Scripture.

I believe that Psalm 87 critiques the Nehemiah text and offers us a model and a vision that is worthy of Jerusalem. It presents God standing at the gate of the city and welcoming all people of the various ethnic backgrounds including some of the staunchest enemies of the ancient Israelites. All of them are welcomed as having been born in the city and are its citizens, "This one and that one were born in it." Jerusalem belongs to them all. The significance of this psalm cannot be underestimated. Jerusalem must not be the monopoly of any one country or any one religion (Ateek, Duaybis, and Shrader 1997). It is equally holy to the three monotheistic religions. It must be shared politically and religiously. Psalm 87 can inspire a vision for the sharing of Jerusalem. It is an amazing tribute to an inspired writer who hundreds of years before the coming of Christ saw the need for an inclusive approach to the city (Ateek 2008, 140–50; *Cornerstone* 2009).

POLITICAL VISION FOR THE RESOLUTION OF THE CONFLICT

Palestinian Liberation Theology does not separate the religious from the political. I have always held that we live our life in its comprehensiveness under God. Our life cannot be easily compartmentalized. We are accountable to God in all that we say and do in all aspects of our lives, the political, religious, social, and economic. Life must be lived in faith, and our love of God and neighbor must govern our actions.

How do we see the future of the conflict and the prospects for peace?

THE GENEROUS OFFER OF THE PALESTINIANS:

As we come to the vision for the resolution of the conflict, it is important to point out that since 2002 the Arab league including the Palestinian Authority have introduced a proposal for the resolution of the conflict on the basis of UN Security Council Resolutions. It accepts Israel on over 75 percent of the area of historic Palestine and makes peace treaties with it, provided the government of Israel withdraws to the 1967 borders and allows the establishment of a Palestinian state on the remaining 22 percent of Palestine. Although the Arab league proposal is very generous, Israel did not even consider it because, in essence, it curbs Israel's greed of attaining the vision of a much expanded Zionist dream. This proposal is based on the demands of international law but the international community of nations has lacked the will to enforce such a solution. Yet long before the generous offer of the Arab League, the Palestinians have been stretching out their hands for peace on the basis of the principles of international law.

Since the articulation of a Palestinian Theology of Liberation, Sabeel has made it clear that the one-state solution is the ideal for our small country, one democratic state that gives all of its citizens equal rights and demands equal responsibilities of Jewish, Muslim, and Christian citizens (Ateek 1989, 165).

Although this is the ideal one-state solution, Sabeel has been promoting the two-state solution in accordance with the demands of international law. When *Justice and Only Justice* was published in 1989, the government of Israel was against the two-state solution. In fact, Israel was practically creating a one-state on the ground under its powerful military, taking advantage of the weakness of the Palestinians and the impotence of the Arab states and the international community. Only in the last two years did the government of Israel begin to talk about a two-state solution, not in accordance with UN resolutions but in accordance with what the government has been carving through its settlement building and the erection of its Separation Wall. In other words, Israel's vision of a two state cannot satisfy the demands of international justice, nor the Palestinian vision for peace. However, in the absence of an international will and the weakness of the American administration, Israel has managed to freeze the international community into inaction while it continues its settlement building and devours Palestinian land.

The two-state solution can still be salvaged but only if the borders of the Palestinian state are those of 1967 as a minimum. This means that any border adjustments must be in favor of the Palestinian state. I have also boldly proposed that, in principle, there should be no objection to allow those Jewish settlers that are willing to live in peace under a Palestinian state to stay and become Palestinian citizens. Jerusalem must be shared and a just solution for the refugees, in accordance with international law, must be found (Ateek 2008, 165–77). Peace based on justice is a realistic possibility if the government of Israel shows willingness to respect and implement the demands of international law rather than impose its own will.

Finally, Palestinian Liberation Theology does not stop with the doing of justice nor with the achievement of peace. It must work for the achievement of reconciliation and forgiveness. There are many people on both sides that are ready to do justice and to be reconciled together in peaceful living (Ateek 2008, 178–87).

KEY THEMES OF PALESTINIAN LIBERATION THEOLOGY IN 2011

There are four prominent themes that have been pursued in the development of Palestinian Liberation Theology. Two are recurring themes and two are new ones.

The recurring themes have to do with the use and abuse of the Bible. Due to ignorance and misinterpretation, we must continue to address any biblical abuse, critiquing exclusive theologies, and emphasizing inclusive theologies of God, people of God, and land; as well as the biblical teaching on justice, peace, and nonviolence. Besides continuing to develop a viable theology of liberation, we have a responsibility to address the liberation of much of the antiquated theologies which our churches have developed or inherited over the last 2000 years (Ateek 2008, 11–14).

A second theme must be the strengthening of the nonviolent resistance movement in Israel-Palestine and the world, especially among people of faith including Muslim and Jewish peace activists. At the same time, we must continue to awaken the consciousness of mainline church members in the West to their responsibility in resisting the evil of occupation and working for a just peace (Ateek 2008, 78–91).

The two newer themes deal with the question of empire which touches on the political and theological aspect of the conflict. (Ateek 2008, 113–14, 148–49) In addressing this, it is clear that it is important to be aware of the place of Israel as an extension of the American Empire. The question of Empire is crucial to peace. It is hoped that Sabeel's 8th international conference, February 23–28, 2011 with its theme, "Challenging Empire: God, Faithfulness, and Resistance" will provide a clearer agenda for pursuing this topic.

Finally, Sabeel needs to strengthen its relationship with the Muslim community especially in the interfaith program that brings together Christian and Muslim clerics. Sadly, many people fear the increasing influence of religious extremists in the Middle East. Islam has been cast as the enemy of the western world and the enemy of freedom and liberation. Islamophobia is a phenomenon that must be addressed. Sabeel has a role to play in tackling the local Christian-Muslim agenda as well as the international one. As Christian Palestinians, we have a responsibility to work with our Muslim brothers and sisters in presenting the true face of Islam. At the same time, we need to work together against extremist Islamists that damage the good relations between our two religions and mar the face of their own religion.

These are key themes that must be dealt with. They touch on politics and religion. At the same time, they are so huge in magnitude that it is difficult to know how best to tackle them in a way that can make a positive difference in our world today. We realize that for empire to exist, it needs an enemy. Unfortunately, Islam has been given that role. There is a great need for Palestinian Muslims and Christians to work together to change western perceptions of both Islam as well as Eastern Christianity (Ateek, Duaybis, and Tobin 2007, 210–20).

IMPACT OF SABEEL

An assessment of the impact of the work and ministry of Sabeel must be left to others, local and international, who have been touched by its ministry and involved in its activities. Such an assessment carries far greater weight and credit than anything produced by "Sabeelers" who can be accused of pretense and exaggeration. Be that as it may, it is possible to say that Sabeel, during its almost twenty years of existence, has made a modest but genuine contribution in the three areas of its work.

Ecumenically, it has transcended denominationalism and brought many Christians of various denominations closer together thus breaking down historical barriers, prejudices, and alienations. Sabeel has provided forums locally and internationally for new biblical and theological reflections and discussions, thus restoring faith and hope for many. Ecumenically, Sabeel has also enhanced women's empowerment and leadership through their active participation in biblical and theological discussions. Sabeel continues to probe, critique, and promote the best in the culture and faith of Palestinians. It is possible to say that Sabeel has earned the respect of many people in the Palestinian community and its presence and contribution are felt and real.

Sabeel's branch in Nazareth has had a similar impact in Galilee especially on the level of ecumenical relations bringing Christians closer together. Sabeel promotes equal democracy for all the citizens of the state of Israel—Jews and Arabs—and stands against discrimination. Through joint programs between the Jerusalem and Nazareth branches, Sabeel connects the different communities together reducing isolationism and building their sense of identity and self-confidence.

In this field of ecumenism, Sabeel has only scratched the surface. We are only at the beginning of a long journey.

In Christian-Muslim relations, Sabeel has been successful in cultivating understanding, respect, and acceptance between Christian and Muslim clerics leading to more fruitful relations. There are genuine possibilities for continued cooperation that can bring the two communities closer together and address sporadic communal problems.

Again, in this field of inter-faith or "life together" as Sabeel calls it, we have barely scratched the surface. We are only at the beginning of a long journey.

On the justice and peace level, hundreds of groups come to visit Sabeel Jerusalem and Nazareth every year to learn about the Christian community of the land as well as the prospects for a just peace. This is in addition to the ongoing work of Friends of Sabeel in various areas of the world that carry on a fruitful work of educating people about the origin and ramifications of the Palestine-Israel conflict and witness to the increasing number of Christians, Muslims, and Jews, locally and internationally that have become advocates for a just peace based on non-violence and the demands of international law. As an example, Friends of Sabeel in the United States have conducted 32 regional conferences over the last seven years with thousands of people participating. Today, Sabeel has clusters of Friends in eleven countries around the world with local leadership that are working as volunteers. Furthermore, Sabeel has organized eight international conferences in Jerusalem, Bethlehem, and Nazareth with hundreds of participants from around the world dealing with cutting-edge themes that relate to justice and peacemaking. At the same time, Sabeel has circulated statements and messages on a regular basis that deal with theology and politics. One of the important actions is the sending of the "Wave of Prayer" every week to all our friends around the world asking them to pray with us at noon every Thursday when the Sabeel staff and friends join together in their weekly worship in Jerusalem. The "Wave of Prayer" contains the burning issues that we need to lift up to God. The impact of the wave of prayer cannot be underestimated.

In this area, we will continue to labor with God and all people of good-will until justice, peace, and reconciliation are achieved for all the inhabitants of our land—Palestine and Israel. Indeed, Sabeel's ministry has touched the minds and hearts of many people.

Sabeel continues to provide a response to theological justifications for the Zionist claim to the land of Palestine. Through lectures, workshops, and publications in Arabic and English, Sabeel has provided a forum for clergy and laypeople to engage in active reflections and discussions; thus connecting people's faith with the reality of their daily lives.

Sabeel will continue to be a movement that "encourages individuals and groups from around the world [and especially in Palestine and Israel] to work for a just, comprehensive, and enduring peace informed by truth and empowered by prayer and action" (Sabeel Purpose Statement, footnote 1).

References

Ateek, Naim S. 1989. *Justice & Only Justice: A Palestinian Theology of Liberation.* Maryknoll, New York: Orbis.

————. 2008. *A Palestinian Christian Cry for Reconciliation.* Maryknoll, New York: Orbis.

Ateek, Naim, Cedar Duaybis, and Marla Schrader, eds. 1997. *Jerusalem: What Makes For Peace! A Palestinian Christian Contribution to Peacemaking.* London: Melisende.

Ateek, Naim S., Cedar Duaybis, and Maurine Tobin, eds. 2005 *Challenging Christian Zionism: Theology, Politics and the Israel-Palestine Conflict* London: Melisende.

————. 2007. *The Forgotten Faithful: A Window into the Life and Witness of Christians in the Holy Land.* Jerusalem: Sabeel Ecumenical Liberation Theology Center.

Ateek, Naim S., Marc H. Ellis, and Rosemary Radford Ruether, eds. 1992. *Faith and the Intifada: Palestinian Christian Voices.* Maryknoll, New York: Orbis.

Ateek, Naim, and Michael Prior, eds. 1999. *Holy Land—Hollow Jubilee: God, Justice and the Palestinians.* London: Melisende.

Cornerstone (A Quarterly Publication by Sabeel Ecumenical Liberation Theology Center) 55. 2009. *Jerusalem: the Heart of the Conflict.*

Kairos Palestine. 2009. *Kairos Palestine: A word of faith, hope, and love from the heart of Palestinian Suffering.* http://www.kairospalestine.ps./

Sabeel Documents. 2004. *The Jerusalem Sabeel Document: Principles for a Just Peace.*

————. 2005. *Morally Responsible Investment: A Nonviolent Response to the Occupation.*

3

Theologies of Liberation in Palestine-Israel and the Struggle for Peace and Justice

Prof. Marc H. Ellis

Does the Birth of a Jewish and Palestinian Theology of Liberation have anything to Say about the Future of Israel-Palestine?

For many years I have been writing on the question of theologies of liberation in Palestine-Israel. This began with my own forays into a Jewish theology of liberation, my first article on the subject appearing in 1984, and coming to fruition in my book *Toward a Jewish Theology of Liberation* in 1987. Independent of my work and knowledge, Naim Ateek's Palestinian theology of liberation was also being written during this same time period. Ateek's Doctor of Ministry thesis on a Palestinian theology of liberation was presented for approval in 1985, with its publication under the title of *Justice and Only Justice: A Palestinian Theology of Liberation* appearing in 1989. Over the decades, our books have often been discussed and linked together, both by those who applaud our efforts and those who denigrate them (Ellis 1987; Ateek 1989).

Unbeknownst to most of our supporters and detractors, the link between a Jewish and Palestinian theology of liberation is actually much closer than assumed. Though written independent of each other, Naim

39

and I have had a personal bond in relation to these theologies that is unusually close and perhaps, because of the time in which it formed, unique. This bond makes a Jewish and Palestinian theology of liberation so close as to be a disturbing to some and for others a hopeful sign to the world.

In some ways, Naim and I have journeyed together. This journey combines an intellectual, spiritual and personal learning process that seems almost antiquated by today's standards. Yet I believe it makes the lessons we learned relevant to time periods beyond our own. Though the optimism of our theologies of liberation seems distant today, it may be time to once again broach the possibility of justice, reconciliation found in the pages of both books. Having come full circle, Jews and Palestinians have reached the point where only beginning again makes sense. Of course, it also may be too late. The pages of a Jewish and Palestinian theology of liberation may attest to both options—that we have to begin again—that it may indeed be too late.

Let me begin with the story of our bonding. It was in May, 1987 that I first met Naim Ateek. I was touring Jerusalem and was asked to give several lectures on the subject of a Jewish theology of liberation. I was an unknown quantity but a Jewish Israeli (born in America), Yehezkel Landau, had visited me at Maryknoll during his own tour of the United States in the summer of 1986 and asked me to come to Israel to visit with him and see the work that he and his fellows were doing to advance peace between Jews and Palestinians in Israel. I had been to Israel twice before, in 1973 and 1984, and both visits occasioned a questioning of my Jewish identity and the place of Israel in that identity. Coming from the perspective of Holocaust Theology, a theology that I studied with my teacher, Richard Rubenstein as it was being born in the 1970s, by the 1980s the linking of the Holocaust and Israel was firmly in place. Yet in my visits to Israel—and my experience of meeting with Palestinians in the West Bank and Gaza—I realized that binding the Holocaust and Israel was deeply problematic. Or, perhaps more accurately, that such binding was leading Jewish Israelis and Jews around the world into the darkest of corners. Could we as Jews emerge from our own dark corner of the universe, the Holocaust, and in pursuit of our own liberation push others into their dark corner of the universe, the ongoing *Nakba* (Ellis 1990)?

Today we know the answer—the answer was no doubt already known by Palestinians—but in my own life it was only emerging as a question. In the years since my second visit to Israel, I struggled to discover my own voice of Jewish dissent. Today, Jewish dissent is widely disseminated but during the 1980s it was hidden in public and certainly confined to dark corridors within the Jewish community. Today a significant number of Jews of Conscience have visited Israel *and* Palestine, traveled among Palestinians and know Palestinians as friends and as comrades in arms. In 1984 when I first went among Palestinians in the West Bank and Gaza, the only Jews who most Palestinians had "met" were Israeli soldiers displacing them and occupying their land. Because of this lack of critical thought and contact, there was little guidance for me as a Jew as to what I should think when, for instance, I sat in the homes of Palestinian families who had lost their children to bullets shot by Israeli soldiers. In refugee camps in the West Bank and most poignantly in Gaza, the framed pictures of the young "martyrs" cried out to me as I sat with Palestinian families in their homes. As an American Jew, whose grandparents were European, what was I to do with the history we had created?

It was in this crisis of history and identity that I first met Naim and came in to contact with a Palestinian theology of liberation. As I was touring with Yehezkel Landau, I noticed that with every Palestinian we met, he negotiated historical injustices and rights, essentially trying to trade Israel's legitimacy for some confession of Palestinian intransigence towards Israel and Jews in general. Landau's negotiating stance seemed silly, trivializing both Jewish and Palestinian history and, of course, the interaction between them. Without being able to name it at the time, I was encountering what I would later name as a "progressive" Jewish understanding of the Israeli-Palestinian conflict. In the years ahead this Progressive Jewish stance would be dramatized by Michael Lerner and his new glossy journal, *Tikkun*. I felt disgusted by these views. Already in Jerusalem I began to distance myself from these views and from Jews that held and promulgated them (Lerner 2003).

My lecture had been scheduled for the Shalom Hartman Institute, a bastion of Progressive Jewish thinking at the time. Headed by a modern Orthodox Jew from America, David Hartman, I was dimly aware of his writing and more aware that he was a constant source for *New York Times* reporters. He was also a key figure in the modern interfaith encounter of Jews and Christians, which was seen then as it is now, as revolving around Western Jews and Christians, Israeli Jews being counted as Western. Later I would write of the Jewish-Christian dialogue as the interfaith ecumenical deal, a deal that needed to be broken, but that was in the future. The main aspect of the Jewish-Christian dialogue turned deal was that the central meeting point of both communities was the affirmation of Christian responsibility for centuries of anti-Semitism that led to the Holocaust and the unquestioned affirmation of Israel as the proper, even providential, Jewish *and* Christian response to the Holocaust. Any criticism of Israeli policies toward Palestinians on the Christian side was and even today is seen as anti-Semitism. On the Jewish side, such criticism is seen as evidence of Jewish self-hate (Hartman 2000).

Unbeknownst to me, Hartman was oblivious to my lecture and when I met him the day before he showed no sign of knowing who I was. Nor did he seem to care. Clearly he was not planning to attend my lecture. Perhaps the title—"Toward a Jewish Theology of Liberation"—was too much for him. After all, in our brief conversation, the tone he took was that he was the expert on all things Jewish. Who was I to lead a charge that went beyond and perhaps even contradicted his well-connected thought and international standing?

Naim wasn't coming to my lecture either or so he had made it known. I was to speak on a Jewish theology of liberation, my completed but as yet unpublished book, and several people around Naim, who met me during the days leading up the lecture or who had read parts of the book in galley form, asked him to be one of the panelists. He refused. Ateek was tired of "liberal" Israeli Jews like Yehezkel Landau who spoke out of both sides of their mouth. He was hardly in the mood for an American Jew of the same persuasion.

Trying to convince Ateek that I was different was of no avail. Nonetheless, he was intrigued by the possibility. Naim decided to attend the session at the Shalom Hartman Institute, which was unaccountably packed out. Since I was unknown to the general public, I could not understand the reason for the overflow crowd. In the packed auditorium, there were only a few Palestinians in attendance. One, who had agreed to respond to me, was Elias Chacour, a Melkite Greek Catholic priest. The other was Naim. Chacour sat next to me at the table from which we spoke. Naim was in the audience. An Anglican priest, he stood out as he wore his priestly attire. As I began to speak, I wondered who the Anglican clergyman was (Chacour 2003).

My lecture was short, perhaps twenty minutes or so. The three panelists were held to ten minutes each. Along with Chacour, the panelists included an American rabbi, who emigrated to Israel and several years after the event left Israel, and the noted Jewish ethicist, Michael Walzer, who was so upset with my views that his hands shook almost uncontrollably as he spoke. With the introduction and seating time for the large gathering, the prepared presentations covered most of an hour. However, the session was so heated that with a few breaks, the session lasted more than three hours. I remember thinking of the tension in the room and the feeling that something was about to explode. Months later, in December 1987, the Palestinian intifada began.

After the evening ended, I was introduced to Naim. He graciously extended an invitation for dinner at his home the next night. Unbeknownst to me, Naim was more than a priest. He was a Canon of St. George's Cathedral that housed the Anglican Bishop of Jerusalem. After a delightful dinner, Naim went to his closest and brought out a manuscript in a familiar-looking Kinko's box. Inside was his dissertation he had completed a few years earlier at San Francisco Theological Seminary. He asked me if I would take the copy and read it before I left Jerusalem. Perhaps then we could have a discussion about the manuscript before I returned to the United States. As I nodded my head, I read the title. It was his first attempt at writing a Palestinian Theology of Liberation.

Encountering (each) Other

Several days later I left Jerusalem with Naim's thesis in hand. I did read the thesis, in one sitting and late into the night, and agreed to take the thesis back to the Maryknoll School of Theology, where I taught and was the founding director of the Institute for Justice and Peace Studies. Maryknoll, the Catholic Foreign Mission Society of America, is popularly known as Maryknoll because its center in upstate New York is located on a knoll and the community venerates Mary. Since its founding at the turn of the 20th century, Maryknoll, as a traditional Catholic missionary society, understood its mission as converting pagans to Christianity. In the 1960s, Maryknoll underwent its own conversion toward the poor and the marginal and soon became the leading publisher of liberation theology in the world through its publishing arm, Orbis. Although I taught full-time at Maryknoll's School of Theology, I also did editorial work at Orbis which was just publishing my own Jewish theology of liberation.

When I left for Jerusalem, Orbis had just undergone a major change in personnel. The incoming director was unfamiliar with liberation theology and, as I soon found it, politically moderate, if not conservative on most issues. When I first discussed Palestinians, he was unsympathetic toward the Palestinian cause, mostly equating Palestinians with acts of terror and largely seeing Israel as innocent. I promised Naim that I would convince Orbis that it should publish his manuscript. I knew that, because of Orbis' international outreach, a Palestinian theology of liberation would quickly become known in liberation circles around the world.

It was an uphill battle but in the end, Orbis agreed to publish the book, though with extensive editorial changes. I prevailed upon Orbis and Maryknoll to bring Ateek to Maryknoll and finance his stay there for six months. Soon he was at Maryknoll where he and I worked on his manuscript with help from the Orbis editorial staff. Thus we were together again, this time in upstate New York, at one of the most significant, difficult and hopeful times in the history of the Israeli-Palestinian conflict. Much had transpired since Naim and I had met just months earlier. It was 1988. The Palestinian uprising was in full swing.

The tension surrounding the Israeli-Palestinian crisis was palpable. The uprising set forth movements among Palestinians and Jews inside and outside of Israel that some days brought utter despair and, other days, elated hopes. Meanwhile, the causalities among Palestinians were many and increased daily. Thousands of Palestinians were imprisoned. Pronouncements of hopes for justice and peace alternated with Israeli violence that shook even the most conservative parts of world Jewry. Now was the time to take sides—on each side. Was it the appropriate season to spend time editing a manuscript that, though implicitly political, concentrated on the theological aspects of the Christian tradition?

Naim and I were on a learning curve. For the most part, Naim studied liberation theology from afar and from books, whereas I traveled with Maryknoll to Asia, Africa and Latin America. Though Naim studied in the United States, his experience of the world was limited. Now he was at Maryknoll, a global crossroads where missionaries and those from the Third World were now speaking for themselves. The world I had lived in for almost a decade was new to Naim. Not only was liberation theology a declaration of freedom for those who had been colonized by Western powers and a dominant European Christianity, liberation theologians were asking profound questions of identity and self-identification. Was Christianity a way of liberation for themselves and their people? Could the oppressive Christianity they inherited be inverted, turned around, almost reinvented, so as to a force of liberation within the confines of their thoroughly colonized Christian institutions?

The world of Latin America liberation theology, the most dominant of the liberation theological regions, was a different world than Naim experienced in Palestine. As a minority religion within a broader and powerful Muslim Palestinian majority and region, Naim's Christianity was necessarily a defensive one. The role of the ancient and contemporary Jews in Latin American liberation theology was also different. Liberation theologians held up the Exodus as the powerful prophetic holy event that freed the prophetic Jesus from a Greco-Roman Jesus who favored the earthly status quo and a heavenly reward for the oppressed. Liberation theologians also saw the Holocaust as a wake-up call for the oppressed Christians of the world to free themselves from the dominating and violent excesses of European Christianity. Though complicated in its articulation, a renewed appreciation of ancient and contemporary Judaism in the context of Jewish history was crucial to origins of liberation theology.

Naim was in a completely different situation, as a Christian leader trying to navigate his own faith community between a dominant Islam and an empowered Jewish community that displaced him, his family and his people. Thus Naim had more to deal with then his own limitations of travel and theological exposure. He was in the middle of a positive revolutionary movement within Christianity that sought to come to grips with its progenitor and eternal Other. This came at a time when Naim and his people were being ethnically cleansed from Palestine by the very same people that liberation theology sought to reconcile with.

Entering the Western Christian discussion of faith and politics from the Middle East, Naim sought Christian partners whose understanding of Christian theology and Christology itself had undergone a vast transformation in light of European—and Christian—colonialism. Understandably, the anti-Semitism that led to the Holocaust and by extension to the founding of the state of Israel that had displaced him, his family and his people, was of less interest or, in another way, of more interest to Naim but form a very different angle of vision. It was difficult for Ateek to understand how Christians in the West could identify with Jews and Israel, an identification that at times overshadowed their solidarity with Palestinian Christians as brothers in Christ.

I witnessed this difficulty in my discussions with Naim and, later, with other Palestinian Christians. For Naim, the great divide was this Western Christian identification with the history of Europe's Jews and an increasingly dynamic embrace of the Jewish roots and continuing Jewishness of Christianity. Identifying Jesus as a Jew was exceptionally emotionally charged. When I first read through of Naim's manuscript in Jerusalem, I noticed his discussion of Jesus as a Palestinian who lived under occupation. True enough. But wasn't Jesus living under occupation precisely because he was a Jew? As well, Western Christian identification with the Holocaust—and thus with Israel—stuck in the throat of Palestinian Christians who were struggling to be free of the use of the Holocaust to justify violence against Palestinian life and land. With his fellow Palestinian Christians, Naim asked why Christians in the West lived in the Jewish-Christian past at the expense of Palestinian Christian life in the present (Ateek, Ellis, and Ruether, 1992).

Naim's experience of Palestine was confined mostly to Israel. As an Israeli Arab—the way he identified himself when I began working with him—he found it difficult, if not impossible, to travel to the West Bank. When he became known for his Palestinian theology of liberation, people meeting him were surprised when they learned he had never traveled to Gaza. It was only years after he published his Palestinian theology of liberation that Naim was able to travel to Gaza. At that time as well, there was often a deep divide, even suspicion, between those Palestinians who remained within Israel after the creation of the state and those who were forcibly removed from the Israel and lived under Jordanian rule and Israeli occupation. Naim experienced these complexities within himself. Thus the first chapter of his *Justice and Only Justice* was a much changed and difficult journey through his own internal political and religious landscape as a Christian, a Palestinian, an Arab and an Israeli. Naim titles that chapter "Encounter" with a subheading, "Who Am I?" (Ateek 1996, 7–17).

Ostensibly a way to introduce the reader to the complexities of Palestinian life under the shadow of Israel's occupation, Naim was encountering himself. Where did his true loyalties lie? Who, in fact, was this Palestinian theologian of liberation? I witnessed an anxiety in his writing and even more so as we wrestled together with the ideas in the manuscript. Of course, the Palestinian uprising itself caused a further wrestling than the one that would have been occurred in the circumstances of bringing these ideas into the public realm. If the future relationship between Jews and Palestinians was up for grabs in the Palestinian uprising, Palestinian identity was also in flux.

The same held true for me. As an American Jew, I wrote a Jewish theologian of liberation to find my voice as a Jew conflicted over the ethical trajectory of Jewish history. Like many other Jews, my received Jewish identity was being challenged. But now, intimately involved with what the Jewish community defined as the Palestinian Other, my learning curve was also developing rapidly. I was being challenged on a variety of fronts. For example, Naim's difficult words about the entire history of Zionism were new to me. They sounded harsh and condemnatory. In some passages, Naim seemed dismissive of Jewish history and life. As well, his high Christology was too strong for my taste and for my understanding of the violence of Christian history. Equally disturbing was Naim's dismissal of Judaism; if not directly, it was certainly implied that with the coming of Jesus, Judaism had ceased to be an authentic way to God.

Naim's views, and my interpretation of them, forced me to think where I was on this journey. I had brought Naim's manuscript back to be published and was now working with him so that he could place the Palestinian cause in the international theological arena. In Naim's view, was there a place for Jews there as well?

Liberation Theologies (against) the Grain

In Naim's theology of liberation, his own Palestinian experience and that of his people are privileged. His own family was displaced in the 1948 war and the hardships his family experienced are detailed in his writing. Several years later when his family returned to their village for a visit, his father was so overcome with emotion that he died of a heart attack. In privileging the experience of his own suffering people, Naim was following the general line of liberation theology where God makes a preferential option for the poor and the oppressed. Yet in a Palestinian theology of liberation, the experience of the Israelites featured in Christian theologies around the world, but now by transposition oppressing his own people, could not be privileged. For Naim, the Old Testament was trumped by the redemptive acts of Jesus the Christ. If the Palestinian struggle was seen in light of God's promise of the land to Israel, Palestinians would have to acquiesce to injustice—as part of God's will. God's preferential option for the poor and the oppressed had to be universal, without reference to the land, striking for justice, even against God's former chosen people as they were now committing injustice.

If Ateek's understanding of liberation theology was against the grain of liberation theology as it had become known, my own Jewish theology of liberation was as well. Much of the European Jewish population in previous centuries had been poor and oppressed. Certainly Jews were marginal to Christian theology or, worse, at the centre of that theology in an exceedingly negative light. The Holocaust represents a culmination of the negative place Jews held in Europe and in Christianity. Moreover, unlike Christian medieval anti-Semitism, the Holocaust was a contemporary event. My father, still alive, served in World War II and ended his service in 1945–1946 in Germany. During my youth I learned about the massacre of Europe's Jews. At university, I studied with Richard Rubenstein who pioneered the theological interpretation of the Holocaust, what later became known as Holocaust Theology (Rubenstein 1966).

Holocaust Theology views the Holocaust as unique and omnipresent. Moving forward in time, it understands the state of Israel as the Jewish—and international—response to the Holocaust. More, as Jewish suffering in the Holocaust was the suffering of an oppressed and innocent people, the empowerment of Jews in the state of Israel, as the necessary response of a decimated people, is innocent as well. Anyone who opposes Jewish empowerment in Israel thereby stands in the negative light of anti-Semitism. They oppose innocence with evil. Not only are Jews innocent in their suffering and empowerment, the state of Israel, at least by Jews, is increasingly seen as redemptive of the Holocaust. The Holocaust and Israel are twinned as innocent suffering and empowered redemption. Who could deny this journey from Auschwitz to Jerusalem (Ellis 2011)?

In my journeys to Israel, I began to see another side of this innocence. In my daily meetings with Naim at Maryknoll, I met the other side of Jewish innocence and redemption face to face. Naim reflected for me the movement of Jews after the Holocaust, from innocence to culpability and from oppression to empowerment. It could be that Jews were except from the complexities and culpabilities of empowerment—Jewish history narrated by Jews asserted this. I began to wonder if Jewish redemption, dependent on the oppression of another people, could be our redemption.

It was becoming obvious to me as well that the defense of this narrative of innocence and redemption, the materiality of Jewish discourse, was increasingly dependent on the use of worldly, specifically American, power. Placing the identifier, Jewish, before a state, as in a "Jewish state," could not remove the imperatives of statecraft, military readiness, a national economy and so forth. Israel was armed to the teeth and often used its military to further its national expansionist objectives. It also exported armaments and entered into military alliances with dictatorial regimes in South Africa and Latin America.

In America, the Jewish establishment was silent about this and other aspects of Israeli foreign and domestic policies. It actively discouraged and tried to censor any aspect of Israeli behavior that ran against the narrative of innocence and redemption. Instead, it promulgated the Holocaust narrative as counter to the Palestinian narrative. It was as if the Palestinians were the perpetrators of the Holocaust or the progenitors of the next Holocaust. In some Jewish quarters, the Palestinians were seen and named as new Nazis (Black 2010).

Coming from a suffering people—historically—Jews in Israel and America were now empowered. The question of liberation for me was then inverted or subverted, calling upon our ancient slave past in the Exodus and asking today what liberation might mean in our empowered position. Surely we could not return to our previous European Diaspora situation as a dispersed often despised minority population among majority and often anti-Semitic cultures. Then again, embarking on a project of displacement after the Holocaust, then continuing it as an empowered state, creating refugee populations and occupying a people, could this be a future for an ethically centered, previously suffering people?

The refusal to admit what we as Jews had done in Israel simply made our empowerment even more suspect. The point I thought was to pause and come to grips with the history of both the Holocaust and Israel in a compassionate and self-critical way. Recognizing the exigencies of Jewish history at the time of the creation of the state of Israel but also recognizing the culpability of the formation of the state, could help Jews critically evaluate the limitations of Jewish empowerment. We could ask whether our new-found power had in fact liberated us, if Israel was our redemption and if Israeli power with the support of the American Jewish establishment had healed Jews of the wounds of the Holocaust. In my Jewish theology of liberation I wondered if our wounding of the Palestinians—and our clinging to narrative of innocence and redemption—had actually deepened our wounds, made it more difficult to heal, and in general had backed us into a place of power for power's sake that promised an endless militarization of the Jewish psyche and Jewish life in general.

So Naim and I moved against the grain of liberation theology as received wisdom, he in the Biblical realm of a chosen Israel promised the land, and me raising the question of a recently suffering and now empowered people. As liberation theology sought to free theology from its own captivity and recover the Jewish Jesus in his prophetic trajectory, Naim desperately held to a high Christology to deflect the recovery of the Old Testament narrative as it privileged the people Israel and its journey to Biblical empowerment. As Edward Said pointed out, in the Old

Testament narrative transported into the present, the Palestinians could only be seen as the Canaanites, thus resistors to the promise.

Though Said, as a secular thinker, held high this designation as a resistor to the conquering empire, Ateek and his fellow Christians narrated that same Jewish religious history as sacred to Christians as well. Palestinian Christians also had to deal with the Church's liturgical cycle, following Israel's path through the desert, applauding their entry into the land and the ethnic cleansing of indigenous people whom some contemporary Jews identified as Palestinians. If Palestinians accepted that identification they had to accept their displacement. If they refused that identification, how could Palestinian Christians define their own Christianity to themselves and in relation to Christians around the world, who were recovering in a celebratory manner their Jewish roots (Ateek 2008).

I was caught in the crossfire of Jewish life to be sure but also in this interfaith movement that I celebrated. Surely, the trajectory of Jewish life had to be opposed and subverted. Conquering another people after our history of suffering was akin to moral suicide. On the practical level, a constantly expanding Israel endangered Jewish lives. Because of its actions in the Middle East, Israel was encouraging exactly what Jewish authorities warned against—another Holocaust. I felt that there had to be a way for Jews to live in the Middle East and the world in a mutually and interconnected empowerment. Jews, as other peoples, could not survive without some form of power. But Jews as a minority population in different regions of the world could not survive as a one-off empire connected only to the United States. Israel had become an empire in the Middle East and was increasingly dependent on the United States, itself a global empire.

What Israel needed was integration into the Middle East and acceptance there. Israeli Jews needed that integration/acceptance. So did Jews in America. Yet as I encountered Naim, I wondered whether that integration/acceptance was feared by Israeli and American Jews. As Jews, at least theologically, we believed we were chosen and set apart as a people. It began to dawn on me that the Holocaust and the state of Israel might be a modern incarnation of this ancient sensibility. Without being set apart in the Holocaust and the state of Israel, the *raison d'être* of Jewish life might dissipate.

Reviewing the Turbulent Halcyon Days

Looking back on my initial encounters with Naim, I find it difficult to translate my feelings as if our encounter was only in the past. I continue to face the question as to what I learned from this encounter and the years subsequent to it. Or rather what have we—Naim and I, Jews and Palestinians—learned?

Since the expansion of the state of Israel continues unabated and the Palestine *Nakba* continues, was this encounter of an unknown Jew and Palestinian worth the time and energy we both brought to it? Has it been worth the thousands of miles traveled since, the applause and denigration we have both received? The situation continues to worsen on the ground for Palestinians. The exile of Jews of Conscience deepens. Does this encounter and our subsequent failure to right the political situation in Israel-Palestine mean that a Jewish and Palestinian theology of liberation was misguided and so inadequate as to be part of the problem rather than the solution? Or are there parts of both theologies that have stood the test of time and could be reconfigured for a future that seems so distant as to be pie in the sky? One day, when the time becomes ripe, could elements of a Jewish and Palestinian theology of liberation might help both peoples choose another path. Could the recent democratic uprisings in the Arab world be this moment?

For sure, the turbulent halcyon days of the first Palestinian uprising are behind us. I use that seemingly contradictory word combination, "turbulent halcyon," because the years, 1987–1993, were ones when great suffering also held out great hope. The hope was the possibility of a Two State solution with more to come over the years. This hope has been dashed. Whatever one's perspective on the Two State/One State resolution of the Israeli-Palestinian conflict, there is no denying that the first Palestinian uprising held out hope for both peoples achieving some kind of ordinary life that could, over time, become a flourishing of both peoples. At least that was the vision of a Palestinian and Jewish theology of liberation. The point here is that though so many issues remained unresolved, the ground of a negotiated settlement would allow further consideration of the political issues—for example, Palestinians refugees and Jerusalem—and other cultural and religious issues—for example, Israel becoming more culturally Middle Eastern and the demobilization of Christianity, Islam and Judaism. Demilitarizing the situation and establishing some kind of ordinary life among Jews and Palestinians could lay the groundwork for a more rational and compassionate grappling with the outstanding issues that might, in the end, bring Jews and Palestinians closer together rather than driving them apart.

Naim's discussion of the need for Palestinians to engage the fact and meaning of the Holocaust and my discussion of the need for Jews to confess to the Palestinian people are two areas that still resonate in the present. So, too, is the need for Jews and Christians to engage their respective histories so as to build bridges of solidarity where division reigns. Later, but already present in embryonic form in my encounter with Naim, is my understanding of the need for Jews and Palestinians to embrace Jerusalem as the broken-middle of Israel-Palestine where two peoples broken by history can gather and create new patterns of life and solidarity. All of these issues were contested then. They are contested now. But clearly there is no way to move forward into a future different than the present without grappling with the many layers of the questions themselves.

It was my confession to the Palestinian people in Jerusalem and my insistence that Jewish leadership in Israel and America needed to make such a confession that prompted Naim's invitation to read his Palestinian theology of liberation. It was my confession that prompted to me to argue for its publication. If Jews needed to confess, Palestinians had the right to speak their own story and lay out the ground from which such a confession could take on life. Unlike the *quid pro quo* with Palestinians that Yehezkel Landau sought from the Palestinians during my journey in Jerusalem, Palestinians had to speak their pain in words of their choosing. Palestinians had to then map out their own healing. After the *Nakba*, what would it take to begin again? Could there be a partnership with Jews? What would that partnership consist of? What steps would have to be taken to reach the kind of accommodation that nourished life?

In some ways, my encounter with Naim showed that the way forward could be contested and achieved—if the will was there. Though Naim and I were generous with each other, and caring, our histories clashed in different ways. Naim was learning to negotiate the Western Christian world and trying to wean Western Christians away from what he believed was a Judaising Christianity. Though I could help him with the task of solidarity with Western Christians, I knew this would happen through their renewed question for justice rather than a shared Christian faith. It was the Holocaust itself and the complicity of Christians in anti-Semitism that led to renewal of Western Christianity—and thus solidarity with Jews—a notion, that for understandable reasons, Naim had difficulty accepting. Paradoxically, it was this renewal that eventually forced Christians to consider the plight of the Palestinians. Clearly, this complicated Christian journey was a source of conflict between Naim and me. My solidarity with the Palestinian struggle for justice could not welcome a return to pre-Holocaust Christian view of Jews.

The Holocaust and its consequences for Jewish empowerment in Israel and America remains a bitter pill for Naim to swallow and for good reason. With the mobilization of Holocaust memory in the West, the Palestinians disappeared or were declared terrorists. When Naim and I first met, suggesting that the Palestinians are a viable people with their own grievances and ethical principles, quickly raised the bogeyman of anti-Semitism. On the other hand, when Naim dealt with the Holocaust through my work, he took on a controversial issue in the Palestinian and Arab world. Citing the Holocaust as a Jewish issue that Palestinians had to take seriously was seen by some Palestinians as waiving the white flag of surrender. In the international discourse, admitting the Holocaust was assenting to Israel's right to exist. Though no one in the world knew more than Palestinians that Israel existed and would continue to do so, that existence had to be negotiated. My confession, if extended to the Jewish world, might facilitate such a negotiation but should Naim and other Palestinians show their hand first?

Though it seems old fashioned today, our underlying work together was itself controversial. Naim braved the label of "collaborator" with Zionists and Jews in general. I was accused of joining forces with an anti-Semite, risking the destruction of Israel and a turning back the clock of Jewish-Christian relations. Naim was accused of abandoning the Palestinian cause. I was accused of setting the stage for another Holocaust. This, as we sat side by side for hours, examining ideas and how to phrase them so our peoples could survive and flourish together in the future.

Our encounter, like Jews and Palestinians who came together during the first Palestinian uprising, went much deeper than the terrain we agreed and disagreed on. Perhaps for the first time, Jews and Palestinians realized that the liberation of one was dependent on the liberation of the other. That the Jews and Palestinians, while partaking of their own particularities, wasn't only their particularity. Something had happened in history. Something was happening in history. Bonds had been formed which created a Jewish-Palestinian particularity as well.

As a first step in the quest for liberation, perhaps this new particularity was most important. Certainly the bonding of many Jews and

Palestinians is on a greater scale today than ever before. I believe this to be true despite the terrible, almost catastrophic political situation of the moment. When these initial and awkward, first attempts will bear fruit I do not know. Or have they already borne fruit, fruit that waits the moment to ripen?

Our encounter also demonstrates that if an expanding terrain of mutual solidarity is established many contentious issues can be negotiated over time. If not resolved immediately through intentional actions, at least some of them might be resolved through the variegated meanderings of history. Despite its appearances, history is open. One never knows when the prophetic wild card will appear or when history will be ready to receive the seeds that have already been planted.

Is There a Future for a Jewish/Palestinian Theology of Liberation?

Tracing the arch of theologies of liberation is complex. Sometimes they seem immediately relevant, other times they seem fated as an irrelevant, though sometimes romanticized, relic from the past. Yet if and when the political scene changes, it is likely that these theologies will have something to say to the present, albeit in a somewhat altered form. On the one hand, the boldness of the early theological formations may startle the reader years after their time has passed. On the other, the ideas whose time has passed may return at a crucial moment. What is seen as irrelevant at a certain moment may be embraced as a sane alternative at another. When the problematic become so overwhelming, simplifying the playing field may be of help. Then, its perspectives rather than answers that suggest a way forward.

Looking back, both the Jewish and Palestinian theologies of liberation were naïve and limited. Naim sought to hold onto a kind of Christian witness and Christological sensibility that was damaged by its own historical culpability. His Christology was therefore fated. It was beyond repair. So, too, the sense of Jewish innocence that, even with strong confession, pervades my Jewish theology of liberation. Like Naim's Christology, my own sense of Jewish ethics was fated. It, too, was damaged beyond repair. One of crucibles of all liberation theologies is a penchant for hanging on and seeking a renewal of traditions. The thought is that with a just insurgency, if it adheres to a traditional framing, the tradition will he heard once again and adhered too. There is an inherently conservative aspect of liberation theology which neither a Jewish or Palestinian theology escapes.

Remaining within the traditional religious framework while pointing out its abuses and calling both communities back to its stated values also limited the political framework that both Naim and I worked within. Thus both a Jewish and Palestinian theology of liberation accepted the Two State framework as the ultimate terminus of the Israeli-Palestinian conflict. Though the Two State solution can be argued as a negotiated compromise that allows Jews and Palestinians the space to reestablish an ordinary life and a political framework that supports equality and respects human rights, in hindsight it is clear that the Two State framework had already been eclipsed as both theologies were being born. Though history is open and the interpretations of history are varied, again looking from our vantage point today, Israel never supported the creation of a real Palestinian state. Furthermore, it was naïve of Naim and me to think that the power of the religious or ethical dimensions of Christianity and Judaism could block Israel's expansionist plans.

Limited to traditional religious categories and hoping for the negotiated settlement of two states, our theologies were too narrow. But having stated the obvious, what other theologies, ethics or politics were more efficacious? What was there beyond the limitations of a Palestinian and Jewish theology of liberation? In the end—which is where we have arrived today, every analysis and hope failed. Traditions on all levels failed. Those who broke on all levels with the traditions failed. The question before us today is understanding that failure and extracting from any and every theology, ideology, ethics, politics and ideas, the possibilities that might point a way forward. Being stuck in any one configuration or arguing for the exclusion of any particular analytic methodology is to accept the present as a fated defeat. The ultimate question about the failure of a Palestinian and Jewish theology of liberation therefore leads us to a future where all hands are on deck and the path that leads beyond the present isn't known in advance. Of course, it also matters little if the future evolution of Israel-Palestine names a Palestinian and Jewish theology of liberation at all.

The democratic stirrings in the Arab world represent a possible opening in this decades-long impasse. On the one hand, a democratic Arab world could be a witness to West that deflates the stereotypes that encourages the sense of Israel as the only democracy in the Middle East. On the other, deposing dictators that have special deals with the United

States and Israel, might force Israel to change its long range of security. Tahrir Square forces Jews to think again of how undemocratic Jewish life has become, to the point where many Jews fear the very form of government that Jews longed for in history and help pioneer. Perhaps soon one of the squares in Jerusalem will be renamed Tahrir Square. There Jews and Palestinians can demonstrate their desire for a democracy that includes Jews and Palestinians. If this scenario becomes a reality, the next years might see an increased relevance for both Jewish and Palestinian theologies of liberation. Naim and I could meet again in Jerusalem. Instead of Naim reluctantly listening to me, both of us could listen to others speak their dreams for the future.

That is where we are. Not far from the origins of a Jewish and Palestinian theology of liberation. Yet also far away. Thinking about the past in the context of the present, I feel only gratitude for my encounter with Naim Ateek, my Palestinian Other who I also know as Brother.

References

Ateek, Naim S. 1989. *Justice and Only Justice: A Palestinian Theology of Liberation.* Maryknoll, New York: Orbis.

———. 2008. *A Palestinian Christian Cry for Reconciliation.* Maryknoll, New York: Orbis.

Ateek, Naim S., Marc H. Ellis, and Rosemary Radford Ruether, eds. 1992 *Faith and the Intifada: Palestinian Christian Voices.* Maryknoll, New York: Orbis.

Black, Edwin. 2010. *The Farhud: Roots of the Arab-Nazi Alliance in the Holocaust.* Washington, DC: Dialog.

Chacour, Elias. 2003. *Blood Brothers: The Unforgettable Story of a Palestinian Christian Working for Peace in Israel.* Ada, MI: Chosen.

Ellis, Marc H. 1987. *Toward a Jewish Theology of Liberation.* Maryknoll, New York: Orbis.

———. 1990. *Beyond Innocence and Redemption: Confronting the Holocaust and Israeli Power.* San Francisco: Harper.

———. 2011. *Encountering the Jewish Future with Wiesel, Buber, Heschel, Arendt and Levinas.* Minneapolis: Fortress.

Hartman, David. 2000. *Israelis and the Jewish Tradition: An Ancient People Debating Its Future.* New Haven, CT: Yale University Press.

Lerner, Michael. 2003. *Healing Israel/Palestine: A Path to Peace and Reconciliation.* Berkeley: North Atlantic Books.

Rubenstein, Richard. 1996. *After Auschwitz: Radical Theology and Contemporary Judaism.* Indianapolis: Bobbs-Merrill. 4

4

Reading the Bible with the Eyes of the *Philistines, Canaanites* and *Amalekites:* Messianic Zionism, Zealotocracy, the Militarist Traditions of the Tanakh and the Palestinians (1967 to Gaza 2013)

Prof. Nur Masalha

Introduction

The militarist land traditions of the Hebrew Bible are theologically problematic and morally dubious (Prior 1998, 41–81). In the narrative of the Book of Exodus, there is an inextricable link between the liberation of the Israelites from slavery in Egypt and the divine mandate to plunder ancient Palestine and even commit genocide; the invading Israelites are commanded to annihilate the indigenous inhabitants of "the land of Canaan" (as Palestine was then called). In the Book of Deuteronomy (often described as the focal point of the religious history and theology of the Old Testament) there is an explicit requirement to "ethnically cleanse the land" of the indigenous people of Canaan (Deuteronomy 7:1–11; see also 9:1–5, 23, 31–32; 20:11–14, 16–18; Exodus 23:27–33) (Prior 1997a, 16–33, 278–84).

Ironically, however, as biblical scholar Robert Caroll argues, so much of the religion of the Hebrew Bible belongs to Canaanite belief and practice; biblical antagonism towards the Canaanites (and Philistines) was partly a way of distancing the "new" Hebrew religion from its Canaanite antecedents (Docker 2008, 103). Contrary to the vitriolic anti-Canaanite rhetoric of the Bible authors, the new biblical scholarship has shown that the biblical portrayal of the Israelites' origins in terms of a conflict between them and the Canaanites or the Philistines is not justification for assuming that such a conflict ever took place in history, in either the twelfth century BC or any other period. Canaanites and Israelites never existed as opposing peoples fighting over Palestine (Thompson 2004, 23; Lemche 1991). Biblical scholar Niels Peter Lemche comments on the invention of the ethnic and racial divide between the Hebrews and Canaanites by the Bible writers during the post-exilic period:

> The "Canaanites" embraced that part of the Palestinian population which did not convert to the Jewish religion of the exiles, the reason being that it had no part in the experience of exile and living in a foreign world which had been the fate of the Judaeans who were carried off to Babylonia in 587 BCE. The Palestinian—or rather old Israelite—population was not considered to be Jews because they were not ready to acknowledge the religious innovations of the exilic community that Yahweh was the only god to be worshipped. Thus the real difference between the Canaanites and the Israelites would be a religious one and not the difference between two distinct nationals (1991, 162n12).

In modern times, however, a whole range of settler colonial enterprises have used the mega-narratives of the Hebrew Bible. The Book of Exodus has been widely deployed as a framing narrative for Western imperialism, while other biblical texts have been used to provide moral authority for colonial conquests in Africa, Asia, Australia and the Americas (Prior 1999). In the seventeenth century the Book of Joshua and other divinely prescribed texts were deployed to justify British colonialism in Ireland: English Protestant puritans used the story of Joshua to equate Irish Catholics with the heathen Canaanites and justify English policies in Ireland (Docker 2008, 126). When, in 1649, Oliver Cromwell invaded Ireland he saw the conquest of Canaan celebrated in the Book of Joshua as the prototype of his war against the Irish; he told his troops embarking at Bristol that they were Israelites about to exterminate the idolatrous Canaanites. In practice Cromwell's men slaughtered those Irish Catholics who refused to surrender their cities, as in the massacres of Drogheda and Wexford (Docker 2008, 126; citing Rawson 2001, 269, 301–2).

The deployment of the biblical text politically and the evocation of the exploits of biblical heroes in support of European settler colonialism are deeply rooted in secular Zionism (Masalha 2007), although liberal Zionists deny that the Books of Exodus and Deuteronomy have any contemporary relevance to the fate of the Palestinian people. But with the rise of Jewish fundamentalism since 1967 the militant traditions of the Bible and the stories of Exodus and Joshua have found an explicit relevance in contemporary Palestine-Israel. The dangers of the simplistic application of the Bible to the largely political conflict in the Holy Land can hardly be overstated. This chapter will explore this and other dangers involved in the task of interpreting the text in the xenophobic political context of Palestine-Israel.

The Palestinians are the indigenous people of historic Palestine. Palestinian nationalism, however—like all other modern nationalisms—with its construction of national consciousness and identity, is a modern phenomenon (Khalidi 1997). The Palestinians, until the 1948 catastrophe, were predominantly peasants deeply-rooted in the land of Palestine. They are culturally and linguistically Arab and largely but not exclusively Muslim. Many Palestinians are also Christian Arabs who have historic roots in the Middle East and a long heritage in the land where Christ lived. Palestinian sociologist Samih Farsoun (1937–2005) writes:

> Palestinians are descendants of an extensive mixing of local and regional peoples, including eth Canaanites, Philistines, Hebrews, Samaritans, Hellenic Greeks, Romans, Nabatean Arabs, tribal nomadic Arabs, some Europeans from the Crusades, some Turks, and other minorities; after the Islamic conquests of the seventh century, however, they became overwhelmingly Arabs. Thus, this mixed-stock of people has developed an Arab-Islamic culture for at least fourteen centuries . . . (Farsoun 2004, 4).Some secular Palestinian nationalists, however, have, anachronistically, advocated deep historical roots for Palestinian nationalism—roots going back over the past three millennia, thus seeing in people such as the Canaanites, Jebusites, Amorites and Philistines the direct forebears and linear ancestors of the modern Palestinians. (Khalidi, 1979, 149 and 253n13)

Biblical prejudice and antagonism towards the Philistines, a people who occupied the southern coast of Canaan, survived in the derogatory meaning of the modern term: "a *philistine* is a person ignorant of, or smugly hostile to, culture" (Eban 1984, 45; Rose 2004, 17). Outside the field of Christian theology, archaeological discoveries and critical Bible scholarship show that the cultural and technological accomplishments of the Philistines were markedly superior to those of the Israelites. The Philistines long held a monopoly on iron smithing (a skill they possibly acquired during conquests in Anatolia), and perhaps the biblical description of Goliath's armor (see below) is consistent with this iron-smithing technology. As former Israeli Foreign Minister Abba Eban commented in his Channel 4 documentary of the 1980s, *Heritage, Civilization and the Jews*, "the Philistines were not barbarians but skilled craftsmen" (Eban 1984, 40; Rose 2004, 17).

Many Zionist-Jewish zealots, including Gush Emunim rabbis and spiritual leaders, have routinely compared Palestinian Muslims and Christians to the ancient Canaanites, Philistines, or Amalekites whose extermination or expulsion by the ancient Israelites was, according to the Bible, predestined by a divine design (Shahak and Mezvinsky 1999, 73). Messianic leading rabbis in Israel have frequently referred to the Palestinians as the "Canaanites," "Philistines" or "Amalekites of today." Many of the Gush Emunim rabbis talk about the "new Canaanite era," and insist on giving the biblical commandment to "blot out the memory of Amalek" a contemporary relevance in the conflict between the Israelis and the Palestinians. Although some Israeli fundamentalists refer to the Palestinians as "Ishmaelites" and to the circumstances under which biblical Abraham "expelled" Ishmael, others prefer to use Joshua's destruction and subjugation of the Canaanites as a model for the determination of Israeli policy towards the contemporary "Palestinian problem." For example, in April 1969, in a statement in *Mahanaim*, the journal of the Israeli Army Rabbinate, a certain Shraga Gafni cites biblical authority for driving the "Canaanite peoples" from the land of Israel and explains the "relevance" of the judgment of Amalek (1 Samuel 15) to the Palestinians:

> As to the Arabs—the element that now resides in the land is foreign in its essence to the land and its promise—their sentence must be that of all previous foreign elements. Our wars with them have been inevitable, just as in the days of the conquest of our possessions in antiquity, our wars with the people who ruled our land for their own benefit were inevitable . . . In the case of the enemies, who, in the nature of their being, have only one single goal, to destroy you, there is no remedy but for them to be destroyed. This is "the judgment of Amalek."

Since 1967 other Jewish fundamentalist leaders have argued that Palestinian Muslims and Christians face the choice between destruction, emigration or conversion to Judaism.

THE LAND TRADITIONS OF THE BIBLE AND SETTLER COLONIALISM IN PALESTINE

The conquest paradigm of the Bible (with its militant land traditions) which inspired settler colonial Zionism, appeared to mandate the genocide of the *indigènes* of Canaan. Of course it is possible to develop a Jewish theology of social justice, liberation and non-violent struggle with strong dependence on the Hebrew prophets—especially with reference to the countertraditions of the Bible found in the Books of Isaiah, Amos and Ruth. Feminist approaches to religious studies, in particular, have explored countertraditions in the Bible focusing on the tension between the dominant patriarchal and masculine discourses of the Bible and counter female voices found in the Book of Ruth—Ruth "the doubly Other"— both a Moabite women and a foreigner (Pardes 1992). But it would be no more difficult to construct a political theology of ethnic cleansing on the basis of other Old Testament traditions, especially those dealing with (the mythologized) Israelite origins that demanded the destruction of other peoples. Clearly interpretations of Scripture whether by settler colonial movements or indigenous peoples resisting colonialism have always had theological and ideological dimensions. Inevitably post-modern feminist interpretations of the Bible can be as ideological as traditional patriarchal and masculine interpretations. But all interpretations of ancient holy texts should be subject to a moral critique in line with modern standards of ethical obligations.

According to the Hebrew Bible, the ancient Israelites shared the belief that Yahweh (Jehovah) was a warrior directly involved in earthly battles. Was Yahweh a "genocidal" god? At least some ancient Israelites believed that Yahweh demanded the complete extermination of the enemy people (Masalha 2007, 271). Biblical scholar Michael Prior (1942–2004)—an outstanding liberation theologian and a Vincentian priest—argued that the mega-narratives of the Hebrew Bible presents "ethnic cleansing" as not only legitimate, but as required by the Deity; that by modern standards of international law and human rights what these mega-narratives mandate are "war crimes" and "crimes against humanity." The strictures against the Canaanites and the politics of reading the Bible in Israel were major themes explored by Prior in *The Bible and Colonialism: A Moral Critique* (1997). This seminal work shows the extent to which colonial interests have been successful in utilizing and manipulating the oral and written theological and political traditions contained in the Bible for their own benefit. An example of such ideological manipulation is the Zionist enterprise in Palestine. Also Western biblical and archaeological scholarship has itself contributed substantially to the de-Arabicization of Palestinian geography and toponymy and to the ethnic cleansing of Palestine (Thompson 2008, 1–15; Masalha 2007, 240–62; Prior 1997; 1997a, 20–21; 1998, 41–81; 1999, 129–55, 1999a, 69–88; 1999b, 2000a, 49–60, 2001, 9–35; 2002, 44–45; 2003, 16–48; 2003b, 192–218; 2004; 2004a, 145–70; 2006, 273–96). Greatly influenced by Edward Said's writings and the idea that our understanding of a text should always be underpinned by our own *worldliness* (Prior 2006, 274–76; Prior 2003a, 65–82), Prior's critique of Western biblical scholarship echoed Said's devastating attack on Orientalism (1978). Prior first came across the idea of reading the Bible "with the eyes of the Canaanites" in a critique of Michael Walzer's *Exodus and Revolution* (1985) written by Said in 1986 (Prior 2006, 273–96; Said 1986, 289–303; Walzer 1985)—although Prior was critical of Said for not pursuing his "Canaanite Reading" of the biblical narrative (Prior 2005, 273–96).

Yet the first person to develop this new perspective was the North American native scholar Robert Allen Warrior, who speaks of how strongly he was compelled by Martin Luther King's Exodus imagery of going to the mountaintop, seeing the Promised Land, and crossing the River Jordan. He writes of being stunned at the realization that native Americans were in fact the Canaanites of the American colonial experience. He writes:

> The obvious characters in the story for Native Americans to identify with are the Canaanites, the people who already lived in the Promised Land. As a member of the Osage Nation of American Indians who stands in solidarity with other tribal people around the world, I read the Exodus story with Canaanite eyes. And it is the Canaanite side of the story that has been overlooked by those seeking to articulate theories of liberation. Especially ignored are those parts of the story that describe Yahweh's command to mercilessly annihilate the indigenous population. (Warrior 1991, 289; Prior 2006, 277)

Warrior observes that the land traditions of the Bible, conveniently ignored by most Western theologies of liberation, provide a model of conquest, oppression and genocide for native Americans, Palestinians and other indigenous peoples. Yahweh the conqueror, who delivers the Israelites from their oppression in Egypt, leads them in their conquest of the land of the Canaanites, the Hittites, the Amorites, the Perizzites, the Hivites, and the Jebusites:

> With what voice will we, the Canaanites of the world, say, "Let my people go and leave my people alone?" And, with what ears will followers of alien gods who have wooed us (Christians, Jews, Marxists, capitalists), listen to us? The indigenous people of this hemisphere have endured a subjugation now a hundred years longer than the sojourn of Israel in Egypt. Is there a god, a spirit, who will hear us and stand with us in the Amazon, Osage County, and Wounded Knee? Is there a god, a spirit, able to move among the pain and anger of the Nablus, Gaza, and Soweto of 1989? Perhaps. But we, the wretched of the earth, may be well advised this time not to listen to outsiders with their promises of liberation and deliverance. We will perhaps do better to look elsewhere for our vision of justice, peace and political sanity—a vision through which we escape not only our oppressors, but our oppression as well. Maybe, for once, we will just have to listen to ourselves, leaving the gods of this continent's real strangers to do battle among themselves (Warrior 1995, 287–95).

Inspired by Warrior's radical critique of Western theologies of liberation, Michael Prior argued that mainstream theologies of liberation was not radical enough in its critique of the biblical narrative or in eliminating oppression of indigenous peoples, especially the Palestinians. To begin with, the Exodus narrative portrays Yahweh as a tribal, ethnocentric, genocidal God, with compassion *only* for the misery of his "own people" (Exodus 3:7–8). In the narrative of the Book of Deuteronomy the divine command to commit "genocide" was explicit; genocide and mass slaughter followed in the Book of Joshua. These highly dubious traditions of the Bible were kept before subsequent generations of Jews and Christians in their prayers. Christians still pray in Psalm 80 (7–9) on Thursday morning: "Restore us, O God of hosts; let your face shine, that we may be saved. You brought a vine out of Egypt; you drove out the nations and planted it [in the Promised Land]. You cleared the ground for it."

To illustrate his thesis Prior cited the following mega-narratives:

a. Although the reading of Exodus 3, both in the Christian liturgy and in the classical texts of liberation theologies, halts abruptly in the middle of verse 8 at the description of the land as one "flowing with milk and honey," the biblical text itself continues, "to the country of the Canaanites, the Hittites, the Amorites, the Perizzites, the Hivites, and the Jebusites." Manifestly, the Promised Land, flowing with milk and honey, had no lack of indigenous peoples, and, according to the narrative, would soon flow with blood. As the Israelites were fleeing Egypt, Yahweh promises Moses and the people: "When my angel goes in front of you, and brings you to the Amorites, the Hittites, the Perizzites, the Canaanites, the Hivites, and the Jebusites, and I blot them out, you shall not bow down to their gods, or worship them, or follow their practices, but you shall utterly demolish them and break their pillars in pieces" (Exodus 23:23–24).

b. Matters got worse in the narrative of the Book of Deuteronomy which is canonized as Sacred Scripture. In fact it contains menacing ideologies and racist, xenophobic and militaristic tendencies: after the King of Heshbon refused passage to the Israelites, Yahweh gave him over to the Israelites who captured and utterly destroyed all the cities, killing all the men, women, and children" (Deuteronomy 2:33–34). The fate of the King of Bashan was no better (3:3).

c. Yahweh's role was central to the destruction of other peoples: "When Yahweh your God brings you into the land that you are about to enter and occupy, and he clears away many nations before you—the Hittites, the Girgashites, the Amorites, the Canaanites, the Perizzites, the Hivites . . . and when Yahweh your God gives them over to you . . . you must utterly destroy them . . . Show them no mercy . . . For you are a people holy to Yahweh your God; Yahweh your God has chosen you out of all the peoples on earth to be his people, his treasured possession" (Deuteronomy 7:1–11; see also 9:1–5; 11:8–9, 23, 31–32).

d. The Book of Deuteronomy tells the Israelites that when they approach towns along the way, they are to offer terms of peace to the inhabitants. If the people accept the peace terms, they are to be reduced to serving Israelites at forced labour; if they refuse, all the adult males are to be killed and the women, children, and animals are to be taken as spoils of war (Deuteronomy 20:10–15). When, however, the Israelites reach the lands where they are to dwell, they are to annihilate the inhabitants entirely so that they cannot tempt the Israelites to worship their gods (Deuteronomy 20:16–18). "But as for the towns of these peoples that Yahweh your God is giving you as an inheritance, you must not let anything that breathes remain alive. You shall annihilate them—the Hittites and the Amorites, the Canaanites and the Perizzites, the Hivites and the Jebusites—just as Yahweh your God has commanded, so that they may not teach you to do all the abhorrent things that they do for their gods, and you thus sin against Yahweh your God" (Deuteronomy 20:16–18).

e. The first part of the Book of Joshua (chapters 2–12) describes the conquest of key cities, and their fate in accordance with the laws of the Holy War. Even when the Gibeonites were to be spared, the Israelite elders complained at the lapse in fidelity to the mandate to destroy all the inhabitants of the land (9:21–27). Joshua took Makkedah, utterly destroying every person in it (10:28). A similar fate befell other cities (10:29–39) everything that breathed was destroyed, as Yahweh commanded (10:40–43). Joshua utterly destroyed the inhabitants of the cities of the north as well (11:1–23). Yahweh gave to Israel all the land that he swore to their ancestors he would give them (21:43–5). The legendary achievements of Yahweh through the agencies of Moses, Aaron, and Joshua are kept before the Israelites even in their prayers: "You brought a vine out of Egypt; you drove out the nations and planted it (Psalm 80:8; see also Psalms 78:54–5; 105:44).

f. This is sometimes justified because the other peoples worship alien gods and thus do not deserve to live. There are similar commands in the Book of Numbers (chapter 31). Later in the biblical narrative, when the Israelites reach Jericho, Joshua orders that the entire city be devoted to the Lord for destruction, except for Rahab the prostitute and those in her house. All other inhabitants, as well as the oxen, sheep and donkeys are to be killed in the name of God (Joshua 6:21). In the First Book of Samuel, Samuel prophesies in the name of the Lord to Saul: "Thus says the Lord of hosts, "I will punish the Amalekites for what they did in opposing the Israelites when they came up out of Egypt. Now go and attack Amalek and utterly destroy all that they have, do not spare them, but kill both man and woman, child and infant, ox and sheep, camel and donkey" (1 Samuel 15:2–3).

The historical and archaeological evidence, however, strongly suggests that such genocidal massacres never actually took place (Masalha 2007), although these racist, xenophobic and militaristic narratives remained for later generations as powerful examples of divine aid in battle and of a divine command for widespread slaughter of an enemy. Regarding the divine demand in the Hebrew Bible to kill entire tribes, the later rabbinical tradition of post-biblical Judaism would view the wars of conquest of Canaan as a unique situation that offered no precedent for later wars. Some later Jewish commentators would interpret the struggle against the Amalekites and Canaanites as a symbolic metaphor for fighting genocidal evil (Lefebure 2002).

Ben-Gurion, the Book of Joshua and the 1948 War for Palestine

Political Zionism emerged in Europe in the late nineteenth century as a basically secular movement, with non-religious and frequently anti-religious dispositions. Although the Hebrew Bible was always in the background as a support, the Jewish state would not be a theocracy. In the late nineteenth century the Zionist programme was generally opposed by both wings of Judaism, orthodox and reform, as being anti-religious (by the Orthodox) and contrary to the universalism of Judaism (by Reform Jewry). Indeed the founding fathers of modern Zionism and the state of Israel were almost all of them atheists or religiously indifferent, although their legitimization of the Zionist enterprise by the biblical narrative and record was always a powerful driving force in gaining international support.

However the biblical paradigm, the story of the Exodus from Egypt and Joshua's conquest of the "promised land" have all become central to the foundational myths of secular political Zionism. From the Hebrew Bible secular Zionism took some central ingredients but gave them different meanings and contexts. These were, according to Israeli sociologist Baruch Kimmeling (1939–2007)

1. The definition of the boundaries of the collectivity as including all the Jews in the world.

2. The target territory, from the a priori perspective that emigration from Europe and establishing a society on another continent and

amidst other peoples is an acceptable and legitimate practice in the context of the colonial world order

3. Large, if selective, selections from the religious symbols of Judaism, including the Holy tongue, Hebrew, and the attempt to secularize it and to transform it to a modern language.

4. The Bible and especially the Books of Joshua, Isaiah and Amos. The Book of Joshua provided the muscular and militaristic dimension of conquest of the land and annihilation of the Canaanites and other ancient people that populated the "Promised Land," while the Books of Isaiah an Amos were considered as preaching for social justice and equality (a kind of proto-socialism) . . . (Kimmerling 1999, 339–63)

Although it was possible to construct a Jewish theory of social justice with strong dependence on the Old Testament prophets, in reality, political Zionism developed a theory of ethnic and racial superiority on the basis of the land and conquest traditions of the Bible, especially on the Book of Joshua and those dealing with Israelite origins that demanded the subjugation and destruction of other peoples. It is hardly surprising, therefore, that the Book of Joshua is required reading in Israeli schools. Although the Israelite "conquest" of Canaan was not the "Blitzkrieg" it is made out to be in the Book of Joshua, this book holds an important place in the Israeli school curriculum and Israeli academic programs partly because the founding fathers of Zionism viewed Joshua's narrative of conquests as a precedent for the establishment of Israel as a nation (Burge 2003, 82). Professor Benjamin Beit-Hallahmi, of Haifa University, wrote in 1992:

> Most Israelis today, as a result of Israeli education, regard the Bible as a reliable source of historical information of a secular, political kind. The Zionist version of Jewish history accepts most Biblical legends about the beginning of Jewish history, minus divine intervention. Abraham, Isaac and Jacob are treated as historical figures. The descent into Egypt and the Exodus are phases in the secular history of a developing people, as is the conquest of Canaan by Joshua. The Biblical order of events is accepted, but the interpretation is nationalist and secular.
>
> The Historicization of the Bible is a national enterprise in Israel, carried out by hundreds of scholars at all universities. The starting point is Biblical chronology, then evidence (limited) and speculation (plentiful) are arranged accordingly. The Israeli

> Defense Ministry has even published a complete chronology of
> Biblical events, giving exacts dates for the creation of the world
> . . .

Claiming this ancient mythology as history is an essential part of Zionist secular nationalism, in its attempt to present a coherent account of the genesis of the Jewish people in ancient West Asia. It provides a focus of identification to counter the rabbinical, Diaspora traditions. Teaching the Bible as a history to Israeli children creates the notion of continuity. It is Abraham ("the first Zionist," migrating to Palestine), Joshua and the conquest of Palestine (wiping out the Canaanites, just like today), King David's conquest of Jerusalem (just like today) (1992, 119). For David Ben-Gurion and other founding fathers of Zionism the invention of a tradition and the synthesizing of a nation meant that the Hebrew Bible was not a religious document or a repository of a theological claim to Palestine; it was reinvented as a nationalized and radicalized sacred text central to the modern foundational myths of secular Zionism. As a primordialist movement of secular nationalism, asserting the antiquity of Jewish nationalism (Smith 1986), inspired by Eurocentric ethnic, völkisch and racial ideologies, Ben-Gurion viewed the Bible in an entirely functional way: the biblical narrative functioned as a mobilizing myth and as an "historical account" of Jews' "title to the land"—a claim not necessarily borne out by recent archaeological findings. For Ben-Gurion it was not important whether the biblical narrative was an objective and true record of actual historical events. It is not entirely clear whether Ben-Gurion assumed that the ancient events Israel was re-enacting had actually occurred. But as he explains:

> It is not important whether the [biblical] story is a true record
> of an event or not. What is of importance is that this is what
> the Jews believed as far back as the period of the First Temple
> (Pearlman 1965, 227; Rose 2004, 9).

However like other founding fathers of the State of Israel, who were secular or atheist Jews, Ben-Gurion made extensive use of "elect people-promised land" ideas and kept stressing the "uniqueness" of the Jewish people. He liked to invoke the biblical Prophet Isaiah who enjoined the Jews to be "a light unto the nations." He was also quick to put the ethnocentric concepts of "promised land-chosen people" to use for their political value, both as a means of attracting believing Jews to the Zionist cause and as a way of justifying the Zionist enterprise in Western eyes and the eyes of world Jewry. The relatively moderate Israeli leader Moshe Sharret, who had served as Foreign Minister and (and for a short period) prime minister in the 1950s, had this to say about Ben-Gurion's ethnocentric Zionism and messianic tendency:

> [Ben-Gurion's] constant stress on the uniqueness of the Jewish people is another aspect of his egocentrism—cultural egocentrism. The third aspect of a messianic mission vis-à-vis Israel and Jewry (Shindler 2002, 64).

Ben-Gurion also, and crucially, argued that he was fighting all Zionist battles with the help of the Hebrew Bible. Already in his first published work, in Yiddish, entitled: *Eretz-Yisrael: Past and Present* (1918), that he co-authored with Yitzhak Ben-Tzvi—later to become the second president of Israel—he argues that the Jewish "return" to Palestine is actually a "repeat" of Joshua's conquest of ancient Palestine (Zamaret 2006). The 1948 Palestine War drew Ben-Gurion ever nearer to the biblical narrative, as seen from his frequent references to biblical figures and biblical battles of conquest. Apparently the Book of Joshua was the biblical text to which Ben-Gurion was most drawn. On more than one occasion Ben-Gurion pointed to an "unbroken line of continuity from the days of Yehoshua bin Nun [Joshua son of Nun] to the IDF" [Israel Defense Force] in and after 1948 (ibid). When he spoke of sweeping Jewish offensives in the 1948 war, he apparently did so in language evocative of the Book of Joshua. The Israeli army, he declared, had "struck the kings of Lod and Ramleh, the kings of Beit Naballa and Deir Tarif, the kings of Kola and Migdal Zedek . . . " (Lazare 2006).

The epic tale of how young David, the future king of Israel, armed with only a slingshot and stones, defeated Goliath, a well-armored giant warrior and "the Philistine of Gath," has become one of the most famous of all biblical fables (1 Sam 17:41–51.). The slain enemy's name has become a synonym for "huge" and in Western culture the phrase "David and Goliath" has become a literary cliché for a struggle between opponents of unequal strength and a cultural confrontation between civilization and barbarism. In the "culture wars" of modern Europe, to the enlightened "chosen few," the "Philistines" embodied the anti-intellectual, vulgar and threatening masses.

In the official Zionist rendition of the 1948 war the events are presented as a battle between a "Jewish David and an Arab Goliath." Central to key narratives in Israeli Zionist culture is the myth which depicts the

Israel-Palestine conflict as a "war of the few against the many." Since the early 20th century Zionist historiography has based this narrative of the "few against-the-many" on the biblical account of Joshua's conquest of ancient Palestine, while mainstream Israeli historians continue to portray the 1948 war as an unequal struggle between a Jewish David and an Arab Goliath, and as a desperate, heroic, and ultimately successful Jewish struggle against overwhelming odds. (Shlaim 2004) The European Zionist settlers brought with them to Palestine the "few-against-the-many" narrative-a widespread European cultural myth which appeared in many variations, including the American western cowboy variation of the early 20th century (Gertz 2000, 5). Turning the Jewish faith into secular ideology, Israeli historians and authors have adopted and reinterpreted biblical sources and myths and have mobilized them in support of post-1948 Israeli objectives (ibid). The few, who overcame the many by virtue of their courage and absolute conviction, were those European Zionist settlers who emulated the fighters of ancient Israel, while the many were those Palestinians and Arabs who were the embodiment of various ancient oppressors. The Zionist struggle against the indigenous Palestinians was thus portrayed as a modern re-enactment of ancient biblical battles and wars, including David's slaying of Goliath, the Hasmonean (Maccabean) uprising against ancient Greece, and the Jewish wars against the Romans, with the zealots' last stand at Masada in 73 AD and the *Bar Kohcba* revolt 67 years later (ibid).

While the "David and Goliath" version of the Israel-Palestine conflict continues to exercise hegemony in the West, since the late 1980s, however, many of the myths that have come to surround the birth of Israel in 1948 have been demolished by revisionist Israeli historians. In my work *Expulsion of the Palestinians* (1992) I have shown that Ben-Gurion entered the 1948 war with a mind-set and with premeditation to expel Palestinians and that the 1948 war against the Palestinians was a form of politicide.

FROM SECULAR ZIONISM TO THE MESSIAH: THE RISE OF JEWISH ZEALOTOCRACY SINCE 1967

Since its establishment in 1948 the Israeli state, which had been built mainly by atheist Zionists, has undergone a slow but constant process of clericalization and orthodoxization, with leading Labour Zionists and founding fathers of the state (notably David Ben-Gurion) seeking an alliance with religious Zionism—thus cementing the alliance between the sword and the Torah, between the secular establishment of Zionism and the Zionist religious parties (Cygielman 1977, 28–37). As Mark LeVine observes,

> Prime Minister Ben-Gurion granted orthodox Judaism sole authority over Jewish life in the new state, which meant that large sums of money were directed to yeshivas and other religious institutions that helped lay the foundation for the "religious revival" that occurred after 1967 (LeVine 2009, 189–90n23).

This partnership between the ostensibly secular Labour Zionism and the forces of religious nationalism, Zeev Strenhell observed, was much deeper than appeared on the surface (Sternhell 1998, 335).

Today there are two distinct strands of Jewish fundamentalism in Israel. The first is represented by the Jewish-Zionist fundamentalist or nationalist-religious camp (also known as the "messianic" camp), and the second by the ultra-orthodox rabbis and non-Zionist religious parties of the Haredim, both Sephardi and Ashkenazi. Furthermore since the 1967 conquests radical religious Zionism has transposed Theodor Herzl's political Zionism from being an altogether secular aspiration to create the sovereign "state for the Jews" (*Der Judenstaat*) into the apocalyptic redemption of the "whole Land of the Bible" (Prior 1997; Prior 1999, 67–102; Prior 1999a; Masalha 2000, 105–62; Masalha 2003a, 85–117). This continuing process of clericalization of the Israeli state, accelerated in recent decades, has serious implications for interfaith relations and society and the state in Israel-Palestine.

Although the deeply secular Herzl had been little concerned with the exact location of the "Judenstaat" and the scope of its boundaries, the Zionist messianic force has been inspired by maximalist colonial-settler expansionism. Yet, as Israeli sociologist Baruch Kimmeling has argued, the shift was bound to take place from the moment European secular Zionist leadership invented a tradition, retitling and reimagining Palestine as the "Land of Israel":

> [Zionism] has to repeatedly explain to itself and to the international community why it chose Palestine, the land retitled as "The Land of Israel," as its target-territory for settlement . . . it was chosen out of ideological-religious motives. This fact not only turned the Zionist project into . . . an essentially religious project, which was not able to disconnect itself from its original

identity as a quasi-messianic movement. The essence of this society and state's right and reason to exist is embedded in symbols, ideas and religious scriptures—even if there has been an attempt to give them a secular re-interpretation and context. Indeed, it was made captive from the beginning by its choice of a target-territory for immigration and a place for its nation building. For then, neither the nation nor its culture could be built successfully apart from the religious context, even when its prophets, priests, builders and fighters saw themselves as completely secular. (Kimmerling 1999; Cook 2006, 174–75)

This major shift from secular to messianic Zionism was reflected in the findings of a public opinion poll conducted in the late 1990s, and cited by Kimmerling. It showed, *inter alia*, that a majority of 55 percent of the Jewish population of Israel believed absolutely in the (mythological) biblical story that the Torah ("matan Torah," in Hebrew) was "given" to Moses on Mount Sinai—only 14 percent rejected it outright as a historical reality. Furthermore, 68 percent believed that the Jewish people were a "chosen people"—only 20 percent rejected this supremacist, ethnocentric belief. Some 39 percent believed in the coming of the Messiah (but they were not asked about the time of his coming); only 14 percent had some doubts about this and only 32 percent completely rejected the messianic idea (Kimmerling 1999, 339–63).

In the 1980s even the leader of the secular Labour party, Shimon Peres, was undergoing a process of orthodoxization. Israeli media reports and pictures showed him going to the Wailing Wall after being sworn in as prime minister and head of the National Unity government in September 1984; then he was observed taking Talmud lessons from a chief rabbi—although these displays of piety elicited some ridicule and derision in the secular press (Beit-Hallahmi 1992, 136).

Jewish religious revivalism and the ascendance of Israel's radical right—which includes both secular and fundamentalist currents—were partly the outcome of the 1967 war which was a watershed in the history of Israel and which had a profound effect on the country's religious and secular camps (Masalha 1997; Masalha 2000, 105–62). Even for many secular Israelis who were indifferent to religion or even opposed to it, the capture of East Jerusalem and the West Bank represented a conversion of almost mystical proportions: "Religious" and "secular," Right and Left, fathers and sons, still felt that they shared historical and cultural rights based on the sanctity of the Jewish heritage [of the Bible]" (Strenhell

1998, 335). Israel's victory created a sense of triumphalist history among many non-believing Israeli Jews who saw the capture of the old city of Jerusalem as a "sign from Heaven." This triumphalist feeling brought to prominence Neo-Zionism and gave rise to messianic Zionism, generating feverish Jewish fundamentalism which in turn contributed to exacerbating Israel's schizophrenic cultural identity and the division between the secular and religious camps in the country (Margalit 1991). In the wake of the war, and the rise of radical religious Zionism, the role of the militant biblical narrative within Zionist ideology and Israeli settler colonialism increased significantly. Radical religious Zionism has since developed into a major political and cultural force, with a considerable influence on the attitudes, commitments, and votes of a large number of religious and secular Israelis. Its organized focus is the colonial-settlement movement of Gush Emunim ("the Bloc of Faithful"), the most influential extra-parliamentary movement in the country, which also activates the entire panorama of Neo-Zionist and secular ultra-nationalists, including some of Israel's most powerful secular leaders (Lustick 1988, ix, 12–16, 153; Newman 1982; Pappe 2000, 33–44; Cook 2006; Friedman 1992; Gorenberg 2000; Inbari 1984, 10–11).

Messianic Zionism in Israel, in its various shades, emphasizes both the "holiness" and "territorial wholeness" of Greater Israel (the so-called "biblical Land of Israel"). In constructing neo-Zionist ideology, national identity is not simply a socio-cultural phenomenon, but a geopolitical and territorial ideal (Pappe 2000, 33–44; Lustick 1987, 118–39). This is reflected in the popular slogan: "The Land of Israel, for the People of Israel, According to the Torah of Israel." As the late Rabbi Tzvi Yehuda Kook, the spiritual leader of messianic Zionism, put it: "The Land was chosen before the people." Hanan Porat, one of the most influential leaders of Gush Emunim, echoed the same view:

> For us the Land of Israel is a Land of destiny, a chosen Land, not just an existentially defined homeland. It is the Land from which the voice of God has called to us ever since that first call to the first Hebrew: "Come and go forth from your Land where you were born and from your father's house to the Land that I will show you" (Lustick 1987, 127).

Although there is a variety of Jewish fundamentalist groups and movements in Israel, they invariably envisage a theocratic regime for Israel based on the *halacha* (the Jewish religious law) and spurn universal, humanistic and liberal values. For them Zionism and the Israeli state (with its army, tanks, aircraft and other weapon systems) are divine agents (Ravitzky 1996).

The political theology of the Israeli messianic trend is based on four major components: a) messianic fervor related to a belief in the territorial "sanctity" of Greater Israel; b) the building of the Temple on the site of the Muslim shrines in occupied East Jerusalem; c) the ethos of a theocratic utopia, reflecting the desire to build a theocratic state based on the *halacha*; d) the establishment of Jewish political sovereignty over Greater Israel (Gorny 1994,150–151).

Moreover, the creation of the Israeli state in 1948 and the conquest ('liberation') of additional territories in the 1967 war are both perceived as constituting part of the divine process of messianic redemption—a process that, according to Neo-Zionists, should not be stopped or altered by any government of Israel (Newman 1994, 533).

The ideology of the messianic current generally conceives a radical and sharp distinction between Jew and non-Jew in Israel-Palestine and assumes basically antagonistic relations between them. For messianic Zionists, the conflict with "gentiles" over Jerusalem, and even war against them, is "for their own good," because this will hasten messianic redemption (Lustick 1988, 120). For the messianics, who embrace the supremacist paradigm of Jews as a divinely "chosen people" (*'am segula*), the indigenous Palestinians are no more than illegitimate tenants and squatters, and a threat to the process of messianic redemption; their human and civil rights are no match for the divine plan and the biblically ordained duty or commandment (Hebrew: *mitzvah*) of conquering, ethnic cleansing, possessing and settling the "Promised Land." Rabbi Tzvi Yehuda Kook, in particular, promoted a racist doctrine of the Jews as a divinely-chosen "superior race," while the Palestinians, descendants of Ishmael (Hebrew: Yishmael; Arabic: Isma'il)), were an "inferior race" (Rachlevsky 1998, 392–93). Ishmael is a figure in the Hebrew Bible and Quran. The Quran views Isma'il as a prophet, and as the actual son that Abraham (Arabic: Ibrahim) was called on to sacrifice. The Bible, however, generally views Ishmael as a "wicked" though repentant son of Abraham; although he is Abraham's eldest son, he was born of his wife Sarah's handmaiden Hagar (Genesis 16:3). Furthermore, Jewish believers maintain that Isaac (the "father of the Jewish people") rather than Ishmael was the "legitimate" son and "true" heir of Abraham; "The distinction between

Yitzhak [Isaac] and Ishmael [the 'father of the Arabs'] is a clear racial distinction," Kook wrote (Rachlevsky 1998, 406).

For Kook and his disciples, Israel must continue the ancient biblical battles over settlement of the "Land of Israel," to be won by a combination of religious faith and military might. The devotion of an increasingly powerful trend to the ethnic cleansing of Jerusalem and Greater Israel, and to messianic redemption, has turned the Palestinians in East Jerusalem—illegally occupied and unilaterally annexed to Israel after 1967—into resident aliens in their own historic city. The same political theology has spawned Jewish terrorism in East Jerusalem and the West Bank. This Jewish terrorism has been reflected in, among others, the violence of *Hamahteret Hayehudit* (the Jewish Underground) and "Terror against Terror" of the early 1980s; the Hebron massacre in February 1994; and the assassination of Prime Minister Yitzhak Rabin on 4 November 1995.

Ethnocratic State, Established Church and Messianic Zionism

Several Israeli scholars, who have documented the ongoing process of clericalization in Israeli since 1948 and the rapid growth of messianic Zionism since 1967, have observed a strong element of religious coercion. Already in 1965 a prominent Israeli scholar, Ya'acov Talmon (1916–1980)—an Orthodox Jewish Professor of History at the Hebrew University of Jerusalem—observed the major role played by the religious establishment in the state and society:

> In Israel today, the Rabbinate is rapidly developing into a firmly institutionalized Church imposing an exacting discipline on its members and facing the general body of laymen as a distinct power. This is not a religious development, but, ironically enough, the outcome of the emergence of the [Jewish] State. The latter has given birth and legitimacy to an established Church (Talmon 1965, cited in Tamarin 1973, 37).

Professor Talmon pointed out that none of this has roots in Jewish tradition or the Jewish diaspora. The theocratic elements in Israeli state and society are often explained in terms of the problems of coalition politics, but the socio-political and cultural reasons are much deeper. Such a theocratic development is hardly surprising in an "ethnocratic state" in which some basis must be established—in state ideology, cultural attitudes, and law—for distinguishing the privileged and dominant Jewish population from the non-Jewish citizens of Israel (Chomsky 1975, 37–38).

In fact since 1948 successive policies adopted by the "ethnocratic" state of Israel—land, ethnic and demographic, legal and political, military and strategic—have aimed at reinforcing the power and domination of Israel's ruling Jewish majority (Masalha 2003; Yiftachel 2006).

However, until 1967, religious Zionism remained relatively pragmatic in its demand for the application of the halacha within Israel as well as in foreign affairs. Since 1967, as several Israeli scholars—including Israel Shahak, Ilan Pappé, Yehoshafat Harkabi, Yesha'ayahu Leibowitz, Ehud Sprinzak, Avi'ezer Ravitzky, Uriel Tal and Shlomo Sand—have pointed out, militant neo-Zionism has become central to Israel's domestic and foreign policies. Moreover, the relationship between the Jewish religion and Zionist state policies has become increasingly intertwined: a radical political theology is deployed in the service of settler colonial policies, and Zionist ethnic cleansing policies as the implementation of Jewish religious commandments (Hebrew: *mitzvot*) (Harkabi 1986, 207). Furthermore, the fanatical messianic force is inspired by maximalist territorial expansionism (Lustick 1988, 107; Shaham 1979; Elitzur 1978, 42–53).

Michael Neumann, a professor of philosophy at Trent University in Ontario, Canada, writes:

> [the late Professor] Israel Shahak and others have documented the rise of fundamentalist Jewish sects that speak of the greater value of Jewish blood, the specialness of Jewish DNA, the duty to kill even innocent civilians who pose a potential danger to Jews, and the need to "redeem" lands lying far beyond the present frontiers of Israeli control. Much of this happens beneath the public surface of Israeli society, but these racial ideologies exert a strong influence on the mainstream. So far, they have easily prevailed over the small, courageous Jewish opposition to Israeli crimes. The Israeli government can afford to let the fanatical race warriors go unchecked, because it knows the world would not dare connect their outrages to any part of Judaism (or Zionism) itself. As for the dissenters, don't they just show what a wonderfully democratic society Israel has produced? (Neumann 2002)

On the whole, the rise of radical neo-Zionism in Israel—unlike the variety of Islamic fundamentalism in Palestine—is not the product of socio-economic or political marginalization. It is, rather, a middle-class phenomenon and the product of state policies, the influence of Zionist elites, and coalition politics. Moreover, because of its middle-class Ashkenazi origins, the powerful settlement movement of Gush Emunim has been the most successful extraparliamentary movement to arise in Israel since 1948, and has had a profound influence upon the Israeli political system (Lustick 1988, 8, 12–15; Schnall 1985, 15).

Its practical colonization of the West Bank has been the main vehicle of the political success of Neo-Zionism inside Israel. In *The Ascendance of Israel's Radical Right* (1991) Sprinzak writes:

> Gush Emunim has changed since the 1970s. From a messianic collective of young true believers who thought they could change the world by concentrated spirituality and pioneering devotion, it has become a movement of dozens of settlements, thousands of settlers, with financial assets and material interest. It has added a maturity and skepticism to its early spontaneity and messianic craze. But Gush Emunim is still a very dynamic force, by far the most viable component of the radical right. It may also be the most effective social movement that has emerged in Israel since 1948 (Sprinzak 1991, 107).

With thousands of full-time devotees (Aronoff 1985), Gush Emunim colonists' real power lies in the organization's extensive settlement network, its thousands of highly-motivated settlers, its dozens of illegal colonies established in the West Bank, and in the Golan Heights since 1967, with their huge financial and material assets, and above all in the activities of its leading personalities in all the political parties of the right. Gush Emunim has drawn crucial support from the Likud, the NRP, Tzomet, Moledet, Tehiya, Matzad, Ihud Leumi (National Union) and Yisrael Beiteinu. Knesset members of these parties identified with Gush Emunim objectives and openly campaigned for their implementation. In 1987, members of the Knesset faction Matzad, all of whom were closely identified with Gush Emunim, succeeded in capturing key positions within the NRP. Furthermore, several leading Gush Emunim personalities, including Hanan Porat, Rabbi Eli'ezer Waldman, and Rabbi Haim Druckman have been Knesset members (Newman 1994, 533; Joffe 1996, 153).

"Kookist" Political Theology

The single most influential ideologue of messianic Zionism was Rabbi Tzvi Yehuda Kook (1891–1982), who was the head of the large Merkaz Harav Yeshiva in Jerusalem. His father was the Chief Ashkenazi Rabbi of the Jewish community in mandatory Palestine between 1920 and 1935, Rabbi Avraham Yitzhak HaCohen Kook (1865–1935). The latter ("Ha-Rav," or "Rabbi Kook the elder"), a prolific author, was the founder of the Zionist religious and messianic ideology. He was a key figure in accommodating the ideology of secular Zionism to classical Jewish orthodoxy, and is held in great regard not only by religious messianics but also by many secular Zionists. He established the Chief Rabbinate of Israel, the *Rabbanut*, and Israel's national rabbinical courts, *Batei Din*, which work in coordination with the Israeli government, having jurisdiction over much law relating to marriage, divorce, conversion, and education. He also built political alliances between the secular Labour Zionist leadership and followers of religious Zionism. He believed, according to his theological system, that the secular and even anti-religious Labour Zionist settlers of the pre-state period were part of a grand divine scheme of building up the physical land, laying the groundwork for the ultimate messianic redemption of world Jewry. The Kooks (father and son) were key figures in Israel's Ashkenazi (religious and secular) establishment (Lustick 1988, 8, 12–15; Schnall 1985, 15). Their demand that the *halacha* guide official policies towards the Palestinian population is widely accepted in religious circles and parties in Israel.

The teachings of the Kooks (father and son) integrated the traditional, passive religious longings for the land with the modern, secular, activist and settler Zionism, giving birth to a new comprehensive theology of Jewish nationalist-religious messianism (Jones 1999, 11–14; Prior 1997a, 20–21; Aran 1997, 294–327). Kookist political theology saw the 1967 war and the occupation of the Old City of Jerusalem as a turning-point in the process of messianic redemption and the deliverance of *Eretz-Yisrael* from what it termed the *Sitra Achra*—literally the (evil) "Other Side" (Jones 1999, 12). Rabbi Tzvi Yehuda Kook himself rushed with his biblical claims towards the West Bank immediately after the 1967 conquests:

> All this land is ours, absolutely, belonging to all of us, non-transferable to others even in part . . . it is clear and absolute that there are no "Arab territories" or "Arab lands" here, but only the

lands of Israel, the eternal heritage of our forefathers to which others [the Arabs] have come and upon which they have built without our permission and in our absence." (in Schnall 1984, 19; Lior 1986)

Rabbi Tzvi Yehuda Kook's politics were described by the Israeli journalist David Shaham as "consistent, extremist, uncompromising and concentrated on a single issue: the right of the Jewish people to sovereignty over every foot of the Land of Israel. Absolute sovereignty, with no imposed limitations"; "From a perspective of national sovereignty," Kook says, "the country belongs to us . . ." Immediately after the 1967 war, Tzvi Yehuda Kook demanded the annexation of the Occupied Territories, in line with explicit *halacha* provisions. He also said at a conference after 1967:

> I tell you explicitly . . . that there is a prohibition in the Torah against giving up even an inch of our liberated land. There are no conquests here and we are not occupying foreign land; we are returning to our home, to the inheritance of our forefathers. There is no Arab land here, only the inheritance of our God—the more the world gets used to this thought the better it will be for it and for all of us (in Pichnik 1968, 108–109).

These statements were made in the presence of senior public figures, including the Israeli President Zalman Shazar, Ministers, Members of the Knesset, judges, chief Rabbis and senior civil servants (in Pichnik 1968, 108–109).

For the followers of Tzvi Yehuda Kook, continuing settler colonialism, combined with the establishment of Jewish sovereignty over Greater Israel and the building of the Temple in occupied East Jerusalem, are all part of implementing the divinely-ordained messianic redemption. Rabbi Shlomo Aviner, a Parisian-born Jew and the former Rabbi of Beit El, a religiously observant Israeli settlement on the West Bank, and currently the chief rabbi of the 'Ateret Cohanim yeshiva in East Jerusalem's Old City—a fundamentalist group campaigning to rebuild the Jewish Temple on the Al-Haram Al-Sharif (the Noble Sanctuary) (Aviner 2000)—called for further territorial expansionism beyond the current Occupied Territories: "Even if there is a peace, we must instigate wars of liberation in order to conquer additional parts of the Land of Israel" (Aviner 1982, 110).

THE HALACHIC STATUS OF GER TOSHAV AND THE PALESTINIANS

Since 1967, Neo-Zionists have debated whether Palestinians residing in the "land of Israel" qualify for the halachic status of *ger toshav* ("resident alien"). In line with this *halacha* concept of *ger toshav*, both Palestinian Muslims and Palestinian Christians are viewed by some Jewish religious nationalists, including many of the Gush Emunim rabbis, as temporary "resident aliens," a population living, at best, on sufferance. While the relatively moderate members of the NRP have categorized the Palestinians as *gerei toshav* ("resident aliens"), the more radical Jewish fundamentalists pointed out that biblical discussion of *ger toshav* refers to only non-Jews who adopt Judaism (Num 10:14).

Jewish fundamentalists have also "reinvented" the celebrated mediaeval philosopher and theologian Moses Maimonides (1135–1204) and metamorphosed him from being a rationalist and universalist philosopher—the most illustrious example of the Golden Age of Arabo-Islamic-Judaic symbiosis—into anti-Arab religious zealot (Masalha 2002, 85–117). The messianics invoke theological orthodoxy and a conservative interpretation of the Jewish *halacha* of Maimonides to justify their attitudes. Quoting selectively and misleadingly from Maimonides' theology, the neo-Zionists conceive a racial distinction between Jew and non-Jew in Israel. They pointed out that Maimonides had made it clear in his law code that the *Torah* concept of *ger toshav* refers to a "righteous gentile" who becomes a Jew (Nisan 1992, 167). That radical position is found in the book of Dr. Mordechai Nisan, a senior lecturer at the Hebrew University of Jerusalem and a supporter of Gush Emunim (1992, original Hebrew 1986). The halachic legal status of *ger toshav* is, according to Nisan, as follows: a gentile who accepts the Seven Laws of Noah (Hebrew: *Sheva mitzvot B'nei Noah*), enjoys a social standing in the "Land of Israel" above a man who is a slave to a Jew:

> The Gentile in Eretz-Israel who accepts the Seven Noahide Laws becomes a *Ger-Toshav* (a resident alien) and, according to Maimonides, enters the category of "the righteous nations of the world." This point is discussed in halachic literature and codified by Maimonides into Jewish Law. The concept of the *Ger-Toshav* refers to a person who has gone through the process of a partial conversion before a Rabbinic court of three. The *Ben-Hoah* assumes a more inferior and limited status if his acceptance of Torah is due to a rational decision alone, but not a Divinely fixed

> obligation. The *Ger-Toshav*, then, is positioned between the *Ben-Noah* and the Jew. He ascends to a level of social and religious performance, he goes through a stage of partial conversion, but limits himself to accepting just the Seven Commandments. The *Tosafot* commentary in the Talmud implies that this individual should go further and consider converting completely to Judaism. However, for the moment, the *Ger-Toshav* assumes a middle position in the Torah order within a Jewish-led society. "The position of non-repentant Gentile remains inferior. He refuses to assume a higher life standard as set out by the Torah and rejects Jewish primacy in Eretz-Israel. Maimonides explicates that non-Jews (*Bnei Noah*) are to endure a lowly status compounded by elements of servitude and special taxes." (Nisan 1992, 163)

Nisan, who has elsewhere expressed a rationalization for and endorsement of Jewish settlers' terrorism against the Palestinians of the Occupied Territories, writes the following passages shedding further light on the Jewish religious fundamentalism and exclusionist premises underpinning his ethnic cleansing imperative:

> At the very dawn of Jewish history, contact with the Land of Israel established the principle that the presence of non-Jews in the country is morally and politically irrelevant to the national right of the Jews to settle and possess the Land . . . The Bible states the Jewish right regardless of non-Jewish presence. Much later, the Rabbinic sages expounded on the patriarchal promise and articulated the following principle: . . . Dwelling in the Land is the Jewish priority and it is in no way restricted, let alone nullified, by a non-Jewish majority population in any given part of the Land. This principle was later codified by Maimonides in his legal work, thus lending his outstanding halachic [religious legal] authority to this Abrahamic national imperative . . . [The view that questions the legitimacy of Jewish settlement in "Judea" and "Samaria"] is a direct denunciation of Abraham, the first Jew, the Father of the Jewish people . . . [who] set the precedent and model for settling there in spite of the fact that the "Canaanite was then in the Land." The Jewish presence in the Land has always had to contend with, and at least partially overcome, an indigenous non-Jewish element in the Land . . . The land is the eternal possession of the Jewish people alone . . . (Nisan 1983, quoted in Chomsky 1983, 444 and 470n3)

In August 1984, Nisan, who supports the replacement of Israel's secular law by the *halacha*, repeated the same ideas in an article in *Kivunim* (an official organ of the World Zionist Organization). Relying on a national-ized and radicalized Maimonides, he argued that a non-Jew permitted to reside in the land of Israel "must accept paying a tax and suffering the humiliation of servitude." In *Toward a New Israel*, Nisan bemoans the tra-ditional Jewish *dhimmi* status under Islam: "the hallmark of the *dhimmi* condition was the precarious and pitiful nature of existence under Mus-lim rule. Subjugated to an inferior status, the Jew paid a special poll tax, the *jizya*" (Nisan 1992, 156). Yet in *Kivunim*, Nisan demands, supposedly in keeping with a religious text of Maimonides, that a non-Jew in Israel "be held down and not [be allowed] to raise his head against Jews." For Nisan, non-Jews must not be appointed to any office or position of power over Jews; if they refuse to live a life of inferiority, then this signals their rebellion and the unavoidable necessity of Jewish warfare against their very presence in the "land of Israel" (Nisan in *Kivunim* 1984, 151–56; Harkabi 1986, 216–17).

For a supporter of Gush Emunim like Nisan, the struggle against the Palestinians is also part of a wider effort to reinterpret Jewish history and redeem Maimonides:

> The struggle over Maimonides between Jews and Arabs is really an instance of the confrontation going back more than a millen-nium, as the Jewish people try to perpetuate their unique reli-gious and national identity within the extensive Muslim/Arab homeland. An awareness of this historic confrontation conveys the profundity of the rejection of modern Zionism by modern Arab nationalism. (Nisan 1992, 173–74)

The "Verdict of Amalek": The Israeli Debate on the "Genocide" Commandment in the Torah

The indigenous Palestinians are viewed by radical rabbis as temporary alien residents, and as a population living, at best, on sufferance. The same rabbis deny that a Palestinian nation exists and strongly opposes the idea of Palestinian rights in Jerusalem. According to them, there is no need to take into consideration the Arab residents, since their residence in the city for hundreds of years was prohibited and was based on theft, fraud and distortion; therefore now the time has come for the Arab "rob-bers" to depart. As Rabbi Aviner explains:

> To what can this be compared[?] It resembles a man entering his neighbor's house without permission and residing there for

many years. When the original owner of the house returns, the invader [the Arab] claims: "It is my [house]. I have been living here for many years." So what? All of these years he was a robber! Now he should depart and pay housing rent as well. A person might say: there is a difference between a residence of thirty years and a residence of two thousand years. Let us ask him: Is there a law of limitation which gives a robber the right to his plunder? . . . Everyone who settled here knew very well that he was residing in a land that belonged to the people of Israel. Perhaps an Arab who was born here does not know this, nonetheless the fact that a man settled on land does not make it his. Legally "possession" serves only as evidence of a claim of ownership, but it does not create ownership. The Arabs' "possession" of the land is therefore a "possession that asserts no right." It is the possession of territory when it is absolutely clear that they are not its legal owners, and this possession has no legal and moral validity (Aviner 1983, 10).

In a similar disposition Rabbi Tzvi Yehuda Kook, who apparently inspired Aviner's apologia, wrote:

We find ourselves here by virtue of our forefathers' inheritance, the foundation of the Bible and history, and there is no one that can change this fact. What does it resemble? A man left his house and others came and invaded it. This is exactly what happened to us. There are those who claim that these are Arab lands here. It is all a lie and falsehood. There are absolutely no Arab lands here. (Kook 1982, 10)

The imagery of the homecoming Jew and the Arab invader permeates the writings of a variety of spiritual leaders and ideologists of Jewish fundamentalism, and implies that the Jew has the right to evict the "alien" Arab "invader." Moreover these ideologues interpret the Zionist assertion of "historical rights" to the land as meaning that the very fact of Arab residence on, and possession of, the land is morally flawed and legally, at best, temporary; therefore, the Arabs must evacuate the land in the interests of the "legal owners" of the country, and depart (Aviner 1983, 10).

Palestinian resistance to the extension of Jewish sovereignty over the "whole Land of Israel" will, according to many Jewish messainics, result in their uprooting and destruction. The late Rabbi Meir Kahane, who acquired a reputation for defining the outer limits of both right-wing fascism and Jewish fundamentalism in Israel, was a major contributor to the rise of militant political theology in Israel in the post-1967 period. After his assassination in New York in 1990, Kahane's funeral in Jerusalem was attended by two Israeli cabinet ministers, two deputy ministers, and by the Chief Sephardi Rabbi who urged the mourners to "follow in Kahane's ways" (Elon 1997, 197). Kahane, unlike some of the rabbis of Gush Emunim, made little distinction between Palestinian Christians and Palestinian Muslims. His racist public campaign thrived on media publicity, and concentrated, also, on the Palestinian citizens of Israel, and not just on the Palestinians of the Occupied Territories. As Kahane declared on another occasion: "No non-Jews can be citizens of Israel," seeking to rescind the citizenship status currently given to Palestinian Christians and Muslims inside the Green Line; if the Arabs refuse to accept the [*halacha*] status of *ger toshav* (paying "tribute" and living in "servitude"), "We'll put them on trucks and send them over the Allenby Bridge . . . we'll use force. And if they fire at our soldiers, we'll kill them" (in Tessler 1986, 31).

Reflecting on the appropriate policy to adopt towards the Palestinians, Rabbi Tzvi Yehuda Kook cited Maimonides to the effect that the Canaanites had three choices—to flee, to accept Jewish sovereignty, or to fight—implying that the decision by most Canaanites to resist Jewish rule justified their destruction (Kook 1982, 19). According to the Hebrew Bible, the Amalekites were a nomadic people who dwelt in the Sinai desert and southern Palestine, who were regarded as the Israelites' inveterate foe, and whose "annihilation" became a sacred duty, and against whom war should be waged until their "memory be blotted out" forever (Exodus 17.16; Deuteronomy 25.17–19). Although the biblical stories mention that the Amalekites were finally wiped out during the reign of Hezekiah in the eighth century bc, rabbinical literature dwells on Amalek's role as the Israelites' permanent arch-enemy, saying that the struggle between the two peoples will continue until the coming of the Messiah, when God will destroy the last remnants of Amalek.

Milhemet Mitzvah (Hebrew: "War by Commandment") is the biblical term for a war during which the Israelite kings would go to war against their enemies—such as the war against Amalek—in order to fulfill a commandment based on the Torah and without needing approval from a Sanhedrin. Some of the religious radicals insist on giving the biblical commandment to "blot out the memory of Amalek" an actual contemporary relevance in the conflict between Israelis and Palestinians. In February 1980, Rabbi Yisrael Hess, the former Campus Rabbi of the religious university of Bar-Ilan, published an article in the student bulletin *Bat Kol*, the title of which, "The Genocide Commandment in the Torah"

(Hebrew: "*Mitzvat Hagenocide Batorah*") leaves no place for ambiguity. The article ends with the following: "The day is not far when we shall all be called to this holy war, to this commandment of the annihilation of Amalek" (Hess 1980). In fact, the association of the Palestinians with the ancient Amalekites was made in a book written in 1974 by Rabbi Moshe Ben-Tzion Ishbezari, the Rabbi of Ramat Gan. Hess quotes the biblical commandment according to which he believes Israel, in the tradition of Joshua from biblical times, should act: "go and strike down Amalek; put him under the ban with all that he possesses. Do not spare him, but kill man and woman, baby and suckling, ox and sheep, camel and donkey" (Hess 1980; 1 Samuel 15:3). Hess adds,

> Against this holy war God declares a counter jihad . . . in order to emphasize that this is the background for the annihilation and that it is over this that the war is being waged and that it is not a conflict between two peoples . . . God is not content that we annihilate Amalek—"blot out the memory of Amalek"—he also enlists personally in this war . . . because, as has been said, he has a personal interest in this matter, this is the principal aim (Hess 1980).

Citing Hess's article, Amnon Rubinstein, a Knesset Member representing then the centrist Shinui Party and a lecturer in Law at Tel Aviv University, commented:

> Rabbi Hess explains the commandment which instructs the blotting out of the memory of Amalek and says that there is not the slightest mercy in this commandment which orders the killing and annihilation of also children and infants. Amalek is whoever declares war on the people of God. (Rubinstein 1980, 125)

Rubinstein points out that "no reservation on behalf of the editorial board, the students or the University was made after publishing this article which was also reprinted in other newspapers" (Rubinstein 1980, 179). However, a subsequent issue of *Bat Kol* (16 April 1980) carried two articles written by Professor Uriel Simon and Dr. Tzvi Weinberg severely criticizing the article of Rabbi Hess. Clearly for Hess Amalek is synonymous with the Palestinian Arabs, who have a conflict with Israeli Jews, and they must be "annihilated," including women, children and infants. His use of the Arabic term *jihad* leaves no doubt as to against whom such a war of "annihilation" should be waged.

These disturbing ideas were not confined to Rabbi Hess, who refers to the Palestinian Arabs as the "Amalekites of today," who "desecrate the Land of Israel." In his *On the Lord's Side* (1982) Danny Rubinstein has shown that this notion permeates the Gush Emunim movement's bulletins. Thus, *Nekudah* of 29 August 1980 (p. 12) carried an article written by Gush Emunim veteran Haim Tzoriyah, entitled "The Right to Hate," which reads: "In every generation there is an Amalek. The Amalekism of our generation finds expression in the deep Arab hatred towards our national revival in our forefathers' land." The same notion propagated by the messianic trend regarding the equiparation of the Palestinians with the Amalekites was widely discussed in the Israeli daily press and even on television. It was also criticized in moderate religious circles (Torah Ve'avodah, 1984). But it was the late Professor Uriel Tal, who was a prominent biblical scholar at Tel Aviv University, and who conducted his study in the early 1980s, who did more than anyone to expose the "annihilationist" notions preached by the rising messianic force in Israel. Professor Tal, who had also done extensive research on anti-Semitism between the two world wars, concluded that these messianic doctrines were similar to ideas common in Germany during the Weimer Republic and the Third Reich. The gist of Tal's research was presented to an academic forum at Tel Aviv University in March 1984 and was subsequently widely publicized in the Hebrew press and Israeli journals.

Tal pointed out that the radical messianic trend promotes a policy towards Palestinians consisting of three stages:

1. the reduction of the Palestinians in Jerusalem and the West Bank to the halacha status of "resident alien";

2. the promotion of Arab "transfer" and emigration (Nisan 1987);

3. the implementation of the commandment of Amalek, as expressed in Rabbi Hess's article: "The Commandment of Genocide in the Torah," in other words, "annihilating" the Palestinian Arabs (Uriel Tal in *Haaretz* [26 September 1984] 27; Kim 1984; Peri 1984; Rash 1986, 77).

Like Uriel Tal, many liberal Israelis found the resurgence of this messianic and anti-Arab trend a chilling prospect. Yoram Peri, an Israeli political scientist, remarked in 1984:

> The solution of the transports and the trucks is not the end of the story. There is a further stage which the proponents of racist Zionism do not usually refer to explicitly, since the conditions

for it are not ripe. But the principles are there, clear and inevitable. This is the stage of genocide, the annihilation of the Palestinian people. (Peri 1984)

Many Jewish fundamentalists make little distinction between the Palestinian citizens of Israel and those of the East Jerusalem, West Bank and Gaza: "Today there is no plan to make Hebron into a Jewish town . . . but if you ["the Arab neighbor"] think that Kiryat Arba will disappear, you had better remember Jaffa [the Arab town which was largely depopulated in 1948] . . . " Another speaker from the Gush Emunim settlement of 'Ofra, Aharon Halamish, was much more straightforward: "It is not necessary to throw bombs into the *casbah* or expel the Arabs. There is nothing wrong, however, with making their life difficult in the hope that they will emigrate . . . Perhaps in the end only those will remain who genuinely want to be loyal citizens of Israel, and if they really do, let them convert" (Jerusalem Post International 1980). Clearly this settler did not believe that many Arabs would agree to "convert" and therefore he suggested the encouragement of Palestinian emigration.

Many religious Zionist figures sought to legitimize discussions of ethnic cleansing. In October 1987, a prominent office-holder from the religious right, Yosef Shapira, a former member of the NRP and a minister in the cabinet of Yitzhak Shamir, referred to "transfer" as a reasonable and viable solution, suggesting that a sum of $20,000 should be paid to a Palestinian family ready to leave permanently (Sprinzak 1991, 346n20). In support of his proposal, Shapira cited a survey his party conducted among rabbis in the West Bank and Gaza Strip, in which 62 per cent of them responded that "we must force them to do so by any means at our disposal and see in it an exchange of population;" 13 per cent favored the encouragement of voluntary emigration (*Nekudah*, November 1987, 37). In the same year, in an article entitled "In Defense of the Transfer," published in *Nekudah* of 14 April 1987 (pp. 16–17), Moshe Ben-Yosef wrote:

> It is kosher to discuss the idea of transfer, and even to put it into effect . . . It is kosher not only because it is an "actual solution," but also because it is required for the vision of the whole Land of Israel . . . The idea of transfer has deep roots in the Zionist movement.

Gush Emunim's main organ, *Nekudah* ("Point") has, since its first appearance in December 1979, been assiduously popularizing the "transfer" idea. By 1986 its circulation had reached 10,000 copies sent to subscribers in the occupied territories and in Israel, including public institutions and public and academic libraries. *Nekudah* also appears in the form of pamphlets with a circulation of 50,000. The November 1987 issue of *Nekudah* discusses the results of a recent questionnaire on "security matters" conducted among rabbis, Yeshiva students and directors in the settlements of "Judea," "Samaria" and Gaza. 86 per cent of the respondents to the questionnaire from the Tzomet Institute in Elon Shvut settlement supported the imposition of collective punishment-on a refugee camp, *hamulah* or family-for Arab inhabitants. 64 percent were of the opinion that the collective punishment should be expulsion. 77 percent of the respondents believed that "Arab emigration should be encouraged," while 85 percent thought that the death penalty should be imposed on Arab "terrorists." Yisrael Harel, a Gush Emunim activist and the editor of *Nekudah*, wrote in January 1988: "half a year ago, 90 per cent of people would have objected to transfer. Today 30 to 40 per cent would argue that it's not a dirty word or an inhuman policy. On the contrary, they would argue it's a way to avoid friction." (Harel 1988). David Rosentzweig of Kidumim wrote in an article in *Nekudah* in December 1983:

> We should urge them [the Arabs] to get out of here. The Arab public must feel that the land (really the land) is being pulled from under its feet . . . the very fact of their presence endangers our life every day . . . For our own safety there is no place for the Arabs with us in this country . . . we must seek a new and revolutionary way to deal with the Jewish-Arab conflict.

Rabbi Yitzhak Levy was born in 1947 in Casablanca, Morocco, and immigrated to Israel in 1957. He served as leader of the National Religious Party and is currently Chairman of the same party. In the period 1996–2008, Levy served as Minister of Transport; Minister of Education and Culture; Minister of Religious Affairs; Minister of Housing and Construction; Minister without Portfolio; Minister of Tourism; Deputy Minister in the Prime Minister's Office; a Deputy Speaker of the Knesset. According to the daily *Haaretz* of 25 February 1998, Levy—who had previously made clear his opposition to allowing Israeli Arab Knesset members the right to vote on the Oslo Accords of 1993—was reputed to have supported "exiling Arabs" in the occupied territories to other Arab states (Jones 1999, 19). More recently, in June 2007, Levy urged the blocking of humanitarian aid reaching Gaza—in effect, starving the population—until captive Israeli soldier Gilad Shalit would be released.

Rabbi Levy is also known to be close to former Sephardic Chief Rabbi Mordechai Eliyahu, another advocate of Greater Israel, who has called for the rehabilitation of Yigal Amir, Yitzhak Rabin's assassin (Jones 1999, 19). In 1983, while serving as Sephardi Chief Rabbi, Eliyahu sponsored a conference with 'Ateret Cohanim Yeshiva on the rebuilding of the Third Temple in Jerusalem. He believes that the Third Temple would descend from heaven amidst flames of fire—at that point the Muslim shrines, the Dome of the Rock and al-Aqsa Mosque, would be burnt and the Third Temple built in their place (Ronel 1984, 12).

Israeli journalists, who have covered East Jerusalem and the West Bank for over three decades, provide some of the best accounts of the ideology of the settlers' movement and its anti-Arab racist concepts, as well as amply documenting its violence in the Occupied Territories (Grossman 1988). In his seminal work on Gush Emunim, Danny Rubinstein concludes that the majority of the Gush Emunim settlers are in favor of expelling the Arab population, describes the anti-Arab feelings that permeate the Gush Emunim meetings and provides excerpts from the settler movement's pamphlets and bulletins: "Hatred of the [Arab] enemy is not a morbid feeling, but a healthy and natural phenomenon"; "The people of Israel have a legitimate national and natural psychological right to hate their enemies"; "The Arabs are the Amalekites of today"; "The aim of the settlements in the Nablus area is "to stick a knife in the heart of the Palestinians" (Rubinstein 1982, 90–93 and 151). For the religious messainics, Jewish sovereignty over the "whole Land of Israel" was divinely ordained, since the entire land had been promised by God to the Jewish people. At least some leading Rabbis interpreted this biblical injunction regarding the Amalekites (1 Samuel 15:2–3) to justify not only the expulsion of local Arabs but also the killing of Arab civilians in the event of war (Aronson 1990, 289).

With the rise of the radical messianic force in Israel in the last three decades, many far-reaching ideas, such as annihilating the "Amalekites, Canaanites and Philistines of today" (have entered mainstream Zionist religious thinking. Inspired by a racist interpretation of some of the traditions of the Hebrew Bible, especially the Books of Exodus, Deuteronomy and Joshua, their discourse presents ethnic cleansing as not only legitimate, but as required by the divinity. It has already been shown that the discourse of ethnic cleansing is widely supported by nationalist religious groups as well as by the Gush Emunim movement, both leaders and members. If the very idea of Arab residence in Palestine is based on "theft," is morally flawed and legally temporary, according to Jewish fundamentalists in Israel, then, Arab removal is the logical conclusion. Rabbi Yisrael Ariel bluntly and explicitly demanded expelling the Palestinians as necessitated by Jewish religious commandments:

> On the one hand there is a commandment of settling *Eretz-Yisrael*, which is defined by our sages of blessed memory also as the commandment of "inheritance and residence"—a commandment mentioned many times in the Torah. Every young student understands that "inheritance and residence" means conquering and settling the land. The Torah repeats the commandment "You shall dispossess all the inhabitants of the land" tens of times, and Rashi [Rabbi Shlomo Yitzhaki, a paramount Bible and Talmud commentator in the 11th. century] explains that "You shall dispossess—You shall expel." The Torah itself uses the term "expulsion" a number of times such as: "Since you shall expel the inhabitants of the country with my help." The substance of this commandment is to expel the inhabitants of the land whoever they may be . . . This is also the opinion of Rashi in defining the commandment. In the same Talmudic passage which mentions the commandment pertaining to the land, Rashi interprets: "Because [of the commandment] to settle *Eretz-Yisrael*—to expel idolaters and to settle [the people of] Israel there." Thus according to Rashi the commandment to settle [the land] aims at the expulsion of the non-Jew from *Eretz-Yisrael* and that it be settled with Jews. (Ariel 1980)

For messianic Zionists, the Palestinians face the same predicament as the Canaanites of the Bible and have little choice but to leave their native land. Hence the approval of Jewish terrorism on the part of many Jewish fundamentalists is the logical and practical conclusion of the political messianic ideology of Greater Israel and is a political instrument designed to force the Arab population into evacuation (Nisan 1990/91, 139–41; Prior 2003, 26–29).

The political theology of the messianic Zionists, including the racist notion of the "Amalek of today," also found an echo in an article published by the Chief Military Rabbi of the IDF Central Command, Rabbi Avraham Zemel (Avidan) who, according to Professor Amnon Rubinstein, gave *halacha* justification for the "murder of non-Jewish civilians including women and children, during war" (Rubinstein 1980, 124). Rabbi Yisrael Ariel, using and abusing Maimonides, justified the campaign of the

Jewish Underground terrorist organizations, implying that the killing of a Palestinian was not murder:

> Anyone who searches through the code of Maimonides, which is the pillar of the *halacha* in the Jewish world, [and searches for] the concept "you shall not murder," or the concept "holy blood," with regard to the killing of a non-Jew-will search in vain, because he will not find [it] . . . It follows from the words of Maimonides that a Jew who kills a non-Jew . . . is exempt from the prohibition "you shall not murder." And so Maimonides writes of murder in the *halachot*: "An Israelite who kills a resident alien is not sentenced to death in the court of law" (Ariel 1980).

An Israeli soldier, who was also a yeshiva student, asked his Rabbi about the subject of *"tohar haneshik"* (the "purity of arms"). From the answer of the rabbi the soldier concluded: "During war I am permitted or even obliged to kill every male and female Arab that happens to be in my way . . . I must kill them even if this involves complication with the military law" (Rubinstein 1980, 124). Professor Rubinstein, who in his book *The Zionist Dream Revisited: From Herzl to Gush Emunim and Back* cites many references made by the spiritual mentors of Gush Emunim to the Arabs as the "Amalek of today," wrote critically in an article in *Haaretz* daily on 3 February 1983:

> We are dealing with a political ideology of violence. It is needless to show how this ideology is expressed in the way the Arabs are treated. The Rabbis of Gush Emunim-except for the few brave ones . . . publicly preach incitement to kill Arab civilians, and those who kill civilians, and are caught and brought to court, are later amnestied by the Chief of Staff [General Raphael Eitan], who believes in the use of violence that the Arabs understand." Those who think that it is possible to differentiate between blood and blood are wrong. The verdict on "Amalek" can easily be extended to the enemies within, the traitors.

Amnon Rubinstein wrote his article against the background of the attacks carried out by the extreme right on the Peace Now demonstrators and the increasing violence in Israeli political life in general as well as the resurgence of the far right and the national religious chauvinists. There is good reason to suggest that the greater the role of the Jewish *halacha* in the political life of Israel becomes, the more vigorously this messianic current will demand that the Palestinian Arabs be dealt with according to halachic regulations—including the imposition of the status of "resident alien" on them; the insistence on diminishing Arab numbers by making life more difficult; the revival of the command to "blot out the memory of Amalek"; the insistence that the Palestinians are the "Amalekites of today" to be dealt with by annihilations; and the repetition of the assertion that the killing a non-Jew is not a murder.

Milhemet Mitzvah and Territorial Expansionism

The neo-Zionist messianic current is inspired by maximalist territorial annexationism (Lustick 1988, 107; Shaham 1979; Elitzur 1978, 42–53); many rabbis in the Zionist religious camp see the Israeli army "operations" against the Palestinians as part of a *milhemet mitzvah* commanded by the Torah against modern Aamlek and the "Canaanites of today." Although at present the colonization drive is confined to the Occupied Territories, according to the late Ehud Sprinzak, the author of *The Ascendance of Israel's Radical Right*,

> When Gush ideologues speak about the complete [whole] Land of Israel they have in mind not only the post-1967 territory, but the land promised in the Covenant (Genesis 15) as well. This includes the Occupied Territories—especially Judea and Samaria, the very heart of the historic Israeli nation, and vast territories that belong now to Jordan, Syria and Iraq. (Sprinzak 1991, 113)

Traditionally Transjordan where, according to biblical myths and legends, the Israelite tribes of Reuven, Menashe and Gad were supposed to have resided, has been the primary focus of Gush Emunim's expansionist ambitions (Lustick 1988, 107), although other expansionist aspirations in all sorts of directions across the Fertile Crescent have also been openly expressed. In the judgment of the late Rabbi Tzvi Yehuda Kook, the spiritual leader of Gush Emunim, the destined borders of the Jewish state would stretch broadly across the whole area: Transjordan, the Golan Heights, the "Bashan" (the Jabal Druze region in Syria), are all part of the "Land of Israel" (Shaham 1979). Echoing the same geopolitical ambitions, Yehuda Elitzur, one of the most influential scholars in Gush Emunim, considered the "promised land" and "patriarchal" boundaries to extend to the Euphrates River, southern Turkey, Transjordan, and the Nile Delta; the lands which Israel is required eventually to conquer, "redeem," "inherit" and settle include northern Sinai, Lebanon and western Syria, the Golan Heights, and much of Transjordan (Elitzur 1978, 42–53).

The 1982 Invasion of Lebanon

Israel's military invasion of Lebanon in 1982 encouraged many religious Jews to discuss "*halachic* imperatives" towards territorial expansion in the direction of Lebanon, regardless of the price. These religious Jews claimed large tracts of Lebanon to be the domain of the biblical tribe of Asher. Beirut was even Hebraicised to Beerot—the Hebrew for "well." Members of the Israeli army's rabbinate issued a leaflet which quoted the "inheritance of Asher" in the Book of Joshua (Shindler 2002, 155). In September of that year the Gush Emunim journal *Nekudah* published "a study" of Yehuda Elitzur, which claimed that the most serious distortion of Israel's borders was in the north-in Lebanon (Lustick 1988, 107). The following month a paid advertisement of Gush Emunim in support of the invasion of Lebanon asserted that south Lebanon was part of *Eretz-Yisrael* and that the 1982 war "brought back the property of the tribes of Naftali and Asher into Israel's boundaries" (Talmom 1965, 37). In the same month messianic rabbis reiterated the same claim in a book entitled *This Good Mountain and the Lebanon*. Rabbis Ya'acov Ariel, Dov Lior and Yisrael Ariel declared southern Lebanon to be the lands of the (mythologized) biblical tribes of Zevulon, Asher and Naphtali. Yisrael Ariel went even further by asserting that the boundaries the Land of Israel included Lebanon up to Tripoli in the north, Sinai, Syria, part of Iraq and even part of Kuwait. In the same month he called for the annexation and settlement of most of Lebanon with its capital Beirut to Israel, at any price:

> Beirut is part of the Land of Israel-about that there is no controversy, and being that Lebanon is part of the Land of Israel we must declare that we have no intention of leaving. We must declare that Lebanon is flesh of our flesh, as is Tel Aviv and Haifa, and that we do this by right of the moral power granted to us in the Torah. Our leaders should have entered Lebanon and Beirut without hesitation, and killed every single one of them. Not a memory or a trace should have remained . . . We should have entered Beirut at any price, without regard to our own casualties, because we are speaking of the conquest of the Land of Israel . . . We should immediately divert the waters of the Litani to the Jordan [River] (*Nekudah*, 12 November 1982, 23).

Forty American rabbis who had been brought to the hills surrounding Beirut to view the Lebanese capital besieged and bombarded by the Israeli army declared that Operation Peace for Galilee was, Judaically, a just war and a *milhemet mitzvah*—a "commandment war" or an obligatory war—a war which resulted in the death of some 20,000 Palestinians and Lebanese. Following the invasion of Lebanon, a leading American Jewish scholar, Rabbi J. David Bleich, suggested that a verse from the biblical Song of Songs (4:8) supported the acquisition of southern Lebanon. Bleich interpreted this as another step towards complete redemption (Shindler 2002, 155). The Ashkenazi Chief Rabbi of Israel, Shlomo Goren, went even further and, following Maimonides, cited three categories of obligatory wars, which included Joshua's battle to clear the "land of Israel" when biblical Israelites crossed into Canaan, the battles against the Amalekites, who became the symbolic biblical enemies of the Israelites down the centuries, and the contemporary war in Lebanon (Shindler 2002, 156). The Lubavitcher Rebbe, the Hasidic leader who held court in Brooklyn and popularized the messianic idea, fiercely opposed Israel's partial withdrawal in 1985 from southern Lebanon, describing the area as Israel's "North Bank" which allegedly had been part of the biblical Land of Israel (Shindler 2002, 193).

Back in 1982, shortly before Israel's invasion of Lebanon and immediately after Israel's evacuation of the settlement of Yamit in northern Sinai, leading Gush Emunim figures, such as Beni Katzover and Rabbis Moshe Levinger and Haim Druckman, formed an organization called Shvut Sinai ("Return to Sinai"), dedicated to campaigning for the reconquest of Sinai by Israel and Jewish rule over it (Lustick 1988, 61). Two years later, in 1984, Ya'acov Feitelson, a Tehiya party member and the former mayor of Ariel, the largest Jewish settlement in the northern part of the West Bank, echoed the same Jewish imperial vision of an Israeli state stretching across the entire Arab East:

> I am speaking of a tremendous vision. We are only in the infancy of the Zionist movement . . . Israel must squarely face up to the implementation of the Zionist vision-a vision that has not changed since the days of Herzl. As is known Herzl never indicated what the borders of the state were to be . . . in his time the settlement [by Jews] of the Syrian desert was discussed. I say that Israel should establish new cities throughout the entire area. I mean really the whole area of the Middle East, without limiting ourselves: we should never say about any place: here we stop. (*Koteret Rashit* [14 November 1984] 23).

In the same year (1984), Rabbi Eli'ezer Waldman expressed opposition to the idea which was then being propagated by Likud leaders, such as Ariel Sharon and Yitzhak Shamir, that Jordan had become the

Palestinian homeland. Waldman and the majority of Gush Emunim opposed any final agreement relinquishing the East Bank of Jordan to non-Jewish rule (Lustick 1988, 107).

This geopolitical vision of territorial expansion across the region could only be ensured by military campaigns and holy wars. In fact the actual settlement drive in the West Bank is viewed and planned as nothing less than a military campaign. Military might, war and warfare are desired and often eagerly sought by many Neo-Zionist groups. War simply represents a time of testing, a sign of strength—a necessary means by which the will of Providence is worked out. Territorially ambitious rabbis and leaders of Gush Emunim share the same attitude to war. Within Gush Emunim, war, leading to Jewish rule over the "whole Land of Israel," is a central component of the purgative process that will bring about messianic times. Emphasizing expansion by military means, Rabbi Tzvi Kook advised the following:

> We are commanded both to possess and to settle [the land]. The meaning of possession is conquest, and in performing this *mitzvah*, we can perform the other-the commandment to settle . . . We cannot evade this commandment . . . Torah, war, and settlement-they are three things in one and we rejoice in the authority we have been given for each of them. (Kook 1982, 19)

In a similar vein Rabbi Shlomo Aviner writes:

> We have been commanded by the God of Israel and the creator of the world to take possession of this *entire* land, in its holy borders, and to do this by wars of defense, and even by wars of liberation. (Lustick 1988, 106)

Hanan Porat, a leading Gush Emunim figure, spoke in 1982 in terms of practical preparations for future opportunities that will arise:

> We must prepare ourselves in terms of our consciousness and by establishing new settlement nuclei, to settle those portions of the Land of Israel that today are still not in our hands . . . nuclei for the Litani area [in south Lebanon], Gilead, Transjordan, and Sinai (*Nekudah* 43 [12 May 1982] 17).

Emphasizing territorial expansion by military means, Rabbi Kook asserted,

> We are commanded both to possess and to settle [the land]. The meaning of possession is conquest, and in performing this

> *mitzvah*, we can perform the other—the commandment to set-
> tle . . . We cannot evade this commandment . . . Torah, war, and
> settlement—they are three things in one and we rejoice in the
> authority we have been given for each of them. (Kook 1982, 19)

In the political culture of the post-colonial world order, Israel is
a society plagued by the problem of identity politics and deep cultural
divisions (Kimmerling 1999, 339–63). On the liberal Israeli side, many
authors voiced strong criticism of messianic Zionism and pointed to the
violent activities of groups such as Jewish Underground and TNT as an
inevitable consequence of the philosophy and activities of Gush Emunim
(Shahak and Mezvinsky 1999; Evron 1995, 223–41; Shlaim 2000; Elon
1997). But the actual reluctance of the state in general and the Likud
administrations in particular to punish those settlers who murdered
Palestinian civilians, as exemplified by the delayed publication of, and
subsequent reticence over, the Karp report on settlers' violence against
Palestinians, only encouraged militant Gush Emunim settlers and their
radical right-wing supporters who were determined to drive the Palestinians out one way or another. The same reticence over widespread settler
violence against Palestinians must also have encouraged those Jewish
fundamentalists who were prepared to use violence against those perceived to be dovish Israeli Jews.

In the 1990s the Oslo process and the Israeli-Palestinian agreements
clearly shocked the messianic current, including the rabbis and leaders
of Gush Emunim, and brought to the surface the deep divisions that had
been developing inside Israeli society in response to the peace talks with
the Palestinians. The establishment of the Palestinian Authority in Gaza
and the West Bank and the appearance of armed Palestinian police and
the sight of Palestinians waving flags all constituted visible evidence of
the weaknesses of the messianic vision of a quick redemption.

In the 1990s the messianic rabbis even turned their hatred on the
"Jewish traitors," whose treason spoiled God's plan and influenced many
Israelis to disregard the divine commandments and to follow the traitors,
who were prepared to give away parts of the "sacred" land. Expressing the
deep divisions inside Israeli society and echoing religious Zionism's traditional hostility towards the symbols of Christianity in the Holy Land,
Rabbi Yair Dreyfus, a settlement leader, declared:

> The true Jews, desirous to live as Jews, will have no choice to sepa-
> rate themselves in ghettos, The new, sinful Canaanite-Palestinian

state [Israel after Oslo] will soon be established upon the ruins of the genuine Jewish-Zionist state . . . God may even make war against this polluted throne of his. The Jews who lead us into that sin no longer deserve any divine protection . . . Our leadership will walk a Via Dolorosa before it understands that we are commanded to resist the [secular] state of Israel, not just its present government. (in Shahak and Mezvinsky 1999, 89)

A Canaanite Reading of the Bible: Religion, Violence and Ethical Obligations

The biblical narrative is meaningless outside its worldly context. The question of Israel-Palestine forced Michael Prior the liberation theologian to recognize and reconfigure the key role of the biblical text within the project of European settler colonialism and empire. Already by 1918 some 85 percent of the earth was in the hands of European colonizing powers, with devastating effects on the indigenous populations of Africa, Asia and Latin American. Invariably the colonizers sought out some ideological principle to justify their deeds, and the Bible has often been, and still is for some (especially the Zionists), a text that redeems territorial conquests (Prior 1999, 130–33).

Inspired by Edward Said's critique of Orientalism, Prior sought to radicalize Christian theologies of liberation in general and Palestinian liberation theology in particular. He also benefited from the emergence of a post-colonial critical scholarship in the two last decades. Biblical "Minimalism," whose key contributors include Philip Davies (1992), Thomas L. Thompson (1987; 1991; 1992; 1999; 2003, 1–15; 2004), Niels Peter Lemche (1988; 1991; 1993, 163–93; 1998; 2000, 165–93; 2003), and Keith W. Whitelam (1996; Coote and Whitelam 1987), has emerged as an identifiable method of scholarship within biblical studies, and argues that the Bible's language is not an historical language. Minimalism has presented serious challenges to biblical scholars, Prior included. It was Prior's personal experiences and study of the Bible in the "land of the Bible" which helped him to see "with the eyes of the Canaanites." Until his death in July 2004 Prior continued to wrestle with the idea that biblical "mega narratives" were politically oppressive and morally reprehensible. Was Yahweh (Jehovah) the great "ethnic-cleanser"? Did Yahweh not instruct the biblical Israelites to rid their "promised land" of its indigenous inhabitants, the Canaanites? Few biblical scholars and those seeking to articulate theories of liberation are prepared to wrestle with these questions.

Despite Prior's extraordinary effort to sustain his main argument, especially with regard to the genocidal themes in the Book of Joshua and other "mega narratives" of the Bible, his thesis came under criticism from various scholars of ancient Palestine, including Professor Bernardo Gandulla, of the University of Buenos Aires. Gandulla, while sharing Prior's critique of the perverse use that Zionism and the Israeli state have made of the Bible to support their ethnic cleansing policies in Palestine, points out that Prior's interpretation of biblical narrative as the epitome of war crimes and crimes against humanity perpetrated against the Canaanite population of ancient Palestine, suggesting that we should "read the Bible with the eyes of the Canaanites," is a wrong interpretation or at least a lyrical metaphor drawn from his appreciation of the text (Gandulla 2005a, 103–4).

As Lemche pointed out, Canaanites and Israelites-Hebrews never existed as opposing peoples fighting over ancient Palestine (Lemche 1991). Although the Canaanites and Hebrews (as well the Philistines and Amorites) may all play the role of "peoples" in the Bible's narrative, they were not ethnic designations of the Bronze or early Iron Age. "Canaanites"—the name was a variation on other biblical names such as the Amorites or Jebusites—were hardly distinguishable and all "three groups" appear in different stories as the original population of Jerusalem. Furthermore in the biblical stories of Samson and Delilah (Judges 14:19–18:2), Saul and David, the "Philistines" are the people of the southern and central coastal plain of Palestine, where they play the role of the Hebrews' enemy, parallel to the role of the Canaanites of the holy war stories of Joshua and Judges. In Genesis, however, the Canaanites live in the Negev, together with the Philistines, Hittites and Amorites, and, in the role of indigenous peoples of Palestine, are friendly to the patriarchs.

Reading the Bible with the eyes of the Canaanites, Gandulla concluded, would only be possible if: (a) the actors of the Hebrew Bible narratives actually existed and were not mere ideological constructions, and (b) if the bloody events described therein, especially in the Book of Joshua, had actually taken place. Certainly, biblical traditions have little or no historical worth because, as Neils Lemche has pointed out, they were not conceived as history even though they contain historical elements since they are a reservoir of collective memory. The biblical narratives represent a set of epic cycles which have all the trimmings of violent conquests written long after the events by a population dominated by Greeks and Romans and driven by the need to legitimize and differentiate themselves from the Greco-Roman elite. Proof of this interpretation can be found in the almost contemporary work of Flavius Josephus (*The Wars of the Jews*) (Gandulla 2005a, 103–4; also 2005).

Gandulla argues that only if we consider that the Palestine of today and the Canaan of the past are one and the same indivisible cultural entity, will it become possible not only to read the Bible but also to understand the ideology of domination from an independent Canaanite viewpoint, in which all who truly defend justice will find a common ground irrespective of what faith they practice. Perhaps this is the message to be discovered in Prior's metaphor (Gandulla 2005a, 103–4).

Yet the Hebrew Bible is neither an historical account of Palestine's past, nor did its authors try to write history. It is a secondary collection of traditions complied by many authors who were theologically and ideologically motivated. The Bible is not history but theology, literature, law and ethics—a work of theology that does contain historical information; but if we want to evaluate this information we should consider when, how and why the Bible was compiled. Since the Bible is filled with literary and theological motifs and themes, it is necessary to understand the author's literary strategy before there is any attempt to use it in an historical synthesis.

Speaking the Truth and Inter-faith Dialogue

In his later writings Prior concentrated on the Bible's provision of alleged moral and theological legitimization for the ethnic cleansing and genocide of the indigenous inhabitants of Palestine. This was the main focus of his major work, *Zionism and the State of Israel: A Moral Inquiry* (Prior 1999b). The heart of the book deals with the biblical and mythical justification for Zionism. Prior takes a liberal approach to biblical scholarship arguing that the biblical claim to the divine promise of land is integrally linked with the claim of divine approval for the extermination of the indigenous people (ibid). The book also exposes the foundational myths of modern Zionism, showing (a) that its roots were in secular East European nationalism of the late nineteenth century and (b) that support for Zionism by religious Jews was a relatively recent phenomenon. Moreover, utilizing the "new" historiography of Palestine and Israel, he convincingly demonstrates that the 1948 Palestinian Nakba (catastrophe) and expulsion of the Palestinians had been intended and planned by the founding fathers of Zionism and the Israeli state from the outset (Masalha 1992; 1997; 2003).

Of course the various religious faiths at their best advocate non-violence, peace, justice and compassion. Prior, however, found incitement to war and violence in the very foundation documents of Judaism, Christianity and Islam. Jews, Christians and Muslims continue to refer to the Scriptures for archetypal conflicts which guide their reactions to threatening situations. In the Hebrew Bible, for instance, there is a dominant strand which sees Yahweh as coercive, "ethnocentric, xenophobic and militaristic" (Prior 1999b, 181). Particularly in their conquest of Canaan, the Israelites are commanded by God to kill and destroy the Canaanites and other indigenous inhabitants of ancient Palestine. Later in the days of the Israelite kingdoms, they are urged to show no pity, but to massacre their enemies. These Hebrew Scriptures eventually were adopted by Christians as the first part of their Bible—described as the Old Testament—and were used to justify atrocities that would not be condoned in the second part of their Bible, namely the New Testament (Morgan 2003). Today, both Christian Zionists in the West and Israeli messianics continue to refer to the Hebrew Scriptures for archetypal conflicts which guide their attitudes towards the indigenous inhabitants of Palestine: the Palestinian Muslims and Christians.

Prior was, inevitably, also critical of the classical works of Latin American liberation theology. Prior went further by arguing that even if one pursues the literature of liberationist theological writers, one would have to search long and hard to find any mention of the Israel-Palestine issue. He argued that the authors of the literature of liberation theology, which emphasizes the Exodus motif as the key for Christian theology, had nothing to say about the fate of the indigenous peoples of ancient Palestine that the biblical Israelites were instructed to dispossess and slaughter.

Still less do the same liberation theologians have anything to say about the settler colonial nature of modern Zionism or the plight of its Palestinian victims. For liberation theologians in Latin America and the West, Prior argued, it was apparently much easier to critique American imperialism in Latin America or monopoly capitalism than to speak the truth about Zionist settler colonialism and ethnic cleansing in the Holy Land.

Some mainstream Christian theologians in Britain and the US criticized Prior's methodology, arguing that he did not regard the Scriptures as the main source of his theology and that he took ethical ideas from secular humanist sources outside the Bible and then used them to critique the biblical texts. They further argued that Prior's radical and subversive approach was difficult to reconcile with the way many religious Jews and Christians (as well as the official teaching of the Roman Catholic Church) try to interpret the "Word of God." Some also argued that for Prior's critique of the biblical narrative to be accepted by a wider audience in the West, it needed to show how principles taken from the Hebrew Bible must themselves guide the interpretation of certain other passages of the Scriptures (such as the conquest narratives) so as to resist a literalist "genocidal" moral mandate.

Prior, of course, would admit that he was also influenced by enlightenment and secular humanist ideas originating outside the Scriptures, especially universal principles of human rights and international law. Although a theologian by training, methodologically his approach was multidisciplinary, grounded in the social sciences and benefiting from a range of secular and religious ideas and sources. When challenged at public meetings, Prior, typically, would respond to his critics by saying that the search for a hermeneutic of the Bible that would be sound theologically would be found in the person of *Jesus the Liberator* (Prior 1995). Also crucially he would argue that the question of Palestine was not just a theological issue; it was essentially a moral and ethical one.

Prior was particularly brilliant at debunking the mythical notion of "redemption" that was deployed in justification for the Zionist colonization of Palestine during the last century. Prior's dedication to truth-telling, his moral courage and pioneering scholarship are manifested in his last edited book, *Speaking the Truth about Zionism and Israel* (2004), with contributions from distinguished authors Professor Naseer Aruri (USA), Professor Rosemary Radford Ruther (USA), Professor Ilan Pappé (currently of Exeter), and South African Archbishop Desmond Tutu. The latter, one of the most influential theologians and critics of the Apartheid regime of South Africa, won the Nobel Peace Prize in 1984. He also chaired South Africa's Truth and Reconciliation Commission in 1995–1998. He had this to write in the Foreword to the Spanish edition of the *Bible and Colonialism*:

> The affairs of the Holy Land have long been a concern for Christians world-wide, and we in South Africa take a particular interest in them. The two countries have so much in common, and the forms of oppression in each demonstrate remarkable similarities. Over the last several years during which problems in South Africa have diminished, matters in the Holy Land have got increasingly worse, and the human tragedy has been multiplied. . . . The transformation in South Africa culminating in the liberation of the 1990s should encourage all those who strive for justice and peace in the Holy Land." (Tutu 2004, 9)

Prior's experience also convinced him that the Jewish-Christian "dialogue" had been hijacked by a Zionist agenda; he carried out extensive research on groups such as Dabru Emet ("speaking the truth"), whose "Jewish-Christian dialogue" was in fact a "monologue in two voices" (Prior 2004a). In his last article, "A Disaster for Dialogue," published posthumously in the Catholic weekly The Tablet (London), 31 July 2004, he powerfully challenged the claim that opponents of Zionism were necessarily anti-Semitic. He also comments that the eighteenth International Catholic-Jewish Liaison Committee, which met in Buenos Aires in July 2004, released a joint statement repeating many of the constant emphases of the Jewish-Christian dialogue of recent years. There were wider global concerns too: economic disparity and its challenges, ecological devastation, the negative aspects of globalization, and the urgent need for international peacemaking. One searches in vain, however, for an interfaith comment on the ever-deteriorating conditions in the Holy Land, and the challenge to justice and charity, or simply to justice and international legality, caused by the situation in Israel. There was not one mention of the Separation Wall dividing Jews and Palestinians. In the same article—and throughout much of his later work—Prior powerfully argued that when liberal Catholics and Protestants in the West variously apply the biblical message of liberation to current situations of political and racial oppression abroad, or to issues of social oppression relating to gender or sexuality at home, their careful avoidance of any reference to apartheid Israel, its Apartheid Wall at the heart of Palestine, and its current ethnic cleansing policies in Jerusalem and in Palestine as a whole is all the more remarkable.

The War Against Gaza: The Army Rabbinate and the War Against the "Philistines of Today"

The Hebrew Bible gave us the legend of Samson and Delilah (Judges 16) and the story of Samson's holy wars against the Philistines, who occupied the southern coastal cities of Canaan, including Gaza. In modern times Valdimir (Zeev) Jabotinsky, the leader of the Revisionist Betar movement, the forerunner of the present-day Likud, developed his concept of militant Zionism in his historical novel *Samson* (1930)—named after the legendary biblical figure who is said to have lived during the period when the Israelites were oppressed by the power of the ancient Philistines of Gaza and other southern coastal cities. In the novel the final message Samson sends to the Israelites consists of two words: "Iron" and "King," the two themes the Israelites were told to strive for so that they would become the lords of Canaan (cited in Bresheeth 189, 123). Jabotinsky's "Iron Wall" doctrine (Jabotinsky, 1923), in particular, with its revival of militarist biblical traditions from Joshua to Samson, and its celebration of modern militarism, has formed a central plank in Zionist attitudes towards the indigenous inhabitants of Palestine, through the early Mandatory period to the 1948 Palestinian catastrophe to the era of the "Separation (Apartheid) Wall" in the occupied West Bank.

Jabotinsky's "Iron Wall" doctrine manifested itself in the devastating military assault launched by Israel against the people of Gaza which began on 27 December 2008—in a campaign codenamed "Operation Cast Lead." Quoting sources in the Israeli defense establishment, the daily *Haaretz* reported that Defense Minister Ehud Barak had instructed the Israeli army to prepare for the campaign more than six months earlier. According to *Haaretz*, "long-term preparation, careful gathering of information, secret discussions, operational deception and the misleading of the public—all these stood behind "Operation Cast Lead" campaign against Hamas targets in the Gaza Strip" (Barak 2009). This widely-expected repetition of Israel's campaigns in Lebanon in 1982 and 2006 was carried out after nearly two years of a silent but no less brutal Israeli siege of the Gaza Strip. The ferocity of Israeli bombings and the ongoing siege of Gaza were little to do with the often *ineffectual Qassam rockets* fired at southern Israel. In fact "Operation Cast Lead" was taking place in the context of a fairly successful ceasefire with Hamas.

The Israeli campaign started with an intense bombardment of the Gaza Strip, including civilian infrastructure, mosques, houses and schools. After 22 days of the offensive against Gaza, Israel declared a unilateral ceasefire. In the days following the ceasefire, the BBC reported that more than 400,000 Gazans were left without running water. As a result of the Israeli bombings, 4,000 Gazan buildings were razed and 20,000 severely damaged. In the three-week war against the people of Gaza—with air strikes aimed at civilian areas in one of the most crowded and destitute stretches of land on earth—1,314 Palestinians were killed, mostly civilians, including 412 children, with the remainder being Palestinian police officers and Hamas fighters. Also 14 Israelis were killed during this conflict, including three civilians. The Israeli strikes not only killed scores of ordinary policemen and destroyed every police station in Gaza, but have killed and injured thousands of civilians; one air strike killed groups of young people in Gaza City on 27 December in a busy street. Seven of the dead were students on their way back home from a UN college for Palestinian refugees.

Deploying the biblical antagonism towards the ancient Philistines of Gaza, the Israeli army rabbinate played an important role in the war against the people of Gaza. On 26 January 2009 *Haaretz* reported on the substantial role of religious officers and soldiers in the front-line units of the army during the Israeli campaign, and on the fact that, for the first time, army units were supported by the significant presence of rabbis in the field. Also, on two occasions, the army weekly magazine *Bamahane* was full of praise for the army rabbinate. The chief army rabbi, Brigadier General Avihai Rontzki, himself joined the Israeli troops in the field on several occasions, as did other rabbis under his command. Israeli officers and soldiers reported that they felt "spiritually elevated" and "morally empowered" by conversations with rabbis who gave them encouragement before the campaign against the Palestinians. In mid-January, a reservist battalion rabbi told the religious newspaper *B'Sheva* that Rabbi and Brigadier General Rontzki explained to his staff that their role was "to fill them with yiddishkeit and a fighting spirit." *Haaretz* reporter Amos Harel writes:

> An overview of some of the army rabbinate's publications made available during the fighting reflects the tone of nationalist propaganda that steps blatantly into politics, sounds racist and can be interpreted as a call to challenge international law when it comes to dealing with enemy civilians. (Harel 2009)

Haaretz obtained some of the army rabbinate's publications through a group of former soldiers called "Breaking the Silence," soldiers who collected evidence of unethical conduct by the army during the campaign. The following are quotations from the material obtained:

> [There is] a biblical ban on surrendering a single millimeter of it [the Land of Israel] to gentiles, though all sorts of impure distortions and foolishness of autonomy, enclaves and other national weaknesses. We will not abandon it to the hands of another nation, not a finger, not a nail of it.

There was also an excerpt from a publication entitled "Daily Torah" studies for soldiers and commanders taking part in the campaign, issued by the army rabbinate. The text is from "Books of Rabbi Shlomo Aviner." The above-mentioned Aviner heads the 'Ateret Cohanim Yeshiva in the Muslim quarter of the Old City in Jerusalem. The following questions were posed in one publication: "Is it possible to compare today's Palestinians to the Philistines of the past? And if so, is it possible to apply lessons today from the military tactics of Samson and David?" Rabbi Aviner was again quoted as saying:

> A comparison is possible because the Philistines of the past were not natives and had invaded from a foreign land . . . They invaded the Land of Israel, a land that did not belong to them and claimed political ownership over our country . . . Today the problem is the same. The Palestinians claim they deserve a state here, when in reality there was never a Palestinian or Arab state within the borders of our country. Moreover, most of them are new and came here close to the time of the War of Independence. (ibid)

The army rabbinate, also quoting Rabbi Aviner, described the appropriate code of conduct in the field: "When you show mercy to a cruel enemy, you are being cruel to pure and honest soldiers. This is terribly immoral. These are not games at the amusement park where sportsmanship teaches one to make concessions. This is a war on murderers." (ibid)

The same view was echoed in publications signed by Rabbis Chen Halamish and Yuval Freund on Jewish consciousness. Freund argues that "our enemies took advantage of the broad and merciful Israeli heart" and warns that "we will show no mercy on the cruel." In addition to these official publications, right-wing groups managed to bring into army bases flyers and pamphlets addressed to Israeli soldiers and commanders with racist messages. One such flyer was attributed to "the pupils of Rabbi Yitzhak Ginsburg"—the former rabbi at Joseph's Tomb and author of the article "Baruch the Man," which praised Dr. Baruch Goldstein, an American born Israeli army physician who massacred 29 Palestinians (and wounded another 150) at prayer in the Ibrahimi Mosque in Hebrew in February 1994. The flyer called on

> Soldiers of Israel to spare your lives and the lives of your friends and not to show concern for a population that surrounds us and harms us. We call on you . . . to function according to the law "kill the one who comes to kill you." As for the population, it is not innocent . . . We call on you to ignore any strange doctrines and orders that confuse the logical way of fighting the enemy. (ibid)

By any standard, the Israeli blitz against Gaza was a crime against humanity, taking place against a largely defenseless civilian population in what has been described as the largest concentration camp in the world. Quoting ancient texts to justify modern crimes against humanity, the Rabbi of Kiryat Arba, Dov Lior, was recently quoted as saying: "A thousand non-Jewish lives are not worth a Jew's fingernail" (Amayreh 2008). According to *Haaretz*, Rabbi 'Ovadia Yosef, a former chief Rabbi and the spiritual leader of the ultra-orthodox Shas party and who is considered by many in Israel as one of the greatest living sages of the Torah, was quoted as telling his followers during a weekly sermon in Jerusalem that Israeli soldiers need to be blessed by God for killing and maiming Palestinians; "Had it not been for them, would we have time to study the Torah?" Clearly these rabbis think that it is only through murder of Palestinians that Jews can sit down and study the Torah. (ibid)

The ascendance of Israel's extreme right (with both its secular and fundamentalist currents) has been exemplified by the meteoric rise of Yisrael Beiteinu, whose leader, Deputy Prime Minister Avigdor Lieberman—a Moldovan immigrant and a member of Rabbi Meir Kahane's Kach party in his youth (Livy 2009)—has been at the centre of Israeli politics in recent years. A secular far right party, Yisrael Beiteinu openly advocates expulsion of the Palestinian citizens, who constitute about one-fifth of Israel's seven million citizens. On the eve of the 2009 general election *Haaretz* published an article entitled: "Lieberman's anti-Arab ideology wins over Israel's teens." Typical of this inflammatory racist rhetoric is the slogan: "Death to the Arabs" which has become as popular a chant among Israeli youth nowadays as the Tikva, Israel's national anthem. Apparently you hear the former far more frequently than the latter in the 2009 election rallies, in football matches and in random gatherings of Israeli youth anywhere near the Palestinian citizens of Israel, especially in mixed cities like Jaffa, Acre, Ramle, and in Upper Nazareth.

At the same time the radical religious right has remained a driving force in the Israeli colonization of the Occupied Territories. Having organized themselves into a militant, well-disciplined force inside and outside the Israeli army, with the encouragement of successive Israeli governments, and having always regarded themselves as being subject to militant divine, biblical and halachic laws, the messianic rabbis and their fanatical followers in Jewish settlements of the Occupied Territories would represent the severest challenge to any Israeli government which might consider ceding West Bank territory to Palestinian sovereignty. Moreover as messianic theology spreads in Israel, with its mystical and fanatical attacks on rationalism, its repercussions for inter-ethnic and inter-faith relations in the Holy Land at large is a major concern.

References

Amayreh, Khalid. 2008. "Ovadia Yosef: The Israeli Rabbi of Hate." *Cross-Cultural Understanding* (5 March). http://www.ccun.org/Opinion%20Editorials/2008/March/5%200o/Ovadia%20Yosef%20The%20Israeli%20Rabbi%20Of%20Hate%20By%20Khalid%20Amayreh.htm (accessed 3 September 2008).

Appleby, R. Scott, ed. 1997. *Spokesmen for the Despised: Fundamentalist Leaders of the Middle East*. Chicago: University Press of Chicago.

Aran, Gideon. 1997. "The Father, the Son and the Holy Land: The Spiritual Authorities of Jewish-Zionist Fundamentalism in Israel." In *Spokesmen for the Despised*, ed. R Scott Appleby, 294–327. Chicago: University Press of Chicago.

Ariel, Yisrael. 1980. "Devarim Kehavayatam" [Things as They Are]. *Tzippiyah I: Anthology of Contemporary Problems, Israel, the Land, and the Temple*. Jerusalem: Hamateh 'Lema'an Ahai ve Rea'ai.

Aronoff, Myron J. 1985. "The Institutionalization and Cooptation of a Charismatic, Messianic, Religious-Political Revitalization Movement." In *The Impact of Gush Emunim*, edited by David Newman, 46–69. London: Croom Helm.

Aronson, Geoffrey. 1990. *Israel, Palestinians and the Intifada*. London: Kegan Paul.

Ateek, Naim S., and Michael Prior, eds. 1999. *Holy Land—Hollow Jubilee: God, Justice and the Palestinians*. London: Melisende.

Aviner, Shlomo. 1982. "Haumah Veartzah" [The People and its Land]. *Artzi* 1 (Jerusalem) 11.

———. 1983. "Yerushat Haaretz Vehabe'ayah Hamusarit" [The Inheritance of the Land and the Moral Problem]. *Artzi* 2 (Jerusalem).

————. 2000. *Lemikdashkha Tashuv: Yerushalayim Ve-Hamikdash* [You Will Return to Your Temple: Jerusalem and the Temple]. Bet El settlement, West Bank: Sifriyat Hava.

Barak, David. 2008. "Disinformation, secrecy and lies: How the Gaza offensive came about." *Haartez* (31 December). http://www.haaretz.com/hasen/spages/1050426. html (accessed 7 February 2009).

Bernal, Martin. 1987. *Black Athena: The Afroasiatic Roots of Classical Civilization.* New Jersey: Rutgers University Press.

Biet-Hallahmi, Benjamin. 1992. *Original Sins: Reflections on the History of Zionism and Israel.* London: Pluto.

Bresheet, Haim. 1989. "Self and Other in Zionism: Palestine and Israel in Recent Hebrew Literature." In *Palestine: Profile of an Occupation,* 120–52. London: Zed.

Burge, Gary M. 2003. *Whose Land? Whose Promise?* Cleveland: Pilgrim.

Chomsky, Noam. 1975. *Peace in the Middle East? Reflections of Justice and Nationhood.* Glasgow: Fontana/Collins.

————. 1983. *The Fateful Triangle: The United States, Israel and the Palestinians.* London: Pluto.

Cook, Jonathan. 2006. *Blood and Religion: The Unmasking of the Jewish and Democratic State.* Ann Arbor, MI: Pluto.

Coote, R. B., and Keith W. Whitelam. 1987. *The Emergence of Early Israel in Historical Perspective.* Sheffield: Sheffield Academic.

Cygielman, Victor. 1977. "The Clericalization of Israel." *New Outlook* 20.7 (October-November) 28–37.

Davies, Philip R. 1992. *In Search of Ancient Israel.* Sheffield: Sheffield Academic.

————. 1994. "A House Built on Sand." *Biblical Archaeology Review* 20:54–55.

————. 2001. "The Intellectual, the Archaeologist and the Bible." In *The Land That I Will Show You: Essays on the History and Archaeology of the Ancient Near East in Honor of J. Maxwell Miller,* edited by J. Andrew Dearman and M. Patrick Graham, 239–53. Sheffield: Sheffield Academic.

————. 2002. "Minimalism, 'Ancient Israel,' and Anti-Semitism." *The Bible and Interpretation.* http://www.bibleinterp.com/articles/Minimalism.shtml (accessed on 30 March 2006).

————. 2003. "Final Comments on Minimalism." *The Bible and Interpretation* (June). http://www.bibleinterp.com/articles/Davies_Final_Comments.shtml (accessed on 25 April 2006).

Docker, John. 2008. *The Origins of Violence: Religion, History and Genocide.* London: Pluto Press.

Eban, Abba. 1984. *Heritage, Civilization and the Jews.* London: Weidenfeld and Nicolson.

Elitzur, Yehuda. 1978. "The Borders of Eretz Israel in the Jewish Tradition." In *Whose Homeland,* edited by Avner Tomaschoff, 42–53. Jerusalem: The World Zionist Organization.

Elon, Amos. 1971. *The Israelis: Founders and Sons.* London: Weidenfeld and Nicholson.

————. 1996. *Jerusalem: City of Mirrors.* London: Flamingo.

————. 1997. *A Blood-Dimmed Tide: Dispatches from the Middle East.* New York: Columbia University Press.

————. 1997a. "Politics and Archaeology." In *The Archaeology of Israel*, edited by Neil Asher Silberman and David Small, 35–34. Journal for the Study of the Old Testament, Supplement series 237. Sheffield: Sheffield Academic.

Evron, Boaz. 1995. *Jewish State or Israeli Nation?* Bloomington: Indiana University Press. Translation of *Hahisbon Haleumi*, "The National Reckoning" (1986).

Farsoun, Samih K. 2004. *Culture and Customs of the Palestinians*. Westport, CT: Greenwood.

Friedman, Robert I. 1992. *Zealots for Zion: Inside Israel's West Bank Settlement Movement*. New York: Random House.

Gandulla, Bernardo. 2005. *Los Hebreos en el Gran Canaán: del Bronce Antiguo al Bronce Tardío*. Buenos Aries: Editorial Canaán.

————. 2005a. "The Bible and Colonialist Discourse." Review of Michael Prior's *La Biblia y el Colonialismo: una crítica moral. Holy Land Studies: A Multidisciplinary Journal* 4.1 (November) 103–4.

Gertz, Nurith. 2000. *Myths in Israeli Culture: Captives of a Dream*. London: Vallentine Mitchell.

Gorenberg, Gershom. 2000. *The End of Days: Fundamentalism and the Struggle for the Temple Mount*. Oxford and New York: Oxford University Press.

Gorny, Yosef. 1994. *The State of Israel in Jewish Public Thought*. London: Macmillan.

————. 1987. *Zionism and the Arabs, 1882–1948*. Oxford: Clarendon.

Grossman, David. 1988. *The Yellow Wind*. London: Jonathan Cape.

Harkabi, Yehoshafat. 1986. *Hakhra'ot Goraliyot* [Fateful Decisions]. Tel Aviv: 'Am 'Oved [Hebrew].

Harel, Amos. 2009. "We will show no mercy on the cruel." *Haaretz* (26 January). http://www.haaretz.com/hasen/spages/1058758.html (accessed on 26 January 2009).

Harel, Yisrael. 1988. Quoted in *Jerusalem Post International* (30 January).

Hess, Yisrael. 1980. "Mitzvat Hagenocide Batorah," [The Genocide Commandment in the Torah]. *Bat Kol* (26 February).

Inbari, Pinchas. 1984. "Underground: Political Background and Psychological Atmosphere," *New Outlook* (June-July) 10–11.

Jabotinsky, Vladimir. 1923. *The Iron Wall: We and the Arabs*. First published in Russian under the title "O Zheleznoi Stene in Rasswyet," 4 November 1923; published in English in *Jewish Herald* (South Africa), 26 November 1937. Online: http://www.marxists.de/middleast/ironwall/ironwall.htm (accessed on 2 June 2006).

Jerusalem Post International. 1980. Cited in *Journal of Palestine Studies* 10.1 (Autumn 1980) 150.

Joffe, Lawrence. 1996. *Keesing's Guide to the Mid-East Peace Process*. London: Cartermill Publishing.

Jones, Clive. 1999. "Ideo-Theology and the Jewish State: From Conflict to Conciliation?" *British Journal of Middle Eastern Studies* 26.1:9–26.

Lefebure, Leo. 2002. *Sacred Violence and Interreligious Conflict: The Background of a Tragedy*. Chicago Studies 41.1 (Spring 2002). http://www.everydayzen.org/teachings/essay_sacredviolence.asp.

Lazare, Daniel. 2002. "False Testament: Archaeology Refutes the Bible's Claim to History." *Harper's Magazine* (March 2002). http://www.worldagesarchive.com/Reference_Links/False_Testament_(Harpers).htm (accessed on 20 April 2006)

Livy, Gideon. 2009. In *Haaretz*, 8 February 2009.

Kahane, Meir. 1980. *Lesikim Be'enekhem* [They shall be Strings in Your Eyes]. Jerusalem: Hamakhon Lara'ayon Hayehudi.

Khalidi, Rashid. 1997. *Palestinian Identity: The Construction of Modern National Consciousness.* New York: Columbia University Press.

Kim, Hanna. 1984. "To Annihilate Amalek." *'Al-Hamishmar* (12 March).

Kimmerling, Baruch. 1999. "Religion, Nationalism and Democracy in Israel." *Constellations* 6.3:339–63. Hebrew version: *Zmanim* 50 (December 1994).

———. 2003. *Politicide: Ariel Sharon's War Against the Palestinians.* London and New York: Verso.

Kook, Tzvi Yehuda. 1982 "Bein Am Veartzo" [Between People and Its Land] *Artzi* 2 (Spring) 15–23.

Lemche, Niels Peter. 1988, reprinted 1995. *Ancient Israel: A New History of the Israelite Society.* Sheffield: Sheffield Academic.

———. 1991, reprinted 1999. *The Canaanites and Their Land.* Sheffield: Sheffield Academic.

———. 1993. "The Old Testament—a Hellenistic Book?" *Scandinavian Journal of the old Testament* 7:163–93.

———. 1998. *The Israelites in History and Tradition.* Louisville: Westminster John Knox.

———. 2000. "Ideology and the History of Ancient Israel." *Scandinavian Journal of the Old Testament* 14.2:165–93.

———. 2003. "Conservative Scholarship-Critical Scholarship: Or How Did We Get Caught by This Bogus Discussion." *The Bible and Interpretation* (September). http://www.bibleinterp.com/articles/Conservative_Scholarship.htm.

Lior, Dov. 1986. "The Arabs and Us." *Artzi* 4 (Spring) 21.

LeVine, Mark. 2009. *Impossible Peace: Israel/Palestine since 1989.* New York: Zed.

Lustick, Ian. 1980 *Arabs in the Jewish State: Israel's Control of a National Minority.* Austin: University of Texas Press.

———. 1987. "Israel's Dangerous Fundamentalists." *Foreign Policy* 68:118–39.

———. 1988. *For the Land and the Lord: Jewish Fundamentalism in Israel.* New York: Council on Foreign Relations.

Macpherson, Duncan, ed. 2006. *A Living Stone: Selected Essays & Addresses.* London: London: Living Stones of the Holy Land Trust and Melisende.

Margalit, Avishai. 1991. "The Myth of Jerusalem." *The New York Review of Books* (19 December). http://www.nybooks.com/articles/archives/1991/dec/19/the-myth-of-jerusalem/?pagination=false.

Masalha, Nur. 1992. *Expulsion of the Palestinians: The Concept of "Transfer" Zionist Political Thought, 1882–1948.* Washington DC: Institute for Palestine Studies.

———. 1997. *A Land Without a People.* London: Faber and Faber.

———. 2000. *Imperial Israel and the Palestinians: The Politics of Expansion.* London and Sterling VA: Pluto Press.

———. 2002. "Reinventing Maimonides: From Universalist Philosopher to Religious Fundamentalist (1967–2002)." *Holy Land Studies: A Multidisciplinary Journal* 1.1 (September) 85–117.

———. 2003. *The Politics of Denial: Israel and the Palestinian Refugee Problem.* London and Sterling VA: Pluto.

———, ed. 2005. *Catastrophe Remembered: Palestine, Israel and the Internal Refugees: Essays in Memory of Edward W. Said.* London: Zed.

Morgan, Barry. 2003. "Religion and Conflict in Recent International Events." Anniversary lecture of the Archbishop of Wales and Bishop of Llandaff, to the Welsh Centre for International Affairs," 20 November 2003. http://www. churchinwales.org.uk/structure/bishops/sermons-and-addresses-archbishop-barry-morgan/b02/ (accessed on 12 February 2005).

Neumann, Michael. 2002. "What's So Bad About Israel?" *Counter-Punch*, 6 July 2002. http://www.counterpunch.org/neumann0706.html (accessed 5 February 2006).

Newman, David. 1982. *Jewish Settlement in the West Bank: The Role of Gush Emunim*, Occasional Paper 16. Durham: Centre for Middle Eastern and Islamic Studies, University of Durham.

———, ed. 1985. *The Impact of Gush Emunim*. London: Croom Helm.

———. 1994. "Gush Emunim" (Bloc of the Faithful). In *New Encyclopedia of Zionism and Israel*, 1:533. London: Associated University Presses.

Nisan, Mordechai. 1983. "Judaism and Politics." *The Jerusalem Post* (18 January).

———. 1984. In *Kivunim* (official publication of the World Zionist Organization) 24 (August) 151–56.

———. 1986. *Hamedinah Hayehudit Vehabe'ayah Ha'arvit* [The Jewish State and the Arab Problem]. Tel Aviv: Hadar.

———. 1990/91. "The Persian Gulf Crisis and the New Order in the Middle East." *Haumah* 102 (Winter) 139–41.

———. 1991. "Arab Hostages." *Modelet*, nos. 28–29 (February-March) 21.

———. 1992. *Toward a New Israel: The Jewish State and the Arab Question*. New York: AMS Press.

Pappé, Ilan. 1992. *The Making of the Arab-Israeli Conflict, 1947–1951*. London: I. B. Tauris.

———. 2000. "Israel at a Crossroads between Civic Democracy and Jewish Zealotocracy." *Journal of Palestine Studies* 29.3 (April) 33–44.

———. 2004. *A History of Modern Palestine: One Land, Two Peoples*. Cambridge: Cambridge University Press.

———. 2004a. "Palestine and Truth, Culture and Imperialism: The Legacy of Edward W. Said." *Holy Land Studies: A Multidisciplinary Journal* 2.2 (March) 135–39.

Pardes, Ilana. 1992. *Countertraditions in the Bible: A Feminist Approach*. Cambridge, MA: Harvard University Press.

Peri, Yoram. 1984. "Expulsion is not the Final Solution." *Davar* 3 (August).

Pearlman, Moshe. 1965. *Ben-Gurion Looks Back*. London: Weidenfeld and Nicholson.

Pichnik, Rabbi, ed. 1968. *Shanah Beshanah, 5728*. [Year by Year]. Jerusalem: Hekhal Shlomo.

Prior, Michael. 1995. *Jesus the Liberator: Nazareth Liberation Theology (Luke 4.16–30)*. Sheffield: Sheffield Academic.

———. 1997. *The Bible and Colonialism: A Moral Critique*. Sheffield: Sheffield Academic.

———. 1997a. "Settling for God." *Middle East International* 565 (19 December) 20–21.

———. 1998. "The Moral Problem of the Land Traditions of the Bible." In *Western Scholarship and the History of Palestine*, edited by Michael Prior, 41–81. London: Melisende.

———. 1999. "The Bible and the Redeeming Idea of Colonialism." *Studies in World Christianity* 5.2: 129–55.

————. 1999a. "The Bible and Zionism." In *Holy Land—Hollow Jubilee*, edited by Naim S. Ateek and Michael Prior, 69–88. London: Melisende.

————. 1999b. *Zionism and the State of Israel: A Moral Inquiry*. London: Routledge.

————, ed. 2000. *They Came and They Saw: Western Christian Experiences of the Holy Land*. London: Melisende.

————. 2000a. "Zionist Ethnic Cleansing: the Fulfillment of Biblical Prophecy?" *Epworth Review* 27:49–60.

————. 2001. "The Right to Expel: The Bible and Ethnic Cleansing." In *Palestinian Refugees and their Right of Return*, edited by N. Aruri, 9–35. London: Pluto.

————. 2002. "Ethnic Cleansing and the Bible: A Moral Critique." *Holy Land Studies: A Multidisciplinary Journal* 1.1 (September) 44–45.

————. 2003. "A Moral Reading of the Bible in Jerusalem." In *Jerusalem in Ancient History and Tradition*, edited by Thomas L. Thompson, 16–48. London: T. & T. Clark.

————. 2003a. "En paz, en el lugar descanso: Una appreciation de Edward W. Said." In *El Legado de Edward W. Said*, edited by Saad Chedid, 65–82. Buenos Aires: Editorial Canaan.

————. 2003b. "The State of the Art: Biblical Scholarship and the Holy Land." *Holy Land Studies: A Multidisciplinary Journal* 1.1 (March) 192–218.

————. 2004. *Speaking the Truth about Zionism and Israel*. London: Melisende.

————. 2004a. "The State of Israel and Jerusalem in the Jewish-Christian Dialogue: A Monologue in Two Voices." *Holy Land Studies: A Multidisciplinary Journal* 3.2 (May) 145–70.

————. 2006. "Reading the Bible with the Eyes of the Canaanites: In *Homage to Edward Said*." In *A Living Stone: Selected Essays and Addresses*, edited by Duncan Macpherson, 273–96. London: Living Stones of the Holy Land Trust and Melisende.

Rachlevsky, Seffe. 1998. *Hamuro Shel Mashiah* [Messiah's Donkey]. Tel Aviv: Yedi'ot Aharonot.

Rash, Yehoshu'a. 1986. "Uriel Tal's Legacy." *Gesher* 32.114: 71–83.

Ravitzky, Aviezer. 1996. *Messianisn, Zionism and Jewish Religious Radicalism*. Chicago: University of Chicago Press.

Rawson, Claude. 2001. *God, Gulliver, and Genocide: Barbarism and the European Imagination*. Oxford: Oxford University Press.

Ronel, Eti. 1984. "Inside Israel: The Battle for Temple Mount." *New Outlook* (February 1984) 11–14.

Rose, John. 2004. *The Myths of Zionism*. London: Pluto.

Rubinstein, Amnon. 1980. *Mehertzel Ad Gush Emunim Uvehazarah* [From Herzl to Gush Emunim and Back Again]. Tel Aviv: Schocken.

Rubinstein, Danny. 1982. *Mi La-H' Elai: Gush Emunim* [On the Lord's Side: Gush Emunim]. Tel Aviv: Hakibbutz Hameuhad.

Ruether, Rosemary Radford. 1998. "Christianity and the Future of the Israeli-Palestinian Relations." In *Remembering Deir Yassin*, edited by Daniel McGowan and Marc H. Ellis, 112–22. New York: Olive Branch.

Ruether, Rosemary Radford, and Herman J. Ruether. 2002. *The Wrath of Jonah: The Crisis of Religious Nationalism in the Israeli-Palestinian Conflict*. 2nd ed. Minneapolis: Fortress.

Said, Edward W. 1978. *Orientalism*. London: Routledge and Kegan Paul International.

————. 1986. "Michael Walzer's *Exodus and Revolution*: A Canaanite Reading." *Arab Studies Quarterly* 8.3 (Summer) 289–303.

———. 1988. "Michael Walzer's *Exodus and Revolution*: A Canaanite Reading." In *Blaming the Victims*, edited by Edward S. Said and Christopher Hitchens, 161–178. New York: Verso.

Said, Edward W., and Christopher Hitchens, eds. 1988. *Blaming the Victims: Spurious Scholarship and the Palestinian Question.* New York: Verso.

Schnall, David J. 1984. *Beyond the Green Line: Israeli Settlements West of the Jordan.* New York: Praeger.

————. 1985. "An Impact Assessment." In *The Impact of Gush Emunim*, edited by David Newman, 13–26. London: Croom Helm.

Shahak, Israel. 1994. *Jewish History, Jewish Religion.* London: Pluto.

Shahak, Israel, and Norton Mezvinsky. 1999. *Jewish Fundamentalism in Israel.* London: Pluto.

Shaham, David. 1979. "*Yedi'ot Aharonot*, supplement, 13 April." In "Zionist Settlement Policy," by Donald S. Will, *Journal of Palestine Studies* 11.3 (Summer 1979) 40.

Shindler, Colin. 1995, 2002. *The Land Beyond Promise: Israel, Likud and the Zionist Dream.* New York: I. B. Tauris.

————. 2002. "Likud and the Search for Eretz Israel: From the Bible to the Twenty-First Century." In *Israel, the First Hundred Years Vol.III: Israel Politics and Society since 1948: Problems of Collective Identity*, edited by Efraim Karsh, 91–117. London: Frank Cass.

Shlaim, Avi. 1996. *Collusion across the Jordan.* Oxford: Oxford University Press.

————. 1996a. "The Last Testament of Yehoshafat Harkabi." *Middle East International* (5 January) 18.

————. 2000. *The Iron Wall: Israel and the Arab World.* London: The Penguin Press.

————. 2004. *The New History of 1948 and the Palestinian Nakba.* http://www.miftah.org/PrinterF.cfm?DocId=3336.

Skutel, H.J. 1983. "Purifying Zion." *Journal of Palestine Studies* 12.2:83–85.

Sprinzak, Ehud. 1977. "Extreme Politics in Israel." *The Jerusalem Quarterly* 15 (Fall) 33–47.

————. 1991. *The Ascendance of Israel's Radical Right.* Oxford and New York: Oxford University Press.

Shraga, Nadav. 2008. "An Eye for an Eye." *Haaretz* 5 (May) http://www.haaretz.com/hasen/spages/980600.html (accessed 3 September 2008).

Smith, Anthony D. 1986. *The Ethnic Origin of Nations.* London: Blackwell.

Sternhell, Zeev. 1998. *The Founding Myths of Israel: Nationalism, Socialism and the Making of the Jewish State.* Princeton: Princeton University Press.

Talmon, Jacob L. 1965. "Who Is a Jew?" *Encounter* 24.5 (May) 28–35.

————. 1965a. *The Unique and the Universal.* London: Secker and Warburg.

Tessler, Mark. 1986. "The Political Right in Israel: Its Origins, Growth and Prospects." *Journal of Palestine Studies* 15.2 (Winter) 12–55.

Thompson, Thomas L. 1987. *The Origin Tradition of Ancient Israel I, Journal for the Study of the Old Testament Supplementary* Series 55. Sheffield: Sheffield Academic.

————. 1991. "Text, Context and Referent in Israelite Historiography." In *Fabric of History*, edited by D. V. Edelman, 65–92. Sheffield:Sheffield Academic.

————. 1992. *Early History of the Israelite People.* Brill: Leiden.

————. 1999. *The Bible in History: How Writer's Create a Past*. London: Jonathan Cape. [American edition, *The Mythical Past*. New York: Basic Books.]

————. 2003. "Is the Bible Historical? The Challenge of 'Minimalism' for Biblical Scholars and Historians," *Holy Land Studies: A Multidisciplinary Journal* 3:1 (May) 1–27.

————, ed. 2003a. *Jerusalem in Ancient History and Tradition*. London: T. & T. Clark.

————. 2008. "The Politics of Reading the Bible in Israel." *Holy Land Studies: A Multidisciplinary Journal* 7.1 (May) 1–15.

Tomaschoff, Avner, ed. 1978. *Whose Homeland*. Jerusalem: The World Zionist Organization.

Torah Ve'avodah [Torah and Work] 6. 1984. Jerusalem.

Tutu, Desmond Mpilo. 2004. "Foreword." In *Speaking the Truth about Zionism and Israel*, edited by Michael Prior, 9–12. London: Melisende.

Yiftachel, Oren. 2006. *Ethnocracy: Land and Identity Politics in Israel/Palestine*. Philadelphia, PA: University of Pennsylvania Press.

Walzer, Michael. 1985. *Exodus and Revolution*. New York: Basic Books.

Warrior, Robert Allen. 1989. "Canaanites, Cowboys and Indians: Deliverance, Conquest, and Liberation Theology Today." *Christianity and Crisis* 49:261–65.

————. 1991. "A Native American Perspective: Canaanites, Cowboys, and Indians." In *Voices from the Margin: Interpreting the Bible in the Third World*, , edited by R. S. Sugirtharajah, 297–95. London: SPCK.

Whitelam, Keith W. 1996. *The Invention of Ancient Israel: The Silencing of Palestinian History*. London: Routledge.

————. 2002. "Representing Minimalism." In *Sense and Sensitivity*, edited by Hunter and Davies, Sheffield: Sheffield Academic.

Zameret, Zvi. "Ben-Gurion's Bible, at: http://www.matan.org.il/Data/UploadedFiles/Free/massekhet_zvizammeret_abs_125.doc (accessed on 15 March 2006)

5

God's Mapmakers: A Theology of Dispossession

Prof. Gareth Lloyd Jones

ON 25 FEBRUARY 1994 Dr. Baruch Goldstein, an ultra-Orthodox Jew of American extraction, entered a mosque in his home town of Hebron in Israeli-Occupied Territory carrying a machine gun. Before he was over-powered and beaten to death, he had shot twenty-nine Muslim worshippers as they knelt in prayer. Today the assassin's grave in a park outside Hebron looks like a garden of remembrance. His massive gravestone, illuminated at night by ornamental lights, refers to him as a saint. The inscription reads: "Having given his life on behalf of the Jewish people, its Torah and its ancestral homeland, he was an innocent, pure-hearted individual." Pilgrims hold services and light memorial candles. Supporters kiss the tomb and stop to pray.

At his funeral Rabbi Jacob Perrin commended his action by stating in his sermon that "one million Arabs are not worth a Jewish fingernail." When Goldstein's son became a bar mitzvah two years later, the officiating rabbi said to him: "Jacob Jair, follow in your father's footsteps. He was a righteous man and a great hero" (*Jerusalem Report* [12 December 1996] 10; cited in Prior, *The Bible and Colonialism*, 149n41).

The British Chief Rabbi, Jonathan Sacks, condemned the massacre in no uncertain terms by declaring that "violence is evil. Violence committed in the name of God is doubly evil. Violence against those engaged in worshipping God is unspeakably evil." Reflecting on Sacks's reaction,

Rabbi Norman Solomon commented, "The problem with Sacks" position is that, much as we may concur with the sentiment, and however many Biblical and Talmudic citations we may amass in praise of peace, we are left with numerous texts that *do* summon us to violence in the name of God, and this makes it difficult to argue against Perrin and the like on purely *textual* grounds" (unpublished lecture "Jewish Sources for Religious Pluralism").

On 4 February 1995 Yigal Amir, the son of an Orthodox Rabbi and a student at the Institute of Advanced Torah Studies in Tel-Aviv, founded by the National Religious Party, assassinated Israeli Premier Yitzchak Rabin. In his defense he claimed that he was acting in the name of God. Because Rabin had signed the Oslo Peace Accords in 1993, which traded land for peace, and shook hands with Arafat, Amir maintained that Rabin endangered the Jewish nation. Rabin's action was that of a traitor. The Torah made provision for such treachery: the sentence was death.

In assassinating Rabin, Amir honored Goldstein. Among the books found in his apartment was one praising his hero's actions. For both men the Palestinians had no rights to their ancestral homeland. Their removal from Hebron, Jerusalem, and the entire West Bank was a *mitzvah*, a commandment which the Jews were expected to honor. Expulsion was part of God's plan. In carrying out their mission, both were confident that they were doing so in obedience to the divine mandate.

These two notorious instances are noted because they point to the religious dimension of Zionism, the chosen topic of this essay. In its origin Zionism was a secular political movement whose pioneers had little time for religion. As such, it had much in common with other 19th century nationalist movements. The First Zionist Congress of 1897 declared that the only solution to the plight of European Jewry was the recovery of a Jewish national identity. The early Zionists believed that Jews would escape persecution only if they returned to Palestine. As Theodor Herzl wrote in his diary, this would mean the expulsion of the indigenous population:

> When we occupy the land we must expropriate gently the private property on the estates assigned to us. We shall try to spirit the penniless population across the border by procuring employment for it in the transit countries, while denying it any employment in our own country. Both the process of expropriation and the removal of the poor must be carried out discreetly and circumspectly. (Patai 1960, 87–88)

Initially this secular dream was firmly rejected by Orthodox Jews on religious grounds. They argued that the Jewish state could be inaugurated only by God's own representative. They could return only if they were led there by the Messiah, who would come in God's good time. The concept of auto-emancipation contradicted the religious tradition. So instead of taking action, they counseled patience.

But as the 20th century progressed, Zionism began to appear as a compelling alternative, even to Orthodox Jews. The Holocaust, the founding of the State, the Six Day War (when East Jerusalem fell into Israeli hands) all contributed to the Orthodox determination to make common cause with political Zionism. They brought politics into line with their theology. They came to believe that the founding of the state was the first step in the coming of the Messiah. They recognized that the Bible, to use Ben Gurion's famous phrase, was their "sacrosanct title-deed to Palestine," and in this they had the support of Christian Zionists. So by the mid-twentieth century there was a theological, in addition to a secular foundation for Zionism. Though late in accepting the Zionist cause, by now the Jewish religious establishment fully supports its achievements.

Because this claim of a right to the land is biblically based, it raises the question of the way one handles a holy book. The issue can be put thus: is it permissible to take particular texts from Scripture without any consideration of the original context and apply them literally to a completely changed situation? Can one dismiss the historical and political developments of 2500 years, and make specific territorial demands, simply by appealing to the Bible?

In considering these questions I shall confine myself to the biblical texts of promise and possession found in the Torah, texts which feature prominently in Zionist Orthodox thinking, and consider them in accordance with the canons of critical biblical scholarship.

Texts of Promise

Of the promises made to Abraham and his descendants, that of land is the most prominent and decisive. It can be traced through the Bible, the Apocrypha, the Dead Sea Scrolls, Rabbinic Literature and the liturgy of the Synagogue. It became a passionately held doctrine of the Jews down the ages and must be given serious consideration in any understanding of the theological role of territory in Judaism. In the words of Abraham Heschel: "The Jewish people has never ceased to assert its right, its title, to the land of Israel. This continuous, uninterrupted insistence, an intimate ingredient of Jewish consciousness, is at the core of Jewish history, a vital element of Jewish faith." The Jews, he says, "asserted their own title to the land" for centuries in their sanctuaries, their books and their prayers (Heschel 1969, 55). Israel is demanded by and belongs to all Jews, including Jews who will never inhabit it, even in their dreams.

The first instance of the promise is in Genesis 13:14 where God says to Abraham: "Look around from where you are towards north, south, east and west: all the land you see I shall give to you and to your descendants. Now go through the length and breadth of the land." What seems to be envisaged is a tract of territory which will provide nomads with a livelihood, namely grazing rights for their animals. It could be argued that the gift of the whole land of Palestine is not envisaged in this primary text; it refers only to the inheritance of Abraham and his family.

It is also noteworthy that although the Bible states that the Canaanites were then living in this divinely-promised land (Gen 13:7); there is no suggestion that Abraham displaced them. We do not read of conquest or ethnic exclusivity. Throughout the Pentateuch the land is referred to as the Land of Canaan, which suggests that it was recognized as belonging to someone else. In fact the only part of it which Abraham actually possessed was the plot he bought from its Canaanite owner in order to bury his wife (Gen 23:17). As the story progresses, God confirms the promise by making a covenant with Abraham giving him and his descendants the land as an "everlasting possession" (Gen 17:8). The covenant makes the promise inviolable and irrevocable. In 35 of the 109 occasions in the Old Testament where land is described as a promise or a gift, the context is a solemn oath made by God.

To ensure that Abraham appreciates the territorial dimensions of what he has been given, after the initial promise the land is more clearly defined. Its borders are delineated in detail by God himself. Just as politicians might refer to historically conditioned frontiers, Orthodox Zionists speak of theologically conditioned frontiers. But although the map-references are quite explicit, they do not agree with one another. In Numbers 34:12 the promised territory stretches eastwards only as far as the River Jordan and the Dead Sea. But in Genesis 15:18, Exodus 23:31 and Deuteronomy 1:7 and 11:24 it goes much further: its eastern frontier is the Euphrates.

It does not require much imagination to appreciate how much political dynamite a verse like Deuteronomy 11:24 contains, if taken literally: "Every place where you set the soles of your feet shall be yours. Your borders shall run from the wilderness to the Lebanon and from the river Euphrates to the western sea." To set the Euphrates as the eastern boundary was to create a totally unrealistic and unrealizable extension. Even so, some early Zionists claimed that the land beyond the Jordan was as much of an inalienable right for Jews as Palestine. But the general acceptance of the border as defined in Numbers, i.e. the Jordan River and the Dead Sea, meant that the title to much of the promised territory was relinquished, presumably for purely pragmatic and demographic reasons. However, because the land has supernatural as well as natural boundaries, the extent of the territory is not a matter of history but of divine mandate, and therefore not negotiable. Because the limits have been set by God the very mention of partition is anathema. The aspirations of a homeless people to have a home in a specific location are synonymous with the divine will.

Texts of Possession

Though the nation is promised that it will dwell in it own land, the actual possession is elusive. Acquisition comes only through conquest. God, speaking through Moses, more than once instructs the Israelites to conquer Canaan, sparing none of the inhabitants. (See e.g. Deuteronomy 7:1–2; 20:16–18.) This is not a mere recommendation, something that should be done if they have the time or the inclination. It is a command to ethnically cleanse the land of its indigenous inhabitants to make room for the chosen people. But Israel cannot be regarded as culpable for the bloodshed, because behind its usurpation of the land lies not only God's promise but also his ordinance.

With the conquest, which is described in the Book of Joshua as being enabled by God, the Israelites' dream becomes the Canaanites' nightmare. At the end of chapter 11 we are told that Joshua "took the whole land, fulfilling all the commands that the Lord had laid on Moses." But notice that here again the land is called "the Land of Canaan," an acknowledgement that the Israelites saw themselves as taking over territory which belonged to other people. Another verse reminds them forcefully of this when God says: "I gave you land on which you had not labored; towns which you had not built; you have settled in those towns and you eat the produce of vineyards and olive groves which you did not plant" (Josh 24:13). Did the writer have a bad conscience over the act of expropriation which he was reporting? Whether he did or not, from the standpoint of historic residence it is clear that the Israelites had no exclusive claim to the land, they simply dispossessed those who lived there before them.

In a text from Numbers which has a markedly modern ring to it, the rationale behind the cleansing is unambiguous: "Then ye shall ldrive out all the inhabitants of the land from before you . . . if ye will not drive out the inhabitants of the land from before you; then it shall come to pass, that those which ye let remain of them shall be pricks in your eyes, and thorns in your sides, and shall vex you in the land wherein ye dwell" (33:52–55 KJV). So the conquest is regarded not only as the fulfillment of the promise made to the patriarchs, and undertaken in obedience to God's command, but also as an eminently practical venture. Settlement may be a holy duty supported by divine legitimation, which provides Zionism with a powerful mystique. But according to the Bible, it also guards against attack. Security dictates settlement. The land becomes a haven preserving the nation from aggression.

As they were used in the past by Joshua, divine promise and command are used today to legitimize conquest and settlement. Because they now perceive the Torah as supporting the Jewish state, many Orthodox Jews in Israel will not support the peace process. On 18 December 1993 the Israeli Chief Rabbi distributed leaflets in every synagogue in the Occupied Territories reiterating that Jews had a God-given right to the land. When he was accused of inciting rebellion, he replied that the supreme law in the land was the Law of Moses: "Any other orders contradictory to the orders of Moses are a rebellion against Moses, against the Torah, against Judaism. There does not exist any kind of rebellion if the refusal is based on obeying the laws of Moses." [Derek Brown, Guardian, 20th Dec 1993, "Jerusalme"] In obedience to the divine diktat, the land is taken from the indigenous population by force, just as it was 3000 years ago. Divine sanction justifies the conquest. Land gifted to a chosen people means that acquisition can be seen as legitimate appropriation. Destiny absolves the deed. But because the promise of land conflicts with the rights of those who already occupy it, mayhem and bloodshed ensue. What is mandate to the one is misery to the other.

An influential colonizing group in Israel is Gush Emunim (Block of the Faithful) formed in 1974. According to D. Landau, their interpretation of the Bible, "which equates the present-day Arab inhabitants of the Land with the Amalekites . . . who lived there in Moses' and Joshua's day, has seeped into current haredi [ultra-Orthodox] theology" (Landau

1993, 159). An example of this equation is to be found in an article published in a student newspaper in 1980 by Rabbi Yisrael Hess, a former campus rabbi of Bar Ilan University. Entitled "The Commandment of Genocide in the Torah," the article states: "The day is not far when we shall all be called to this holy war, this commandment of the annihilation of the Amalekites." The rabbi regards the Palestinians as the "Amalekites of today." (Hess 1997, 208) He preaches a theology of dispossession when he applies the commandment given to the Israelites that they "must without fail blot out all memory of Amalek from under heaven" (Deut 25:19) to the Palestinian Arab population of today.

Like their ancient forebears, Palestinians should be shown no mercy, for they are theologically illegitimate tenants who threaten the Jewish process of redemption. They are regarded as "a barbed hook" in the eye and "a thorn" in the side of the state. Palestinian "human rights are no match for the divine imperative. Armed with the inerrant certainty of the *Torah,* which not only justifies violence, but gives the divine mandate for it, and the glorious example of Joshua, The Gush pursues its policy of settling, in disregard for the indigenous population" (Prior 1997, 164). But even if the modern Amalekites are not annihilated, a concerted attempt will be made to "expand the settlements and settle a million Jews on the West Bank before the turn of the millennium, so that territorial compromise becomes impossible and eventual annexation becomes the obvious conclusion" (Prior 1997, 163).

Before we leave these texts of possession, it should be noted that mediaeval Talmudic and biblical commentators among the Jews refused to accept that the biblical command to exterminate could be applied to the distant future and used to legitimize violence centuries later. In the words of Michael Walzer,

> this means that "right-wing Zionists who cite the biblical passages are practicing a kind of fundamentalism that is entirely at odds with the Jewish tradition. For Judaism . . . is not found in the text so much as in the interpretations of the text." (Walzer 1985, 144)

Critique and Evaluation

The promise made by God to Abraham dominates and determines Jewish thinking about the land. Its fulfillment through the conquest of Canaan and the whole sale annihilation of the indigenous inhabitants became a seminal and dynamic force in Israelite history. But how should references to promise and possession be understood? How is the biblical record to be assessed? One answer is by practicing selection.

A significant contribution of modern biblical study has been to highlight the polyphonic nature of the Bible by drawing attention to inconsistencies and contradictions on several important issues. It has demonstrated how often authors were inspired not by a zeal for pure truth, or accurate theology, but by polemics against other writers whose emphasis they sought to correct. There are conflicting images of the divine. God is portrayed as a wrathful and bloodthirsty warrior who engages in genocide and confiscation of land in some books, but as a loving and universal redeemer in others. Texts of exclusion are balanced by texts of inclusion, those of nationalism by those of universalism. Next to texts of terror and ethnic cleansing are those of charity and tolerance. Reference has already been made to the divergence in the passages which define the land; one text sets the eastern boundary at the Jordan, the other sets it at the Euphrates. The account of the conquest of Canaan given in the Book of Judges is far more congenial than that found in the Book of Joshua and in Deuteronomy 7 and 20. After reading about Joshua's xenophobia, Ruth, Jonah and some of the prophets present a very different attitude towards foreigners. Israel's history as narrated in the books of Samuel and Kings is rewritten and interpreted from another perspective in Chronicles.

Since one of the Bible's distinguishing marks is its multi-voiced character, picking and choosing is the name of the game which we all play when we handle it. The selectivity we employ says something about us: about the assumptions we make, the theology we profess, the culture to which we belong, the family in which we have been nurtured. It can indicate what color and what gender we are. If you are a regular reader of a copy of the Bible which you have had for many years, one can tell a lot about you simply by noting which parts of the text are well thumbed. The existence of favorite passages will invariably give the game away.

Like many Diaspora Jews, Jacob Petuchowski, a former professor at the Hebrew Union College, Cincinnati, does not share the religious Zionists' veneration for the land. He accuses them of making a highly selective use of Scripture. Commenting on Judaism's link with a specific location, he writes:

> When pro-Israeli apologists refer to the importance of "land" in biblical religion, our first question should be whether these apologists really want to set Judaism back to its biblical phase,

i.e. whether they also long for the reintroduction of animal sacrifices, the official toleration of slavery, the death penalty for certain ritual transgressions, and the constitution of a theocratic state. Or do we have here simply an emphasis on the role of the "land" for biblical religion torn right out of its context—as though in its further Jewish development this religion had not gone through a variety of stages which finally led to an independence of the Jewish religion from the "land"? (Küng 1992, 562)

The focus in these questions is on the distinction between the abiding essence of a faith and the changing situation. We have a fixed text, yes, but we have changed minds, new occasions, and different contexts. With reference to this crucial issue of contextuality in connection with the land, Hans Küng asks pertinent questions:

What counts—historical realities or the ancient biblical texts? The frontiers which have become historic or the frontiers promised in the Bible? Do not historical developments in fact forbid any direct and anachronistic application of just any biblical passage to the present? . . . One asks oneself, in the question of frontiers, what is God's revelation and what is nationalistic ideology? (Küng 1992, 560)

Another issue raised with regard to the texts of promise and possession is their historical value. While they can be confidently described as facts of belief, the degree to which they are facts of history is more problematic. Experts in the research disciplines relating to the Bible are divided over the historicity of its early narratives. There was a time when it was confidently believed that archaeology buttressed the Bible. But in the last four decades biblical archaeologists have seen one settled assumption after another concerning ancient Israel questioned. Scholars are now virtually unanimous in believing that the Pentateuch does not contain a record of what actually happened. In their opinion, little can be learned from the Bible about Israel's origins. Many are of the opinion that archaeology points to a very different conclusion about the Israelite conquest of Canaan from that described in the Book of Joshua.

To cut a long story short and to summarize what many biblical scholars, Jewish and Christian, believe, the words of the Jewish historian Norman Cantor must suffice: "Until the glorious day dawns of archaeological verification for the line of Abraham, we have to stipulate that all of Jewish history of the first millennium BCE . . ., as told in the Bible, is one of the great masterpieces of imaginative fiction or artfully contrived historical myths of all time. From empirical evidence, it did not happen." He concludes, "the wisest course" with regard to the "mythical migrations of the patriarchs" is silence (Cantor 1995, 5 and 17).

If this is the case, myth and legend are being used by religious Zionists as a blueprint for action. And that surely presents a problem. If the historicity of the narrative is untenable, how is it possible to hold to the view that God promised Abraham and his descendants a specific piece of land? If the account of the conquest in Joshua is not factual, how can it be used to legitimize occupation? If the biblical texts are judged to be epic, legend or myths of origin (the kind of folklore which is found in almost every society), how can they be used to support a view which is based on the belief that the justifying text is history?

Finally, the need for evaluation. When it is recognized that the Bible has been used as an instrument of oppression against one group or another, and that it has been interpreted in order to justify that which in any civilized society is unjustifiable, it becomes necessary to evaluate it according to the criteria of morality and ethics. Discussing feminist theology, Elizabeth Schüssler Fiorenza, a leading American theologian, writes:

> If scriptural texts have served—and still do—to support not only noble causes but also to legitimate war, to nurture anti-Judaism and misogyny, to justify the exploitation of slavery, and to promote colonial dehumanization, then biblical scholarship must take responsibility not only to interpret biblical texts in their historical contexts but also to evaluate them. (Schussler-Fiorenza 1999, 28)

Responsibility must be taken for the moral and political results of accepting without question certain biblical passages and refusing to assess them. The ideological nature of the biblical narrative must be recognized. The text must be critiqued and subjected to a moral evaluation as well as interpreted.

The moral problem posed by regarding the ethnic cleansing of Canaan as a divinely ordered practice, and thereby assumed to be God's will, is highlighted by the eminent ancient historian G. M. de Ste Croix:

> I can say that I know of only one people which felt able to assert that it actually had a command to exterminate whole populations among those it conquered; namely Israel. Nowadays Christians, as well as Jews, seldom care to dwell on the merciless ferocity of Jehovah, as revealed not by hostile sources but by the very literature they themselves regard as sacred. Indeed they

continue as a rule to forget the very existence of this incriminating material . . . There is little in pagan literature quite as morally
revolting as the stories of the massacres allegedly carried out at
Jericho, Ai, and Hazor. (Said 1988, 166)

This "incriminating material" is a prime example of the way in
which revelation clashes with natural morality, the way in which the
Bible is at variance with human rights, and the law of God contradicts
international law.

To highlight the dilemma further, compare and contrast the divine
directive with this one made almost 3000 years later:

I have issued the command—and I'll have anybody who utters
but one word of criticism executed by a firing squad—that our
war aim does not consist in reaching certain lines, but in the
physical destruction of the enemy. Accordingly, I have placed
my death-head formations in readiness—for the present only
in the east—with orders to them to send to death mercilessly
and without compassion, men, women, and children of Pol-
ish derivation and language. Only thus shall we gain the living
space which we need.

That order, preserved in the Holocaust museum in Washington, was
issued by Adolph Hitler on 22 August 1939 to make room for the master
race. In origin, the directive to exterminate the Canaanites and that to
eliminate the Poles could not be more different. The former was written
by the finger of God, the latter by a sadistic megalomaniac; the former is
enshrined in the literature of two great religions, the latter forms part of
the record of Nazi brutality. But different though they may be in origin,
the expected result is identical.

Because Scripture is so influential, it is of crucial importance that
it is not simply interpreted, but evaluated and critiqued. The need for
evaluation is nowhere more apparent than when morally offensive passages are put to the kind of use noted above, and the Bible is used as an
instrument of oppression. Responsibility must be taken for the moral and
political results of accepting without question the violent narratives in it
and refusing to assess or evaluate them. Its ideological nature must be
recognized, and it must be admitted that there is much in it which is not
worthy to serve as a model for imitation. Sometimes faith, in whatever
God you care to mention, is just criminally wrong.

Conclusion

At one time Zionism was non-territorial. It called for a national home for Jews, but did not insist on Palestine. The weight of religious tradition, however, forced its early leaders to change their minds. Gradually the movement came to see itself as fulfilling the biblical promise of a specific land. But possession comes only via dispossession.

The consequences of a theology of dispossession become the regrettable costs of holy war. They are spelled out in a newspaper article by Abraham Burg who served as Speaker of the Israeli parliament from 1999 to 2003. His words are perhaps a fitting conclusion:

> Israel, having ceased to care about the children of the Palestinians, should not be surprised when they come washed in hatred and blow themselves up in the centers of Israeli escapism. They consign themselves to Allah in our places of recreation, because their own lives are torture. They spill their own blood in our restaurants in order to ruin our appetites, because they have children and parents at home who are hungry and humiliated. We could kill a thousand ringleaders a day and nothing will be solved, because the leaders come up from below—from the wells of hatred and anger, from the infrastructures of injustice and moral corruption. If all this were inevitable, divinely ordained and immutable, I would be silent. But things could be different, so crying out is a moral imperative. ("The End of Zionism," *The Guardian* [15 September 2003])

References

Cantor, Norman. 1995. *The Sacred Chain*. New York: HarperCollins.

Heschel, Abraham. 1969. *Israel: An Echo of Eternity*. New York: Farrar, Strauss, Giroux.

Landau, D. 1993. *Piety and Power: the World of Jewish Fundamentalism*. London: Secker and Warburg.

Hess, Yisrael. 1997. *A Land without a People: Israel, Transfer and the Palestinians 1949–96*. London: Faber and Faber.

Küng, Hans. 1992. *Judaism: the Religious Situation of our Time*. London: SCM.

Patai, R., ed. 1960. *The Complete Diaries of Theodor Herzl, Vol 1*. New York: Herzl.

Prior, M. 1997. *The Bible and Colonialism: a Moral Critique*. Sheffield: Sheffield Academic.

Schussler Fiorenza, Elisabeth. 1999. *Rhetoric and Ethic: the Politics of Biblical Studies*. Minneapolis: Fortress.

Said, E. W., and Hitchens, C., eds. 1988. *Blaming the Victims: Spurious Scholarship and the Palestinian Question*. London: Verso.

Walzer, Michael. 1985. *Exodus and Revolution*. New York: Basic Books.

6

The Quest for Peace with Justice in the Middle East: Christian Zionist and Palestinian Theologies

Prof. Rosemary Radford Ruether

THIS ESSAY WILL DISCUSS competing theologies in relation to the Middle East conflict between the state of Israel and the Palestinian people and their quest for control of their land and for their civil rights. It will focus primarily on competing theologies among Christians, both in the West and in Palestine, as these theologies interact with the Jewish community, both in Israel and in the West. The Jewish voice is also increasingly divided, in defense or in critique of the policies of the state of Israel. Christians interact with these divergent Jewish voices, as they seek to overcome the legacy of Christian anti-semitism and its horrific results in the Holocaust, but also in the debate in relation to the state of Israel. At the same time Palestinian Christians seek to unite their historically divided community to speak with one voice against their oppression and the ethnic cleansing of their land by the state of Israel and to provide an alternative vision of a future Palestine for Israeli Jews and Palestinian Christians and Muslims.

I begin with an exploration of the theology of Christian Zionism, particularly as this has shaped mainstream Western Christianity. I will not focus on the more fundamentalist and millenarian forms of Christian Zionism, important as these are, but rather the often unnoticed and un-named themes of Christian Zionism which have shaped the behavior and politics of the main bodies of Western Christianity. These expressions of

Christian Zionism are deeply entwined with Western Christian imperialism toward the Middle East, represented by then British empire and now by American empire.

These forms of Christian Zionism are deeply rooted in British and American identification of themselves as elect nations, heirs of God's election of Israel. This election was seen as including a duty to patronize the Jewish people as a nation by restoring them to their national homeland in Palestine, under the aegis of global Christian empire, British or American. In the anxiety of Western Christian theologians after the Holocaust to reject classical Christian supercessionism, this role of restorationism in 17th to 20th century Christianity, rooted in the Puritan tradition, has often been ignored.

In restorationism, the relation of Christianity to the Jews remains one of universalism to particularism, but instead of negating Jewish particularism and demanding that it obliterate itself into Christian universalism, it seeks to restore Jews to their status as a nation in their national land, under Christian imperial patronage. It is assumed that thereby they will operate as collaborators with Christian empire in the Middle Eastern context.

As Barbara Tuchman has shown, *The Bible and the Sword: England and Palestine from the Bronze Age to Balfour* (Tuchman 1968) the British had long identified with Israel as God's new elect people. 17th century English Puritans entertained hopes that converted Jews, under the patronage of the English, would be restored to their homeland in Palestine, thereby becoming the precursor of a coming millennium (Sharif 1983). These ideas were revived and developed by new evangelical groups, such as the Plymouth Brethren, under John Nelson Darby, in mid-19th century England (Sizer 2004, 50–52).

But such views were not only found among sectarian groups. They also shaped an evangelical party in the Anglican Church and became influential in British imperial politics in the Middle East, leading eventually to the Balfour Declaration in 1917. A key figure here is Lord Anthony Cooper, Lord Shaftesbury. This story has been detailed in Donald M. Lewis' 2010 book, *The Origin of Christian Zionism: Lord Shaftesbury and Evangelical Support for a Jewish Homeland* (Lewis 2010).

Shaftesbury was an earnest believer in an evangelical interpretation of Biblical prophecy, in which the restoration of the Jews to their homeland was a prerequisite for the return of Christ and the establishment of the millennium on earth. He worked all his life from the 1830s to his death in 1885 for this great event. He was also connected with the highest British political leaders of the day, such as Lord Palmerston, British Foreign Secretary, and sought to translate his enthusiasm for Jewish national restoration in Palestine into terms intended to recommend this to British imperial interests in the Middle East.

Shaftesbury was a leading actor in the decision of the Church of England to establish as Anglican bishopric of Jerusalem. Shaftesbury, as a leader in the London Society for Promoting Christianity among the Jews, envisioned a vast redemptive project in which unconverted Jews would return to Palestine, in the process becoming Anglican Christians. These two events would prepare the way for the Second Advent of Christ. The first incumbent chosen for this Anglican See of Jerusalem was intentionally a converted Jew, the Reverend Dr. Michael Solomon Alexander, professor of Hebrew and Arabic at at King's College, London.

In Shaftesbury's vision of the future age of redemption, Christ would return to reign over restored Israel of Anglican Christian Jews. The Jews Society, as it was called, had the restoration of the Jews to their national existence in Palestine as an integral part of their purpose. Shaftesbury also opposed the Emancipation Bill that would have removed disabilities from Jews to full participation in English political and cultural life. Thus his enthusiasm for the return of the Jews to Palestine went hand in hand with his refusal to accept their full equality as citizens in his own nation.

Although Shaftesbury died in 1885 before seeing a restored Jewish nation in Palestine, the influence of Christian restorationist ideas continued into the next generation of British politicians. Lord Arthur Balfour met with leaders of the developing Jewish Zionist movement, such as Chaim Weizmann, and was aware of their demands for Palestine as the only appropriate homeland for Jews. After World War I, the British collaborated with the French to develop Mandate territories in the former Ottoman territories in the Middle East. On the eve of British General Allenby's entrance into Jerusalem to establish the headquarters of the British Mandate there, Balfour issued the Balfour Declaration declaring the support of Britain for "national home for the Jewish people."

In defending this decision in 1922 before the House of Lords, Balfour made clear the intertwining of British imperial and Christian religious interests. He proclaimed that the decision sprang, not only from its political usefulness, but even more from the deep debt of gratitude which Christians such as himself and those of the House of Lords, should feel toward the Jews as the progenitors of their religion:

> . . . the policy we initiated is likely to prove a successful policy.
> But we have never pretended that it was purely from these ma-
> terialist considerations that the declaration originally sprang. . .
> It is in order that we may send a message that will tell them that
> Christendom is not oblivious to their faith, that it is not un-
> mindful of the service they have rendered to the religions of the
> world, and most of all to the religion that the majority of Your
> Lordships' house profess, and that we desire to the best of our
> ability to give them that opportunity of developing in peace and
> quietness under British rule, those great gifts which hitherto
> they have been compelled to bring to fruition in countries that
> know not their language and belong not to their race? That is the
> ideal which I desire to see accomplished, that is the aim which
> lay at the root of the policy I am trying to defend, and though
> it is defensible on every ground, that is the ground that chiefly
> moves me. (Dugdale 1937, 2 and 58)

How Palestinians were supposed to feel about this declaration of
their homeland as the "national homeland of the Jewish people" is not
discussed. The Declaration does say that it is clearly understood that
"nothing shall be done which may prejudice the civil and religious rights
of the existing non-Jewish communities in Palestine." Yet referring to
them only as "non-Jewish" implies that they have no particular national
identity or claims on this land themselves.

The United States inherited this British support for Palestine as
a "national homeland for the Jewish people" and played a critical role
in converting it into a Jewish state. Americans also possess a religious-
nationalist identification of themselves as a new "elect nation" (Radford Ruether 2007, 26–32), and the Puritan tradition linking this with
restoration of the Jews to their national homeland. Groups promoting
restoration abounded in the 19th century US. One of these was the 1891
Blackstone Memorial organized by William Blackstone, author of the
popular apocalyptic book, *Jesus is Coming* (1878) and signed by 413 leading Americans, such a John D. Rockefeller, Cyrus McCormick, J. Pier-
pont Morgan, and leading senators, clergy and newspaper editors. This
Memorial was sent to President Harrison recommending that he create
a restored state for the Jews in Palestine (Blackstone 1977). Significantly,
American Jewish leaders themselves deeply opposed this initiative, seeing it as a ploy to divert Jewish refugees fleeing pogroms in Russia from
coming to the United States (Steinstern 1963, 5 and 11–31).

But it was after World War II and the Jewish Holocaust that an American President had the opportunity to push forward a resolution in the United Nations partitioning Palestine and giving 55% of the land for a Jewish state." The US also stood by while the 45% allotted for a Palestinian state disappeared, 23% taken into the Jewish state, and the rest occupied by Jordan and Egypt, with a million Palestinians dispersed as refugees. The US has given unstinting support to Israel since that time, both through three to four billions of dollars in yearly aid and continual verbal affirmation. Although claiming to be an "honest broker" for the rights of both groups, no one examining this history can doubt that it is the state of Israel which is overwhelmingly America's primary ally and concern.

What is America's interest in this support for Israel, a one-sided support so entrenched in American political culture that virtually no politician can dare criticize it even slightly without jeopardizing their position? I would argue that here too we find a deep inter-twining of American political and religious identity and interests. On the one hand, particularly since the 1967 war established Israel's military preeminence in the Middle East, the United States has seen Israel as helping to maintain its balance of power in the region. Mostly importantly, the armies of the two countries are deeply intertwined, with constant sharing of military tactics and armaments. Jeff Halper, Israeli critic of Israel's occupation, sees this close identification of the two military systems as the real "elephant in the room" that tie the two states together.

But the religious identification of American Christians with Israel as a Jewish state is also very deep. Most American Christians would agree with the statement that God gave the land of Palestine to the Jewish people as a permanent and exclusive donation. This supposedly Biblically-based claim in effect deprives Palestinians of any national rights to the land. This Biblical land claim is the primary basis for most American Christians' identification with Israel.

This belief has been supplemented, particularly since 1967, with a Christian post-Holocaust theology that claims that Christian responsibility for the Holocaust demands repentance in the form of unstinting support for Israel. This is couched both in terms of a kind of payment or compensation for Christian sins against the Jews, and also as the necessary protection of the Jewish people against any future Holocaust. The guilt and repentance argument is particularly important in mainline churches, while being a less compelling factor for millenarian evangelicals attracted by the combination of the exclusivist land claim and the belief that restoration of the Jews is about to usher in the redemptive millennium. The repentance argument typically takes the form of a devastating rebuttal of any effort of Christians who are aware of injustice to the Palestinians to criticize Israel. Any critique of Israel is typically met with an intense outcry from Jewish spokesmen to the effect that this Christian group is "anti-semitic," threatening the security of the state of Israel, and are even seeking to "destroy" the state of Israel. A sector of Christians within these churches has been cultivated over the years through Christian-Jewish dialogue and Christian post-Holocaust theology to reinforce this outcry.

Christian post-Holocaust theology was developed from the 1970s to today by an influential group of Christian theologians, mainly western Protestants, as an effort to root out anti-semitism from Christian theology and thus overcome what they saw as the primary misinterpretation of Christianity that led to the Holocaust. Theologians such as Paul Van Buren, K. Kendall Soulen and Clark M. Williamson are representative of the post-Holocaust theology that seeks to overcome anti-semitism in Christianity (Van Buren 1983; Soulen 1996; Williamson 1993).

These theologians see the theology of supercessionism as the critical issue leading to anti-semitism. Thus any idea of Christianity as superseding Judaism as a universal fulfillment in a "new covenant" overcoming an inadequate particularist and tribal Judaism must be rejected root and branch. These theologians believe that the way to do this is to reaffirm the primacy of God's election of the Jews as the heart of a single covenant that has not been superseded but continues to define human history. Christianity, far from superseding Judaism, has been added in as auxiliary to Judaism's world mission in this single covenant.

For these theologians God's gift of the land to the Jews as a permanent and exclusive donation is central to this gratuitous election of the Jews by God. Christianity can repent of anti-Semitism only by affirming this exclusive donation of the land to the Jews and wholeheartedly supporting it against all threats to Jewish security and wellbeing in its promised land. Jewish critic of this post-Holocaust Christian theology, Mark Braverman, sees this effort of Christian renewal as actually blocking possibility of a Jewish renewal which must take the form of a questioning of the exclusivism of Judaism which has been renewed through modern Jewish empowerment in the state of Israel. In Braverman's words:

> A theology that attempts to correct for Christian superces-
> sionism by preserving or incorporating God's election of Is-
> rael ultimately replaces Christian supercessionism with Jewish
> exceptionalism. And if Christian triumphalism as expressed
> in supercessionism led to the ovens of Auschwitz, then Jewish
> triumphalism as expressed in political Zionism has led to the
> ethnic cleansing of Palestine. (Braverman 2010, 114)

This kind of post-holocaust theology of Christian repentance for anti-Semitism has become major force in a number of mainline western Churches, in collaboration with the Jewish establishment. The effect of their influence is that Christians calling for some parallel justice for Palestinians are either silenced entirely, or else a very compromised statement is finally issued by the denomination that removes any call for real change in Israel frontline projects of occupation and land confiscation, while fervently affirming the church's commitment to the security of the state of Israel. In effect, any critique of Israel in Western Christian churches, especially in the United States, but also in Canada and Europe, has been effectively silenced by the combination of these forces.

However, in recent years (2004–2010) this situation of silencing of Western Churches has begun to shift slightly, although not yet decisively. This has been caused by two factors. First, Israel's policies toward the Palestinians in the occupied territories has grown increasingly extreme, building the separation wall that confiscates major sections of land and water inside the 1967 truce line, fragmenting the Palestinian communities with curfews and checkpoints, so that it becomes ever more difficult for them to carry on daily life, and making a two state solution ever less possible by removing the contiguous land base for such a state. Those Western Christians in communication with Palestinians have intensified their efforts to educate other Christians about the dire injustice of this situation for Palestinians.

A second key factor is the emergence of a sector of American Jews alarmed by this growing injustice who have come to redefine their own allegiance to Israel, seeing that such allegiance must include some deep change on the part of Israel to accommodate Palestinian rights, either in the restoration of land for a possible two state solution or else by acceptance of a one-state bi-national solution. For them Israel is destroying itself by becoming unsustainably aggressive. A transformation of this culture is necessary both to save Israel and to allow a just solution for the Palestinians.

Critical groups have grown among Israeli Jews, some of whom have become activists in resistance, such as Jeff Halper, founder of the Israeli Committee against (Palestinian) House Demolitions (Halper 2003). Critical Palestinian Christians have also organized as a group and have sought to make their voices heard. Palestinian theologians, such as Naim Ateek and Mitri Raheb (Ateek 1989; Raheb 1995), have developed expressions of Palestinian liberation or contextual theology.

In 2009 a group of Palestinian Christians issued a collective Kairos statement enunciating their cry for justice and their vision of a just future for both peoples and three religions in the one land These four groups, critical Christians and Jews in the United States (and elsewhere in Canada and Europe) and critical Israeli Jews and Palestinian Christians, have bonded and work together. The interconnection of these four groups has begun to create a sufficiently strong common front that it has begun to threaten the hold of Christian Zionism in US mainline denominations.

American Jew Mark Braverman sees as a major obstacle in this quest for a theology of peace in the Middle East the confusion of two different discussions: Jewish-Christian interfaith dialogue and quest for a just resolution of the Israeli-Palestinian conflict. Jewish-Christian interfaith dialogue is primarily a Western discussion, rooted in the centuries of Christian hegemony in the West and the type of Christian theology toward the Jews shaped in that context. By contrast, Christians and Jews in the Middle East from the 7th century lived in a totally different context, both being minority religions under Islam.

Western Jewish-Christian inter-faith dialogue started with the shock of the Holocaust. This caused Christians to want to learn about injustice to Jews by Christians and to appreciate a more authentic Judaism, rejecting anti-semitic supercessionism and affirming the autonomous authenticity of Judaism. However this dialogue has been constructed in a one sided way, in which Jews are not expected or intended to learn anything from Christians, but simply to shame Christians into a position of overt or covert acquiescence to Jewish demands in regard to Israeli policies in the Middle East. Braverman, by contrast, sees himself as transformed by conversation with Christians. Jews like himself have come to critique their own doctrine of election, with its implied exceptionalism, and have been called to a more pluralist universalism.

For Braverman, Jewish-Christian interfaith dialogue must cease being used as a covert tool to silence critique of the state of Israel and its policies toward Palestinians. The Israel-Palestine conflict is not primarily about relations between religions, Judaism, Christianity or Islam. Rather is it an issue of socio-political relations between peoples, of justice and injustice. All three religions and their cultures have traditions to critique injustice and to call for genuine justice toward peoples. These are the traditions that have to come into play to create a just coexistence between Israeli Jews and Christian and Muslim Palestinians who need to share the historic land of Palestine in peace and justice.

For Braverman these two discussions and their false confusion came to a head in the recent General Assembly of the Presbyterian Church meeting in Minneapolis in July 2010. The Presbyterians have developed an increasingly strong critical group seeking justice for the Palestinians. In 2004 this critique took new form in a call for active disinvestment from those parts of the Israeli economy that serve the occupation. This call echoed the successful strategy of disinvestment that was used against the apartheid state of South African in the 1980s. It also repositions the critique of Israel as a critique of an apartheid state. Jewish defenders of Israel were alarmed and mobilized their Christian Zionist allies among Presbyterians to try to kill this idea of disinvestment.

The Presbyterian Middle East Study Commission was mandated to study this conflict. It came up with the carefully worded document, "Breaking Down the Walls," to be voted on in the 2010 General Assembly.

A strong group of defenders of Israel, representing the Simon Wiesenthal Center and the Jewish Council on Public Affairs, together with Presbyterians for Middle East Peace, a Christian Zionist group of Presbyterian pastors and seminary professors, worked determinately to demonize the statement by the Study Commission. It was decried as anti-semitic, as betraying the historic friendship of Jews and Presbyterians, and as seeking to destroy the state of Israel. The Palestinian Christian Kairos document, which the Study Commission recommended for study among Presbyterians, was also decried as anti-semitic and supercessionist.

But unlike earlier years, this time there was a counter group of Jews attending the Presbyterian Assembly, members of the Jewish Voice for Peace, and Mark Braverman, who supported the Presbyterian Study document and counteracted the arguments of the Jewish establishment and its Presbyterian defenders. The result? The Presbyterian Study document, with some modification, passed the Assembly. Presbyterians committed themselves to an effort to end violence on both sides, a call to Israel to relocate the separation wall on the 1967 truce border, equal rights for Palestinian citizens in Israel, cessation of practices such as collective punishment, home demolitions and deportation of dissidents. Use of disinvestment was maintained. The Palestinian Christian Kairos document, as a study document for Presbyterians, also continued to be recommended.

In Braverman's view, the tactics of silencing of Christian critique of Israel, through combined Jewish establishment and Christian Zionist pressure, failed. It failed, not because Presbyterians have become anti-semitic, but because many have learned better what is actually happening in Israel-Palestine and have decided where the line between injustice versus justice and possible peace between the two people actually falls. Others see the Presbyterian document that passed as more compromised and the forces of conflict between those who want to silence the churches and those who want to speak out for justice as still very unresolved.

At this point I will turn to another group of voices in this quest for a theology of peace for the Middle East, that of Palestinian Christians, whose voices have been mostly ignored or suppressed in the West, but whose Kairos document was recommended as a study document for the U.S. Presbyterian Church in 2010.

Palestinian Liberation theology, as developed in the work of Naim Ateek, Palestinian Anglican priest and founder of the Sabeel movement in Palestine and its international supportive organizations, has a number of key characteristics. It is a contextual liberation theology. That is, it arises from the particular context of the Palestinian experience of oppression and ethnic cleansing by the state of Israel and seeks liberation from this situation of injustice. It is thus a theology that arises in a particular land, the land of Israel-Palestine, and addresses the situation of the peoples of this particular land, even while rooted in universal principles and a universal God.

It is an ecumenical and inter-faith theology. That is, it seeks to bring together all Palestinian Christians in the land of Palestine who have been divided into many churches, going back to the many historical schisms from the 4th century to modern times, Catholic, Orthodox and Oriental Churches, and the variety of Protestant churches. It seeks to overcome these divisions in an ecumenical Palestinian local church, speaking with one voice. It is also interfaith in that it seeks to bring together Christians, Muslims and Jews as three peoples of the Abrahamic faith, to work together for justice and peace in the one land of Israel-Palestine.

It is Biblically-based: it draws on the vision of the Bible for justice, liberation and peace, while also seeking to overcome the misuse of the

Bible to advocate separation and negation of some people by others, It sees Christian Zionism as the prime expression of the misuse of the Bible to promote racism, violence and injustice, based on the belief that God chooses one people and gives them exclusive rights to the land against the other peoples of the land. Palestinian liberation theology seeks to show why this theology of Christian Zionism is a distortion of Biblical faith.

Palestinian liberation theology is a theology of non-violence. It follows Jesus' way of non-violence and seeks the path of reconciliation between peoples. It is an anti-imperial theology. It critiques all theologies of empire, whether the Roman empire in the Biblical context, or modern empires, such as the British or American empires. It stands in the tradition of the theology of liberation from empire of both the Hebrew Scripture and the New Testament and applies this critical vision to the political situation of today.

Central to Palestinian liberation theology is its understanding of God. God is not a racist who chooses one people as his favorite elect people and seek to bless them with the land, power and prosperity at the expense of the rest of the people of the land. Rather God is a God of all peoples, of all nations, a God who created the whole earth and all the peoples and lands in it. This God seeks justice and peace for all people, not in an abstract way, but in terms of the particular historical situation of each people in their context and relationships.

As a Christian theology Palestinian liberation theology sees Jesus Christ as a criterion of interpretation of the Biblical message. It emphasizes not only how Jesus Christ represents God, but also exemplifies the fullness of his humanity in his historical context and reality. Its looks to Jesus Christ as a Palestinian Jew living under the occupation the Roman empire of his day. It follows Jesus Christ in his way of non-violent resistance to imperial occupation. It is not supercessionist of Judaism but rather both affirms the continuing validity of the prophetic traditions of Judaism, and also affirms the distinct experiences of the Christian faith.

These themes of Palestinian contextual and liberation theology are reinforced by the Kairos document issued by a group of Palestinian theologians of various Christian churches on December 11, 2009 from Bethlehem. It is called a Kairos document to affirm that this is a critical moment when God is speaking in the crisis of human events and calling us to repentance and transformation. This term recalls the South African liberation struggle in which its Kairos document called the people of South Africa and the world to overcome the historical injustice of apartheid.

This Palestinian Kairos document names Israel's occupation of Palestinian land as a sin against God and humanity, for it deprives Palestinians of dignity and basic human rights and prevents both Israelis and Palestinians from being able to see God in each other's faces. It does not oppose Israel's right to exist, but rather opposes an occupation which prevents the two people from living in peace and justice with each other. It also calls for religious liberty for all people of the land in their various religious traditions. It does not accept either a religious exclusivism which would define Israel as a Jewish state, or the views of those who would make a future Palestinian state an Islamic state.

The Palestinian Kairos document is clearly committed to the way of non-violence as the only way to overcome violent injustice. It calls for non-violent resistance to violence as the way to "put an end to evil by walking in the ways of justice." It is a statement that is grounded in hope despite the times of discouragement and frustration with a political process that has failed for more than sixty years to deliver a just solution to the conflict, but instead has allowed the problem to grow continually more extreme. It is a cry of hope issued in the context of absence of hope under the oppression of Israeli occupation that has grown continually worse, a cry of hope based on faith in God despite all contrary realities.

These contrary realities include a depressing list of negative and worsening facts: the separation wall erected on Palestinian land that confiscates land and water, and turns towns and villages into prisons; Israeli settlements that ravage the land, control natural resources and prevent hundreds of thousands of Palestinians from making a living; daily humiliations to which Palestinians are subjected, as they seek to make their way to jobs, schools or hospitals; the separation of members of the same family, who are not able to live together because of lack of identity cards; lack of access to their holy places, as Christians or Muslims; the plight of refugees, many of whom have been living in impoverished camps for more than sixty years; Palestinian prisoners thousands of whom languish in Israeli prisons; disregard of international law by Israel; the continuing effort to ethnically cleanse the land of Palestinians by giving young people no hope and thus encouraging their emigration; and finally the fragmentation of Jerusalem which prevents the city from being a center of peace, but makes it instead the heart of the conflict.

Central to the hope what grounds Palestinian theology is faith in God, the one God who is the creator of the universe and loves all of his creatures equally. They also affirm faith in God's eternal Word, the Lord Jesus Christ, who came with a new teaching casting new light on the themes of Hebrew scripture. This is a living word that continues to cast new light on each period of history, manifesting to Christian believers what God is saying to us now.

Palestinians believe that their land has a universal mission. The promises of land, election and people of God open up to include the whole of humanity, represented concretely by the presence of three religions, Judaism, Christianity and Islam, and two peoples, Israeli and Palestinians. By seeking to liberate this land from injustice and war and make it a land of reconciliation for all its people, God calls this land to represent the reconciliation of all peoples in their diversity. Thus the mission of this land itself must be based on a rejection of any exclusivism which gives one people or one religion special rights that exclude the others. Theologies of exclusivism must be rejected.

The way to this reconciliation must be through peaceful non-violence. One cannot resist evil with evil. Civil disobedience is one expression of non-violent resistance. This includes strategies of divestment and economic and commercial boycott of the products of the occupation. The struggle is not finally about Palestinian against Jew, but justice against injustice. Jews, Christians and Muslim, Israelis and Palestinians must find a united front in this struggle for justice for all peoples of the land. God is not an ally of one people or religion against another, but does take the side of justice against injustice. It is on this basis that people of faith in the one God of all three religions stand together seeking to make a state for all its citizens, which respects both distinctiveness and equality of each people who must find a common life together.

This Kairos document of the Palestinian Christian people speaks for a reconciliation of particularism and universalism, of both religion and ethnic identities. It rejects both an enclosed particularism of the election of one people that excludes the others. It also rejects a supercessionist universalism that condemns local particularity and turns universalism into the imperialism of world empire, universalizing one nation and religion, under whose rule all other particularities must be subjugated. Rather it embraces a universality through multi-particularity of people who together learn to live together in justice and peace.

Christian Zionism, including the western Post-Holocaust theology which started with good intentions but ends in Christian Zionism, represents a false direction in Christian thought. It supports the combination of Jewish exceptionalism and western world empire. Its result is endless world war. Palestinian liberation theology, by contrast, represents the basis for an authentic theology of hope, justice and peace for the Israeli-Palestinian conflict. Israelis and Palestinians, Jews, Christians and Muslims, can find a new meeting point through the development of this perspective, with its clear affirmation of the three religions and two peoples finding a home together in one land and under the one God who created and affirms them all together.

References

Ateek, Naim. 1989. *Justice and Only Justice: A Palestinian Theology of Liberation.* Maryknoll, New York: Orbis.

———. 2008. *A Palestinian Christian Cry for Reconciliation.* New York: Orbis.

Blackstone, W. E. 1977. *Palestine for the Jews.* New York: Arno.

Braverman, Mark. 2010. *Fatal Embrace: Christians, Jews and the Search for Peace in the Holy Land.* Austin: Synergy.

Dugdale, Blanche. 1937. *Arthur James Balfour.* New York: Putman.

Halper, Jeff. 2003. *Obstacles to Peace: A Critical tour of the Jerusalem/West Bank Interface.* The Israeli Committee against House Demolition.

Lewis, Donald M. 2010. *The Origin of Christian Zionism: Lord Shaftesbury and Evangelical Support for a Jewish Homeland.* Cambridge: Cambridge University Press.

Raheb, Mitri. 1995. *I am a Palestinian Christian.* Minneapolis: Fortress.

Ruether, Rosemary Radford. 2007. *America, Amerikkka: Elect Nation and Imperial Violence.* London: Equinox.

Sharif, Regina. 1983. *Non-Jewish Zionism: Its Roots in Western History.* London: Zed.

Sizer, Stephen. 2004. *Christian Zionism: Road Map to Armageddon.* Leicester: InterVarsity.

Steinstern, Joseph. 1963. *Reform Judaism and Zionism 1895–1984.* New York: Theodore Herzl Foundation.

Soulen, R. Kendall. 1996. *The God of Israel and Christian Theology.* Minneapolis: Augsburg.

Tuchman, Barbara. 1968. *The Bible and the Sword: England and Palestine from the Bronze Age to Balfour.* New York: Minerva.

Williamson, Clark M. 1993. *A Guest in the House of Israel: post Holocaust Christian Theology,* Louisville: Westminster John Knox.

Van Buren, Paul. 1983. *A Christian Theology of the People of Israel.* New York: Seabury.

7

Transcending Monotheism and a Theology of Land

Prof. Lisa Isherwood

> One should not underestimate what it means to live in a country where fields and rivers and hills conserve old and human feelings . . . even the landscape takes on a different quality if you are one who remembers. The scenery is then never separate from the history of the place, from the feeling for the lives that have been lived here. (Thomas 1971, 64)

LOOKING AT THE 20TH century we can see it as a time when a search for roots for a sense of place was a common experience in the lives of individuals, peoples and nations. There seemed to be a longing for a pure place, a safe place especially in answer to existential crisis. For some this place was found in the "truths" of fundamentalist religion which saw a monumental rise globally. In some forms of this type of believing there was also the promise of material security through a prosperity gospel accompanying the sense of home within the given truths of the religion whatever religion that may be. For others this sense of place was a land, a place to call one's own and in which to at least believe oneself to be safe. There is no doubt that a sense of belonging to one place is an important dimension of life and one that enables us to feel fully human and part of a society that has been forged through the interaction of people and place. For others there was a connection of two aforementioned aspects, the desire for land security and safety along with a sense that there was a divine truth in this desire for a certain piece of land and the sense of self and belonging that this sacred space alone can validate. This of course raises many questions amongst which is the relationship of the particular to the universal, how do particular local places relate to the whole and does God prefer one place to another, does God only become available to certain people in certain places and what happens to those who were previously there or wish to remain there and not hold the same convictions about the divine? The colonial history of the world is scattered with tragic examples of how this divine mandate to land has been worked out and many of the articles in this book demonstrate it very well.

Many contemporary scholars have addressed the issue by looking at whether a God would indeed make such land mandates for people and how this relates to notions of sacred and profane land. Can we speak of holy places or do we acknowledge that the whole world is sacred made as most claim by the Creator God? This may seem a simple question and to many attributing any kind of divine origin or spiritual significance to one nation over another perhaps appears antiquated. However, this can never be true for many believers who believe God to have gifted land, nationhood and divine purpose. Indeed, for many people throughout history the nation has been understood essentially as a religious reality. It is also true that clinging to one divine when one's place in a land was under threat has also been a strategy of people throughout history.

We should not lose sight of the way in which the nomadic Jewish tribes had used monotheism that is as an identity statement amidst the cultures and religions in which they wandered. However, of course it is also true to say that scholars also believe that it was never a strict monotheism in that it did acknowledge the existence of other gods but rather wished to state the superior power of their own one God. There are additional issues of course such as does that God have power outside the land in which He wishes his people to dwell, this is shown when the Psalmist asks, "how shall we sing the Lord's song in a strange land?" What I am hoping to highlight is not that monotheism as a concept is wholly negative, as we see for the nomadic Jewish tribes it grew up from their experience and enabled them to remain within a meaningful identity. Of course it was not an exclusive identity since we note throughout the Hebrew Scriptures how intermarriage and the like took place and how cultures met not always in an antagonistic manner. There appeared to be room for integration into the Jewish identity and of course conversely scholars are now showing that with such integrations also came change in time. It is when these boundaries become fixed and impermeable that Schneider and others argue monotheism becomes the tyrant it appears to have been for centuries. When under the influence of state power, culture and philosophy the story of God becomes the story of totality, of a closed system, of the One that it excludes the "other" and becomes a rigid and impenetrable story of ONE (Schneider 2008, 3). Monotheism came to signal civilization and advancement and it is in this capacity that it became a central component of empire in the hands of a variety of European states. Moltmann has argued that this is inevitable as monotheism sits best with theocracy, one cannot be without the other (ibid., 20). The logic of the One suggests that we are able to distinguish between the truth and falsehood which is ideal if one wishes to set up a theocratic society. It is also very useful if like Aquinas you wish to set down a substantial theology, influenced by the writings of Aristotle, which demonstrates that the world itself reveals the unchanging One, the Unmoved First Mover, the One that relegates all other knowing to fiction and myth in its supreme presence. Sameness becomes the basis for establishing what is real from what is unreal and theological ontology becomes reductive with the result that "the other" is lost (ibid., 88), given no existence or demonized. Stasis becomes the nature of the Divine, the same yesterday, today and tomorrow, sustaining a world that is the same yesterday, today and tomorrow. This is of course we have to acknowledge very appealing to many people who understand safety as the ultimate purpose of religion, they live in a world that does not change with a God who does not change and what they have to do is live by the rules that do not change. However it takes very little investigation to realize that none of the aforementioned is true, the world changes, the rules change both theological and ethical over time and one assumes that this implies the divine may change although this has been masked by dualistic metaphysics as our understanding changing. We may also wish to challenge the notion that religion is the ultimate security blanket as Goss demonstrates embodying love is rather counter to keeping safe. For Goss an ethic of what he terms "communal survivability" is not necessarily good enough in ethics and theology.

Of course the notion that the One dictates what is civilized and acceptable may be argued to be at play in the Jewish and Palestinian situation. I was struck when watching the film "The Land Speaks Arabic" by an elderly Palestinian man who was pondering on his life and the way it had so drastically changed since the Nakba; a time when those who had experienced an unimaginable trauma displaced those who were grafted on to the land through generations of interaction and storytelling. Looking back he said that he had Jewish girlfriends and people had got along in their country within a religious mix, the problem he felt was the introduction of European Jews into this Middle Eastern culture. For him this was not actually a religious question at all but rather a cultural one, these in-comers did not know the land or the people in it but they came with a sense of divine salvation and therefore justification in their hearts. Strangely in believing they were reclaiming a land that had been promised to them they believed through Bible stories they were using land and the divine in a way that it might be argued had not been used before. That is to say the One gives identity when land is an issue but land may also give room in the One for multiple dwelling. I am sure it has been argued many times before that at a psychological level having experienced what was so fresh and cut so deep those incomers needed to mould once again an identity so scarred and smashed and we know there was a European and American political agenda behind the move that was not necessarily pro-Jewish. And so I suppose we could be asking "in what ways do *they* sing their Lord's song in a strange land?" In what way can those who have been planted in an environment that did not grow them begin to understand the divine still as one who gives them security and a sense of self but allows the same for others? I do not wish to address the question from a psychological or even purely political point of view rather I would like to examine what part strict monotheism played and plays in the situation and whether we may transcend this in a bid for a peaceful future.

The One and the Many?

So I suppose the question is whether there is indeed room in the One for the diverse many? As a liberation theologian this piece will be informed by those from that tradition. Most are Christian or post-Christian but this is not because I assume they have the answer rather I hope how they address the question may offer something to those most fully engaged in the debates of land and place in Palestine/Israel.

Schneider believes she has an answer and that is that within the logic of the ONE there can be no room for multiplicity and one may even argue diversity (ibid., 192). For her the choice is clear do we settle for the world of categories and abstractions that the ONE presents us with or do we embrace what she calls the multiplicity which is the diverse nature of embodiment. An embodiment that refuses categories as bodies do not tend to come as one rigid category with one set of identity marks and ways of being in the world. Schneider points out that a fundamental goal of love and peace cannot be satisfied under the regime of the ONE. In accordance with other feminist theologians she suggests that love needs another, it cannot be without encounter and it cannot be ethical unless it recognizes the presence of others as they are. Heyward spoke powerfully of this saying that it was the desire to love and be loved that drew the divine from the heavens and into relation through incarnation. We do not see here any hint that a wayward people needed the outpouring of God in order to offer redemption, which may be understood as full and flourishing humanity, to the few. It was God's desire to love and be loved that brought about this outpouring and it is the continued desire that means the divine will never retreat to the heavens and the place of Absolute Oneness, in such a move all relation is lost, all possibility of loving and being loved. For Schneider this way of seeing things signals a notion of the divine so based in love that it is willing to show up and fully risk, nothing less will do (ibid., 206). It is this and this alone that changes things, that brings peace. The ONE brings safety as we have seen but outpouring love changes things. Schneider speaks plainly when she says, "to follow God who became flesh is to make room for more than One it is a posture of openness to the world as it comes to us, of loving the discordant, plentipotential worlds more than the desire to overcome, to colonize or even to 'same' them'" (ibid., 207). Divinity is free, most of all from theology and doctrine and the sameness they impose while bodies however well policed are never free from divine trespass! Of course this is the language of a Christian theologian and so as it stands has little relevance except to those Palestinian Christians who are looking for new ways ahead. However, I hope to demonstrate later that there is a similar approach possible offered by the Hebrew Scriptures which of course have a different theological underpinning but offer radical ways ahead.

There have been many theologians who have addressed the issue of transcendence and all cannot be mentioned here but one who must be, if only briefly, is Dorothee Soelle whose work will never allow the divine to escape to the outer reaches of reality and who always understood theological questions to be both deeply embedded in the personal sense of identity but always political. This is relevant in the present context to counter the arguments of those who would say that if God has given the land then whatever injustice or even atrocity occurs in the pursuit of that end is of no consequence as it is the will of God. There are of course many biblical accounts that could be cited to support such a view but many who hold it see no need to argue beyond the perceived will of God regardless of biblical argument.

It is self-evident that Soelle's work, much of which grew from reflection on her own people's treatment of Jews and others during the Second World War, was dedicated to creating a new social order and this she did through political action but also through theological creation, a task she understood as crucial to counter dispassionate theological dogma and individualistic theology which she saw as a component of patriarchal theology and "capitalist spirituality." We could see how both these components have played a part in the politics of Israel/Palestine with the overarching God of land offering it to the people who will "develop" it most! As Soelle's work progressed we see the God of transcendence becoming a spirit of transformation among us, one who enables us to transcendent the places we find ourselves in to move to another way of liberative being. In *The Silent Cry* Soelle is planting theological seeds for a life that transcends popular understandings of both spirituality and politics. Here we see how a reworking of theology can indeed offer new ways to at once challenge the existing order of hierarchical monotheism with its divisions and categories and instead offer a model that will sustain the individual in their struggle through offering an empowering understanding of transcendence rather than a system that feeds other metanarratives. The repositioning of transcendence as a spirit amongst people which enables them to overcome existing orders can never play into the hands of metanarratives since the realities of lived experience do not fit such bounded and rigid categories. Indeed they are never stable enough to fit such large stories, that is to say what is placed amongst people is always changing and being temporarily molded by the spirit of the time, the breath of God in the midst of the fuller becoming of God and people.

In Soelle's work traditional views of transcendence are seen as just as dangerous as the metanarrative of monotheism since it supplies a crucial component in that narrative- distance! If we are to keep the concept and think theologically then we must she insists see it as moving among us, a notion that Carter Heyward has more recently taken up. For Heyward transcendence is here and now in the lived reality of our lives as we move beyond limited and destructive ways of thinking into new ways- it is important to realize that there is no fixed and pre-ordered place to which we move, it is rather the ability to move, to change, to incorporate that is the vital part for theological thinking that is meant to change the world Heyward like others moans the combination of monotheism and transcendence since it brings in a static world, a world of the One God and his removal to a safe and indisputable distance. Like Soelle this is not the god Heyward knows but it is the One she sees that lies at the heart of discord and injustice. Of course this God that may not be questioned is not traditionally placed in a Jewish concept of the divine, a concept that allows for a lot of talking back and negotiating as we see in many parts of the Hebrew bible (Stone 2005).

In the approach of Soelle there is no challenge to monotheism as such although of course the location of the divine does change the face of monotheism significantly. That is to say if God is between and among us then we do have to think rather differently than if that God is above, beyond and untouchable and completely unknowable, but right in all things and for all time. It is the argument of Maaike de Haardt from the Netherlands that monotheism itself is the root cause of many of our ways of thinking and being and as such is a threat to our global relationality (de Haardt 2010). Just as Francis Fukiyama was signaling the grip of savage capitalism when he declared that history has ended, there is not space for development only repetition and the spread of one ideology so de Haardt argues that it is the singularity of the creator and creation that has set in place very destructive mono- thinking in the world leading to destruction and alienation. We become locked into what she sees as a unilateral relationality where the power is all on one side and does not reside in us as subjects. For de Haardt this is clearly demonstrated in the story of the sacrifice of Isaac which has become foundational for culture. For her the core problem is this unconditional absolute obedience to God as the only authentic way to express faith which sets in place a psychology of abuse. A psychology that does not question the hierarchy of obedience and suffering- one in short that can live with the consequences of the worst excesses played out in the name of God. The hierarchy of obedience to and suffering for that is inherent in this form of monotheism has been pointed out many times in the history of feminist theology for example but has not always led to questioning the ethical implications of continuing with monotheism itself (Korte & de Haardt 2009). What has been more usual is a debate around the notion of co-creation and co-creativity within a process model of relationality between the divine and humans. One in which it has been argued the absolute nature of God has been questioned and slightly altered. However for de Haardt this also falls short as it is she claims a largely male centered model which fails to move from the inherent problems of mono- generativity- she believes there remains an unequal notion at the heart of even the process model that leads to a system that actually takes for granted that hierarchy and therefore service and suffering are inevitable. That whatever the relationship there remains a core that is more equal than the other equal parts, it is this mono-centre that has to be obeyed whatever the consequences, appoint she illustrates by referring to the story of the sacrifice of Isaac.

It is in the work of Catherine Keller that de Haardt sees some way ahead from the mono-generativity of monotheism through an engagement with the Deep or the multiplicity of difference in relation that God is thought to be (see Keller 2003). Keller looks to Genesis and speaks of the tehomic ethics she sees at work in the early pages, a movement of the divine that is deep and dark and chaotic, one that does not set itself in place for exclusion and categories. Keller argues that the cosmos did not emerge from Platonic forms but rather from tehomic chaos, there was no blueprint, but rather the glorious outpourings of surprise and novelty. She offers a proposition for a tehomic ethic and it is that we bear with the chaos, neither liking it nor fostering it but recognizing that there is the unformed future (ibid., 30). This unformed future is made up of repetition but from very early in cosmic development this repetition always adds something new, in every repetition is a transgression, our bodies and that of the cosmos are in constant flux, as they regenerate they change, they are in essence transgressive. It seems little less than perverse to insert an unchanging God with a worked out plan into this enfleshed human and cosmic picture. This movement of the divine is far too wild for categories and far too deep for settling on ONE manifestation and world order. Keller offers an encouraging interpretation which rehabilitates much that has been excluded from theologies and world views due to being seen as chaotic and beyond what the divine may be. Not only that she points out that transgression is also a fundamental way in which both we as bodies and the world itself appears to work and this gives hope that even the most fixed and static categories in theology may be changed, if they refuse they appear to going against the nature of things. The absolute God seems at odds with creation.

Keller like Edward Said before her reminds us that beginnings are always relative, contested and historical whereas origins are absolute and power laden. Beginnings then give the theologian the chance to decolonize this space of origins in creation and the inevitable creator who sits apart and to challenge as Catherine Keller puts it "the great supernatural surge of father power, a world appearing zap out of the void and mankind ruling the world in our manly creator's image" (ibid., 6). We are thrown back to cosmic beginnings, to void and chaos and we are asked to make our theology from that ground. To understand who we are and who we might be from tohu vabohu, the depth veiled in darkness. Once we give agency to void and chaos there can be no creation out of nothing as our power laden dualistic origin. Creation ceases to be a unilateral act laden with power and prohibition and the divine speech in the pages of Genesis is no longer understood as a command uttered by the Lord and warrior King who rules over creation, but as Keller tells us "let there be" is a whisper of desire and what comes forth emanates from all there is rather than appearing from above and beyond—from that place of absolute power. Keller offers the opportunity for people to re-think the way in which they are all related, in the dark in the depth of continued becoming rather than as the chosen of an almighty deity whose voice alone is the command for how the world should be arranged.

However de Haardt still remains uncomfortable as she feels even these theologies that she admires are attempting to find models that fit some pre-existing theological frame at the same time as attempting to overcome models that have dominance and power at their heart. It is here that she makes her main point which is that perhaps we need new practices that change the still dominant imperialistic abusive unilateral relations, language and reality under which we live. Practices because she is not sure to what extent ideas, concepts and theologies impact on social reality but of course she acknowledges that they do. The challenge to monotheism then that she offers is to a way of living that stems from deeply rooted notions that are so deep that they have largely been forgotten but still impact on the way society and international relations and economics are shaped. Of course we will always reflect and think but it seems for de Haardt that the way ahead is to "live" ourselves to a new space, a new shape of being that challenges the violence to women, children, "others" and the planet which might be argued to be the logical extension of mono-thinking. It is by placing ourselves in the now not under the yoke of an absolute and all powerful deity that we may move towards more relational ways of being together. Certainly de Haardt's approach to monotheism seems very radical indeed seeing very little to recommend it and much that it has been responsible for in terms of dysfunctional living- it allows for too many unilateral relationships which rarely if ever satisfy all involved.

A relatively new voice in the transcendent debate is that of Mayra Rivera who approaches the question through a postcolonial theology of God and speaks of the touch of transcendence. Right from the start she makes her position plain God is beyond our grasp but not beyond our touch just as we find in human touch, we touch but can never fully grasp the other creating what she suggests is a "intimacy of transcendence" (Rivera 2007, 2). Situated as her argument is in postcolonial theology she demonstrates how the dominant imperial theologies have never acknowledged anything beyond themselves. While using the disembodied nature of the ONE God to set in place the masculinist imperial symbolic it at the same time stops the world, both physical and symbolic, at its own narrow vistas. Rivera of course is also aware that falling into the untouchable, vertical transcendence that usually follows on is no place to go for those who sit beyond this vista, those who have not been seen or acknowledged as inhabiting land and ways of life that fall beyond. It is precisely because of this that she sees the need for a form of transcendent theology that breaks down the mono stranglehold. For her there is nothing abstract about transcendence as in the hands of the powerful it even controls the creation of time and our spatial perceptions. Her argument is that western industrialism needed to move beyond the rhythms of natural time and impose a universal time in order to maximize the profits it wished to extract and to disconnect people from their land and their natural ways of being. While she is not speaking directly to Palestine I think the connections are clear to see. This also separated the public and private sphere with the private time being seen as feminized and trivial while public time was of the greatest importance, the masculinized time of uninhibited production and detached transcendence (ibid., 8). Perhaps too we can see how the hard working Jewish immigrant to Palestine was seen as male while the original inhabitants were somewhat feminized in the view that they were lazy and unproductive, more concerned with relationality to land and family than to the "real" world of production.

Rivera also argues that horizontal transcendence has divided space itself with what is north as being understood as closer to God while the south is nearer the depths of stagnation and even depravity. In accordance with Derrida she believes that such overarching systems of knowledge produce rather than discover all encompassing foundations, they create the illusion of totality and suppress anything that is at odds or as Rivera sees it anything that is beyond. It is this view of the world she wishes to challenge but she does not wish to assume transcendence is external to the world and therefore human flourishing is subordinate to higher divine principles. Nor does she believe that talk of immanence denies and makes small talk of transcendence. She states her hope in "the ineffable affinity that links all creatures in open relations of mutual transformation which may help us to envision the beyond in the world without losing sight of the transcending character of all creation. This world is indeed more than it appears, calling us to apophatic alertness. God, the creatures and even we exceed all our representations" (ibid., 38).

Along with Gutierrez and others she is happy to declare the profane no longer exists but contrary to how this has been understood it is not an elimination of transcendence but rather a refusal to understand it as identifying God with the status quo. A very important notion when considering questions of the divine and the delegation of rights to land. Transcendence is understood to be in history because if we see God as external then any theological claim that salvation lies in a re-making of history, undoing injustice and replacing it with inclusive and just systems in the here and now is a false hope and an empty theology. It is the possibilities lying in the living of history in the material body that allows for the great hope of human kind, things may happen that have never happened before, "newness is not just discovered as being already present in nature, nor is it externally imposed upon reality. Genuinely new things come into existence from the actualization of possibilities through collective choice" (ibid., 43). Rivera claims that this notion of historical transcendence found in the work of Ignacio Ellacuria is dynamic allowing for contextual structural difference without implying dualism and for intrinsic unity without strict identity categories imposed. In this understanding Jesus can be said to be the supreme form of historical transcendence as he is present in material form as the dynamic outpouring of God, signaling that divine transcendence is not distance and absence but actual material presence. As Rivera says we should "aspire to a love that overcomes its consuming impulses and opens itself to be touched by the other" (ibid., 140). This seems to be a call to theology as much as to individuals. Theology should be touched by what transcends it and thus be transformed it should live in the "unceasing symphony played by the infinite creativity of life" as Gebara puts it and always reach not beyond but deeper and wider (ibid., 141). Derrida and Spivak refer to "hauntings" by which they mean encounters with those who are not present, those who are dead or not yet born, as places where we are called beyond ourselves and asked to embrace possibilities for the future. Ethics, politics and theology all seem to need such haunting in order to understand what is missing from our great schemes and metanarratives, who is not present and what difference consideration of them would make. It could well be argued that the land itself in Palestine/Israel has inherent in it those hauntings, those calls to a different futures based on those who have lived there and those who wish to live flourishing lives in that land. As testimonies suggest there is a time embedded in that land when identities were not the main issue, when people who lived there related to each other and the land as co-inhabitants. There would be some contemporary theologians who would suggest that listening to the land itself may well be the place to begin a new way of living together.

The historical understanding of transcendence is a great deal better than the traditional and the notion of the touch of transcendence and the intimacy thereof is very appealing both being suggestive of breaking through totality into a face to face encounter that changes systems. Of course there is still the problem that face to face may enable humans to think differently but those who wish to appeal to a divine authority may still find themselves appealing to an unchanging absolute whose commands and desires are set in stone. However, I believe that Genesis 32 is just one example of where a different understanding of the divine may be found, one that opens up possibilities. Here we find the story of Jacob wrestling with an angel which is commonly understood to be the divine, it is a fierce struggle in which both are altered.

This passage which has so often been read as fixing the nature of the divine does not actually read "I am what I am" but rather "I will be who I will be" a statement made in the midst of a struggle, a fight between a named person [Jacob], through naming we do assume some level of identity, and a stranger one who appears terrible and even terrifying in "his" otherness, almost beyond all that humans may know, an angel. They exhaust one another in this struggle and the human has a wound inflicted which means that he is unable to walk as he once did, but there is no real conclusion to this struggle and the name asked for by the human is as open ended as the struggle "I will be who I will be" no commitment to a fixed essence or even one implied in naming but an open flow of becoming in answer to a question that sought fixedness. Far from setting anything in stone least of all the God who is commonly understood to be the angel in this story there are endless possibilities placed in the telling, there is agency but openness to the movement of becoming that is relational. Relational and far from simple, there is struggle and even menace in this becoming for both the divine and the human, threat is ever present and no satisfaction in the end, indeed we may even say there is no end. No name is ever given and the human is left physically changed, not crippled, but not able to walk as once. The encounter has actually meant that his relationship with his body has been alerted and he is set a challenge to incorporate this into his future of physical landscapes. How is he to navigate his way now? The encounter with this stranger has left him less sure footed and it may be argued more aware of his own body and environment which now has to be considered when making a journey. Further of course Jacob also undergoes a name change, to Israel, a name signaling he has striven with God and with men. It is something to ponder that this struggle with God and men resulted in a change of name, a change then perhaps of how one sits in the world given the importance that names are felt to have in many cultures and particularly at the time of the story. Yet the angel, God, remains a form of becoming not a fixed identity through a naming. In many ways a representative of what Braidotti (1994) calls nomadic subjectivity because this becoming is capable of taking form and engaging within concrete contexts but remains fluid and untamed- there is a note of defiance and energy in the "I will be what I will be" that is not present in "I am who I am" which seems more resigned and static. I would dare to say there almost seems a relief that no identity is being imposed on the divine and the freedom to be and to change is allowed in that struggle.

I would suggest that for those who wish to use a biblical starting point for claims of land ordained by an absolute God they may do better to read this story. Of course it is open to many interpretations but for the purpose of this chapter it is the resistance to static naming and by extension to rigid systems on behalf of the divine that is of importance. There is room for change and that change appears to involve human struggle too, I believe this is a good starting point for any theology and it may also be a way to forge theology and social systems that allow movement in Palestine/Israel.

References

Braidotti, Rosi. 1994. *Nomadic Subjects.* New York: Columbia.
Grey, Mary. 1989. *Redeming the Dream. Feminism and the Christian Tradition.* London: SPCK.

Haardt, Maaike de. 2010. "Monotheism as a Threat to Relationality." In *Through Us With Us In Us: the Challenge of Relational Theologiesin the 21st Century*, edited by Lisa Isherwood and Elaine Bellchambers, 181–96. London: SCM.

Hampson, Daphne. 1996. *Swallowing a Fishbone: Feminist Theologians Debate Christianity*. London: SPCK.

Heyward, Carter. 2003. "Crossing Over: Dorothee Soelle and the Transcendence of God." In *The Theology of Dorothee Soelle*, edited by Sarak K. Pinnock, 221–38. London: Trinity.

Keller, Catherine. 2003. *Face of the Deep: a Theology of Becoming*. London: Routledge.

Korte, A-M, and Maaike de Haardt, eds. 2009. *The Boundaries of Monotheism: Interdisciplinary Explorations into the Foundations of Western Monotheism*. Leiden: Brill.

Rivera, Mayra. 2007. *The Touch of Transcendence: A Postcolonial Theology of God*. Louisville: Westminster John Knox.

Ruether, Rosemary Radford. 1983. *Sexism and God-Talk*. London: SCM.

Schneider, Laurel. 2008. *Beyond Monotheism: A Theology of Multiplicity*. London: Routledge.

Soelle, Dorothee. 1996. *Theology for Sceptics: Reflections on God*. Philadelphia: Fortress.

Stone, Ken. 2005. *Practising Safer Texts*. Edinburgh: T. & T. Clark.

Thomas, Ned. 1971. *The Welsh Exremist: A Culture in Crisis*. London: Victor Gollancz.

8

Beyond Interfaith Reconciliation: A New Paradigm for a Theology of Land

Dr. Mark Braverman

THE CHRISTIAN CONFRONTATION WITH the Nazi genocide produced a radical re-evaluation of theology with respect to Christianity's relationship to the Jewish people. Motivated by the urgent need to atone for the sin of Christian anti-Judaism, this revisionist movement focused on the repudiation of replacement theology. This revisionism has had profound implications for the current discourse on the political situation in historic Palestine. It directs and frames "interfaith" conversations in the West and promotes church policy designed to protect relationships with the Jewish community at the cost of the church's social justice mission with respect to human rights in historic Palestine. On a deeper level, this revisionist theology serves to support Christian triumphalist tendencies. Whereas the confrontation with the Nazi Holocaust presented an opportunity to confront this quality in Christianity, Christians instead chose to focus on anti-Semitism as the primary Christian sin. As a result, Christian triumphalism is actually reinforced, through an identification with a rehabilitated Judaism and an affirmation of the exclusivist nature of God's covenant with the Jewish people. In addition to this reversion to particularism, Christianity's spiritualization of the land has been disavowed, and a superior Jewish claim to the land is legitimized. In this chapter I discuss the implications of these issues for the development of a theology of land that supports equality and the transcendence of national boundaries. I call on the academy and global church to lead in this project.

A NEW TRIUMPHALISM

As a Jew born into a religiously observant family in post-World War II America, I was raised in a potent combination of Rabbinic Judaism and political Zionism. I grew up immersed in the Zionist narrative of the return to the Jewish homeland. I was taught that a miracle—born of heroism and bravery—had blessed my generation. The State of Israel was not a mere historical event—it was redemption from millennia of marginalization, demonization, and murderous violence. The legacy of this history was a sense of separateness—a collective identity of brittle superiority for having survived, despite the effort, "in every age"—so reads the Passover liturgy—to eradicate us. The ideology and mythology of the birth of the State of Israel partook of this legacy of separateness, vulnerability, and specialness. I embraced it.

Until I saw the occupation of Palestine and learned the other narrative. Until I realized that the colonial project that I was witnessing in the West Bank, progressing without brakes and with massive funding from my own government, was the continuation of the ethnic cleansing that had begun in earnest in 1948 and that had been planned almost from the beginning of the Zionist project. I returned home to the United States with two questions burning within me: "Why is my people doing this?" and "Why is the Christian world helping us to do it?"

As part of my attempt to answer these questions, I have come to several realizations. First: it is clear that politics have failed to bring about a just resolution of this conflict. I now believe that only a civil society-based movement of nonviolent protest against the policies of the State of Israel will produce the political resolution required to bring justice to the Palestinian people and peace and security to the people of the land—including my Jewish sisters and brothers in Israel. Second: I believe that the church—on an ecumenical and global basis—has a key role to play in providing the spiritual energy and leadership that is needed to ensure the growth and ultimate success of this movement. Finally, only when Christians are liberated theologically to act faithfully, in accordance with their witness to this injustice, will the church be able to fully answer the social justice imperative that calls out to it so clearly. Like the Jews of first century Palestine, we are living in prophetic times. At no time have we been in greater need of the voices of the prophets, including that of Jesus of Nazareth, who, like the prophets, spoke—and acted—in direct response to the injustice that plagued his people.

In Bern Switzerland, American theologian Harvey Cox challenged the assembled at the World Council of Church's Palestine Israel Ecumenical Forum conference on "Promised Land" with this question:

> What do we really mean by "promised land?" How has the term been hijacked and used for various political reasons, when maybe that is not the significance of the texts at all? Ancient Israel is often confused with modern Israel. They are not the same. We can talk about an integral relationship which must be there theologically between Christians and the Jewish people. Jesus was Jewish; the whole background of Christianity comes from the Jewish people, but the Jewish people and the modern State of Israel, though they overlap in certain ways, are not the same, and therefore we have to be thoughtful and self-critical about how that theme is dealt with. (Cox 2008)

Cox's bold statement sets before us the most urgent theological issue of our time. Awareness of Israel's current and historic denial of Palestinian rights has been growing among Jews and non-Jews alike. American voices, both secular and from the faith communities, are joining those of religious and political figures across the globe in calling Israel to account for decades of hostilities and for the current political stalemate, and in naming my own government's complicity in financing and diplomatically supporting the policies and actions that stand in the way of peace. Paralleling this important change in political awareness is an equally crucial shift from a theology occupied with the evil of anti-Semitism to one concerned with a theology of land.

THE CHRISTIAN SIN

I paid a visit to a professor of theology at the seminary of a major Protestant denomination in Washington DC. As the author of articles and books in the post-supersessionist tradition, he has taken on the blatantly anti-Semitic aspects of Christian doctrine, as well as strongly reaffirming the special relationship between God and the Jewish people. I told him that I felt we had a lot in common: that as a Jew, I was committed, as was he as a Christian, to rooting out destructive practices and doctrines in my religious tradition. I described my horror at discovering that my people, in pursuing our ethnic nationalist project, were betraying the most fundamental and cherished elements of our ancient tradition. I said that without question, Christians had to confront the anti-Jewishness of replacement theology—but that I was concerned that in the rush to atone for anti-Semitism, progressive Christian theology was supporting the abusive practices of the Jewish state by supporting a superior Jewish right to historic Palestine. I expressed my concern that this stream in progressive Christian thought served to furnish theological legitimacy to Israel's land grab and to its past and ongoing ethnic cleansing, and that it suppressed criticism of Israel's human rights violations and thwarted honest, productive dialogue about the Israel-Palestine situation.

The professor's response was swift: "That's an old story," he said to me. "It's the story of an archaic, tribal Judaism and an enlightened, universalist Christianity. We don't tell that story anymore." He stated that even if this "old story" had not been discredited by virtue of its blatant anti-Semitism and its responsibility for millennia of persecution of the Jews, it was passé, having been demonstrated to be theologically unsound. I was stunned by this reaction. Yes, anti-Jewish Christian doctrine deserved to be discredited in view of its pernicious effects. But I had expected more receptivity to a discussion of this issue. Theology, I pointed out, had to be in conversation with history. Did the crimes committed against the Palestinian people and the ongoing insecurity visited upon the Jewish citizens of Israel as the result of a quasi-messianic movement merit opening up the topic, despite the possibility that some would cry anti-Semitism? But the professor seemed closed to a nuanced discussion. Anything, apparently, that carried even a whiff of Christian anti-Jewishness, or that might possibly be perceived as such, had to be summarily discounted. Atoning for anti-Semitism trumped all other discussions.

My exchange with the professor that day is far from an isolated case. In our current political climate, it seems acceptable for Christians to look critically at elements of their own faith and history that have caused harm, especially when these have been cornerstones of their doctrine. But it is not permissible to extend this conversation into any critical examination of the behavior of Jews or their institutions. While Christian sins are fair game, criticism of Judaism or things Jewish is simply out of bounds.

It is not hard to understand how this has come to pass. Sixty five years ago, Christians stood before the ovens of Auschwitz and said: "What have we done?" Since then the Christian world has been engaged in a purposeful, passionate, and often painful process to examine its own theology and to reconcile with the Jewish people. But this effort has gone beyond cleansing the faith of anti-Jewish doctrine. In an effort to find an antidote to the toxic anti-Jewish beliefs known variously as "replacement theology" and "supersessionism," Christians in the West have embraced a theology that effectively supports the superior Jewish claim to the land. It represents a regression to an archaic view of God as dwelling in a geographical location and favoring a particular people. It has put the Christian faith, which came to move mankind away from particularism, on a slippery slope to the endorsement of a dangerous, anachronistic ideology of land possession and conquest.

A CRY FOR PURIFICATION

The Christian project of atonement for its sins against the Jewish people has created an industry of Christian-Jewish interfaith scholarship that has profound implications for Christian attitudes toward the Jewish people and the global discourse about the State of Israel. The historical, psychological and spiritual ground zero of this project is the wartime and postwar reaction of the German Protestant church to the Nazi era. In his 1998 collection, *Jews and Christians: Rivals or Partners in the Kingdom of God?* Belgian theologian Didier Pollefeyt traces this movement, reflecting on the "ground that has been covered in Jewish-Christian relations" since the Second World War. The chapter in Pollefeyt's collection by German Protestant theologian Bertold Klappert describes the situation of the German Confessing Church in the postwar era. Klappert describes how, confronted with the scale of the crime against the Jewish people, the focus of German Protestant theology had shifted from concern about the faithfulness of the church to its theological core as opposed to the demands of the state, to a penitential focus on Christianity's culpability for the Nazi genocide. Listen to Klappert's quote from his teacher and member of the original Confessing Church, Hans Joachim Iwand. In a 1959 letter discussing the Church's "academic and theological guilt" for Auschwitz, Iwand asks:

> Who is going to take this guilt away from us and our theological fathers—because there it started? . . . How can the German people that has initiated the fruitless rebellion against Israel and his God become pure? (Iwand 1997, 43)

In this cry for purification we can discern the central motivation and future direction for a revised Christian theology, a theology that took root not only in postwar Germany but in the Western world at large. Indeed, the history of Christian anti-Jewish doctrine and actions has became a consuming concern for Christian theologians. "Anti-Jewishness," wrote contemporary Protestant theologian Robert T. Osborn, "is *the Christian sin.*" (Osborn 1990, 214; emphasis added) Catholic theologian Gregory Baum, writing about the church's effort to reconcile with the Jewish people and rid itself of its deeply-rooted anti-Jewish biases, declared that "if the Church wants to clear itself of the anti-Jewish trends built into its teaching, a few marginal correctives won't do. It must examine the very center of its proclamation and reinterpret the meaning of the gospel for our times" (Baum 1997, 6–7). Baum—and in this he is joined by a preponderance of other writers, both Christian and Jewish—tied the need for this daunting project to the impact of the Nazi Holocaust:

> It was not until the holocaust of six million Jewish victims that some Christian theologians have been willing to face this question in a radical way . . . Auschwitz has a message that must be heard: it reveals an illness operative not on the margin of our civilization but at the heart of it, in the very best that we have inherited . . . It summons us to face up to the negative side of our religious and cultural heritage. (Baum 1997, 7)

The work of American theologian Paul van Buren was key in setting the stage for this powerful stream of Christian-Jewish reconciliation and a powerful philo-judaic push in American progressive Christianity. According to van Buren, forging a positive relationship with Judaism and the Jewish people is nothing less than the reimagining of what it means to be Christian. "If the church stops thinking of the Jews as the rejected remnant of the people Israel," writes van Buren, "if it starts speaking of the continuing covenantal relationship between this people and God, then it will have to rethink its own identity" (van Buren 1984, 23). Calling attention to the ways in which Christianity had allowed itself to be built on a foundation of anti-Judaism, van Buren set out to correct this theological error by framing God's covenant with the Jewish people as the basis for the Christian revelation. "Christianity must refer to Judaism in order to make sense of itself," writes van Buren. This is in the service of the "church's reversal of its position on Judaism from that of anti-Judaism to that of an acknowledgement of the eternal covenant between God and Israel" (1984, 85).

The issue of the Promised Land figures prominently in this theology. According to van Buren, Christians may participate in the spiritual Jerusalem with the Jews, but the Jews hold the deed to the actual real estate, and the return of the Jews to possess that very same Promised Land confirms this. Consider the following passage from a 1979 interfaith symposium, "The Jewish People in Christian Preaching." Why, asks van Buren, after eighteen centuries, should Christian leaders "turn Christian teaching on its head" with respect to the Jewish people?

> The Holocaust and the emergence of the state of Israel . . . are what impelled them to speak in a new way about Jews and Judaism. . . .the Israeli Defense Force sweeping over the Sinai and retaking East Jerusalem was what could not possibly fit our traditional myth of the passive suffering Jew. The result is that events in modern Jewish history, perhaps as staggering as any in its whole history, have begun to reorient the minds of increasing numbers of responsible Christians. (van Buren 1984)

It is not so much the jarring echo of the mythology of a "new Jew" that shocks and concerns me, nor the one-sided, triumphalist narrative of the 1948 and 1967 wars. What is more disturbing is the theological undertone, the biblical drumbeat, in the appearance of two words in this passage: Sinai and Jerusalem. But there is more going on here than a glorification of Jewish power and the Jewish vision of the Return to Zion: it is that now Christians can join in this triumph, and absorb this historical event into their own vision of what it means to be faithful to God's plan. These events of our time, continues van Buren, reflect "the will of the holy one of Israel, that the greatest of all love affairs of history between God and God's people continue, but that God provides also a way for Gentiles, as Gentiles, to enter along with the chosen people into the task of taking responsibility for moving this unfinished creation nearer to its completion" (1984, 25).

This is an astonishing reversal in Christian thought. This revised theology perpetuates the triumphalism that helped create the very sin that Christians are attempting to correct. Chosenness has been returned to the Jewish people, and then claimed as well for Christianity as heirs to this privileged status. We have here a kind of Judeo-Christian triumphalism—a significant step backward from the spiritualization of the land and the universalization of the parent faith that characterized the original Christian vision. And this is not a theological quibble—this shift carries huge consequences. First, it provides theological justification for a massive and an ongoing abuse of human rights. Second, it blocks Christian actions, on both individual and institutional levels, to address this wrong by opposing Israel's actions as a state.

In the introduction to his book, Pollefeyt proposes to "reflect the critical questions we must confront in framing a theology that can help us in the modern age." Pollefeyt has assembled an impressive collection, but in his goal of laying out the groundwork for an alternative to substitution theology, he errs in looking backward, rather than forward. In his introductory chapter, Pollefeyt brings in Rabbi Irving Greenberg's now well-known dictum: "No statement, theological or otherwise, should be made that would not be credible in the presence of the burning children." Greenberg's principle has achieved the status of an ultimatum, holding Christianity and indeed Western civilization hostage to the historic victimization of the Jewish people. Pollefeyt writes that if Christianity, "even after Auschwitz, can only bring its message at the expense of the life and well-being of the Jewish people, then Christianity is simply immoral and unbelievable . . . " (1997, 20). It is true that historically Christianity did establish itself at the expense of the Jews, with disastrous consequences throughout history. But now, in *this* historical context, there is a terrible cost in narrowing the focus in this way. Baum's statement that "Auschwitz has a message that must be heard" is correct. But this must be seen as applying to civilization as a whole, to all the holocausts born of religious particularity and ethnic and nationalist supremacy. This penitential Christian focus on the sins against the Jews—what I, with apologies to Dietrich Bohnhoeffer, would call *cheap penitence*—becomes problematic in the current historical context, because it serves to support the very particularity that the early Christians had come to confront in the time of Rome. Who are the burning children? Of course, we must see them as all children. But in practice, this is not so. In practice, the lives of Jewish children have preference over Palestinian children. In practice, Jewish suffering has become the benchmark, defense of Jewish claims and fears the primary focus. And in the current context, the considerable forces that support the interests of the Jewish state above all others are more than willing to exploit this Western Christian attitude.

There are fundamental theological issues raised here. The approach presented by Pollefeyt and others reviewed here rests on the assumption that Christianity was established in the negative—as a replacement for Judaism. This is not the case. Christianity in its earliest days was meant to continue Judaism, not supplant it. History and circumstances got in the way of that project of Jesus' followers and laid the groundwork for replacement theology. But there is a core of Christianity that has nothing to do with the toxic campaign against the Jews that insinuated itself into the faith early on and that has been the source of so much suffering over the centuries. In atoning for their triumphalism, Christians have succeeded only in reinforcing it through their endorsement of the Jewish people's nationalist project. This is a betrayal of the core of Christianity. We need to pick up the trail where it was lost, back in the first century, when an itinerant Jewish mystic brought his people together in opposition to the evil of the Roman oppressor and in resistance to the oppressive practices of their own theocracy in Jerusalem. In this regard I refer you to the work of John Dominic Crossan, Walter Wink, Richard Horsely, Norman Gottwald, Neil Elliot and others, who understand the Gospels as the record of a movement of social transformation and of nonviolent resistance to oppression.

It is the crisis of the land today that brings us to this point, and it is the articulation of a new theology of land that is the crucible in which this work will be done. Before I turn to this, however, I will first discuss the major barrier that confronts the church in taking up this work in earnest. I have termed this "the interfaith trap."

THE INTERFAITH TRAP

As described above, the postwar years produced confessional statements by various German Protestant churches as they struggled to come to terms with the consequences of Christian anti-Jewish doctrine. For the Roman Catholic Church, Vatican II in 1965 was a watershed event, as the Church undertook a long overdue examination of its attitudes toward the Jewish people. Christian-Jewish "interfaith" dialogue was originally undertaken to break down age-old barriers of fear and mistrust between the two communities. Today, however, this dialogue now follows clear rules that serve to insulate Christians from any perception of anti-Jewish feeling and to protect the Jewish community from any possible challenge to unqualified support for the State of Israel or the validity of the Zionist project. These rules are playing out in the academy, in the pews, in interfaith relations on the highest levels, and in everyday encounters. They are rendered more powerful by never being stated or acknowledged.

CAPTURING THE ACADEMY: THE RULES FOR CHRISTIAN-

JEWISH DIALOGUE

Fundamentally, there are two rules:

1. "Sensitivity" to "the Jewish perspective" and Jewish self-perception (as defined for all Jews by one group who claim to represent the whole) is paramount. This is a variation on the burning children principle—sensitivity to Jewish experience determines the direction and nature of the discourse.

2. The superior right of the Jews to the land is not to be challenged.

Two brief examples illustrate this phenomenon:

Ruth Langer is a Reform Rabbi and Associate Professor of Theology at Boston College. In 2008 she published a paper entitled "Theologies of the Land and the State of Israel: The Role of the Secular in Jewish and Christian Understandings." In the paper Langer invokes the first rule described above—that Christians accept "Jewish self-understanding" regarding Jewish identity and the land of Israel as definitional and unassailable. For Langer Jewish self-experience is characterized by two basis elements: (1) The Jewish attachment to the Land of Israel as a Jewish homeland is an essential element of being Jewish—it cannot be questioned. (2) Related to this is the Jewish experience—which Langer presumes to describe for all Jews—of being a people apart. Langer argues that the failure of the Enlightenment to bring Jews fully into Western society and to establish the Jews as a religious group like any other is evidence that this quality of Jewishness is essential and inalienable. She ignores the range of diversity of Jewish experience on both these axes. According to Langer, any Jew who disagrees with her description of Jewish experience is in flight from his or her Jewish identity, like those Jews who historically sought to assimilate in order to curry favor and advantage with the dominant Christian society in which they lived, or worse, those who actually converted to Christianity. And, points out Langer, it was a vain attempt anyway: Although many Jews had attempted to shed their particularism, and with it the identification with the idea of a return to Zion or any sense of seeing themselves as a separate nation, economic and social marginalization and sporadic violence forced them back into a separatist, and ultimately nationalist, stance. The Nazis, of course, provided final and tragic support for those who advance this analysis.

This argument from history is central in defending the Zionist project against those who would question its validity, sustainability, morality, or logic. "Christians," writes Langer, "must strive to learn by what essential traits Jews define . . . Christian-Jewish dialogue. In terms of. . .the development of adequate theologies of the land and state of Israel within the context of the contemporary dialogue, this is a crucial first step." (2008, 16–17)

The use of the historical argument to control the so-called "dialogue" between Christians and Jews takes second place only to the imperative of repudiating replacement theology. In the June 2009 edition of *Cross Currents*, a quarterly on religion with a progressive and interfaith bent, published an issue titled "The Scandal of Particularity." The title of this issue, which features articles by Jewish, Catholic and Protestant authors, suggests a critical analysis of the claim of any religion to a superior or exclusive path to God. In fact, however only Christian particularity is targeted in the publication. The entire issue follows closely the rules of interfaith "dialogue" described above, providing a theological and spiritual basis for the Jewish claim to the land. In one article, William Plevan, a Rabbi and student of theology at Princeton, draws heavily on the anti-supercessionist work of Orthodox Jewish theologian Michael Wyschogrod. "Wyschograd argued" writes Plevan, "that the central theological concept of Judaism is God's election of Israel to God's beloved people. While God demands that Israel observe the commandments and while certain beliefs about God's nature may be implicit in the Biblical record, the essence of divine election is not the commandments or any beliefs about God, but rather God's preferential and parental love of the carnal family of Israel, the flesh and blood descendants of Jacob" (2009, 217). According to Plevan, this exclusivist core is essential to interpreting the message of the Gospel, claiming that "the incarnation of God in Jesus Christ actually has roots in Jewish ideas, such as God's presence in the people Israel." The Temple, although physically gone, is preserved as symbol of landedness and Jewish exclusivity. A piece by Rabbi Nina Beth Cardin entitled "The Place of "Place" in Jewish tradition" claims that although the land has a spiritual and psychological meaning, this "nod to the universal does not cancel out the particular." Jewish life, asserts Cardin, is "all bound up in that particular bit of land on the east coast of the Mediterranean Sea" (2009, 214). The land of Israel is the gift of God to the Jewish people, its *nahalah*—inheritance.

Wyschogrod is popular in Christian circles as well. Indeed, American Christian theologians are in a rush to endorse this kind of Jewish particularism by adopting, whole cloth, the writing of this Jewish triumphalist theologian. Those who choose not to are simply remaining silent.

A number of the articles by Christians in this issue of *Cross Currents* also draw heavily on Wyschogrod, as well as on the work of Kendall Soulen, the theology professor I introduced earlier in this paper who took exception to my analysis of Jewish exceptionalism. P. Mark Achtemeier, a Presbyterian pastor and Associate Professor of Systematic Theology, contributes a piece entitled "Jews and Gentiles in the Divine Economy." "History," he observes, "has. . .dramatically failed to unfold as supercessionist theologies would have led one to expect" (2009, 147). Citing Soulen and Wyschogrod, he holds that the persistent survival and cultural vitality of the Jewish people is evidence of God's enduring love for his entire creation. This theme carries through the entire issue, a publication purportedly devoted to the "scandal of particularity!" Clearly, in today's academy a strict double standard applies. In the rush to interfaith reconciliation, "anti-" or "post-supersessionism" appears to have less to do with cleansing Christianity of particularity and more to do with establishing Jewish particularity as a fundamental theological principle.

CLOSING THE DEAL: THE LAND PROMISE

A centerpiece of the *CrossCurrents* issue is the article by John T. Pawlikowski, a prominent Catholic theologian and Director of the Director of the Catholic-Jewish Studies Program at the Catholic Theological Union." In his piece, entitled "Land as an Issue in Christian-Jewish Dialogue," Pawlikowski asserts that the Vatican's 1993 recognition of the State of Israel was pivotal in correcting Christianity's historic anti-Judaism. With that act, he wrote, "the coffin on displacement/perpetual wandering theology had been finally sealed" (2009, 199) Pay attention to what is being done here: recognizing the Jewish state corrects Christian theology! But there is more: Pawlikowski goes on to repudiate Christianity's spiritualization of the land, taking issue with "efforts by Christian theologians to replace a supposedly exclusive Jewish emphasis on "earthly" Israel with a stress on a "heavenly" Jerusalem and an eschatological Zion" (2009, 199). He continues: "[T]his tendency has the effect of neutralizing (if not actually undercutting) *continued Jewish claims*. The bottom line of this theological approach was without question that the authentic *claims to the land* had now passed over into the hands of the Christians. Jerusalem, spiritually and territorially, now belonged to the Christians" (2009, 199, emphases added).

I find this an astonishing argument. In the original Christian vision-ing—and this was a revolutionary and critically important development — Jerusalem itself became a symbol of a new world order in which God's love was available to all of humankind. The Christian vision clarified the meaning of the land promise in the covenantal relationship, removing any ambiguity about possession or ownership. But Pawlikowski was now maintaining that this spiritualization of the land was a betrayal of God's covenant with the Jews—that it had deprived us of our birthright. Ac-cording to him it was now incumbent upon Christians to honor the claim of the Jewish people to the Holy Land, and indeed to Jerusalem itself. But this is not Christianity! The whole point of spiritualizing the land was to deconstruct, using the full power of the prophetic tradition, the idolatry of Temple and land possession—in Walter Brueggemann's terms, the royal consciousness that seeks only to maintain itself at the expense of community life and social justice.

In the Gospel accounts (Mark 13:2, Matthew 24:2), Jesus stands before the Temple and says: "Not one stone will be left upon another!" Translation: *this old order is over.* And in the Gospel of John (John 2:21), when Jesus says "Destroy this Temple and in three days I will raise it up," the narrator, just to make sure we get the theology right, explains: "He spoke of the temple of his body." *Body of Christ:* one body—mankind made one, whole, united in one spiritual community. Christians, in an act of penitence and collective drive for purification, are now actively engaged in a deconstruction of this core element of their faith. We have to be very concerned about this — generations of mainstream pastors and theologians in the West have been educated in versions of this revised theology. This is the theology called into service by the Jewish establish-ment and elements within the churches themselves to oppose faithful, prophetic efforts within denominations to take faithful stands against companies profiting from the occupation and theft of Palestinian land. These are the arguments used to muzzle and intimidate clergy and secu-lar leaders from speaking out against the State of Israel's human rights violations. The Christian impulse for reconciliation has morphed into theological support for an anachronistic, ethnic-nationalist ideology that has hijacked Judaism, continues to fuel global conflict, and has produced one of the most systematic and longstanding violations of human rights in the world today.

A THEOLOGY OF LAND

A theology of land that is responsive to the current crisis is important not only because of its relevance to the Israel-Palestine conflict. The issue of the land focuses the most urgent theological issue of our time: the particular vs. the universal. As such, it poses two fundamental theological questions: What is God's love? What is faithfulness to his plan? Today, as Harvey Cox pointed out in the passage quoted above, the theology of land has been hijacked. It has become the captive of the penitential impulse of the Christian world on a religious level, and, on a political level, brought into the service of the preservation of the interests of the few and the powerful. Theologically, the land has become, in a very real sense, the coin of the realm. And so we must pose the question: What is the meaning of the land promise? In our search for an answer, we begin by stating what land in the Bible is not: it is not territory. Rather, it is an evolving construct having to do with the nature of God's plan and the divine relationship with humankind.

CONTEXT, MEANING, AND THE SCRIPTURAL NARRATIVE

The issue of context becomes critical in this discussion. In a recent paper, Professor of Systematic Theology George Sabra notes the increased prominence of contextual theology in the last four decades (Sabra 2010). With respect to our topic, he identifies three "clashing" contexts. Early Christian tradition provided the first context, in which the People of God was clearly the Church, replacing the "Israel" of the Old Testament. The second context is represented by the post-Nazi era Christian revisionist effort to reinstate the primary relationship of the Jewish people with God, emphasize Jesus' closeness with the Jewish practice and establishment of his time, and affirm the theological significance of the State of Israel. The third context, in Sabra's view arising in reaction to the second and in particular to the establishment of the State of Israel, is the trend among some Middle Eastern theologians to downplay or even deny the theological significance of the continued survival of the Jewish people and of the State of Israel. In all cases, Sabra notes, the notion of People of God and the view of the land it self is clearly colored by the experience and political agenda of the subjects. While recognizing that all theology is done in and responds to its historical context, Sabra cautions against the trend to have the contextual be determinative of the theology and biblical interpretation. "We must attempt to transcend our contexts," he writes, "so that the gospel may be visible across, through, but also sometimes *in spite* of our contexts. For that, a dialogue of contexts is necessary so as to transcend one's immediate context" (2010).

The work of Old Testament scholar Walter Brueggemann provides an example of an approach that follows Sabra's prescription. In his work on the land, Brueggemann presents the land as both metaphor and as a stage upon which the drama of the divine-human relationship is enacted. The land, writes Brueggemann, is a powerful force for "wellbeing characterized by social coherence and personal ease in prosperity, security, and freedom" (2002, 2). It is rootlessness, not meaninglessness, he writes, that creates the crisis of faith for the people. Indeed, in the Old Testament narrative it is particularly with the loss of the land—in exile—that the people discover who they are and undergo the painful struggle to come to terms with the true meaning of the covenant. Like Sabra, Brueggemann calls on us to remain grounded in the narrative provided by scripture as we seek to understand the meaning and transformative power of theology with respect to the notion of peoplehood and the role played by the land.

The importance of a theological response to context is reflected in the development of Brueggemann's thinking about this topic. Although earlier in his writing Brueggemann appeared to grant the Jewish people a special (albeit conditional) entitlement to the land (Braverman 2010), recently he has brought his theology of promise into conversation with contemporary events. "This ideology of land entitlement," he points out, "serves the contemporary state of Israel" (as quoted in Braverman 2010, xv). It is an ideology, he continues, that is "enacted in unrestrained violence against the Palestinian population . . . It is clear that the modern state of Israel has effectively merged old traditions of land entitlement and the most vigorous military capacity thinkable for a modern state" (ibid., xv). For Brueggemann, this is not an isolated observation targeted at the Israeli regime; it is part of his overarching vision of how power corrupts and how land promise can become land entitlement in service to systems under the sway of royal consciousness. "It is clear," writes Brueggemann, "that the same ideology of entitlement has served derivatively the Western powers that are grounded in that same ideological claim and that have used that claim as a rationale for colonization . . . The outcome of that merger of old traditional claim and contemporary military capacity becomes an intolerable commitment to violence that is justified by reason of state . . . *That is, land entitlement leads to land occupation*" (ibid., xv; emphasis in original).

AN EVOLVING CONCEPT

The concept of the land in the scriptural narrative reflects this evolutionary trajectory. We must see this scriptural narrative as one unified story, beginning in Genesis and continuing through Revelation. It is a story in which the concept of land persists as a powerful and evolving theme, a theme that is central to the narrative and that reflects a response to historical context. The original land promise sets in motion a dramatic story of the transition from the tribal to the universal, from a concept of a territory possessed and conquered to that of the establishment of a global order of social justice. This is where the notion of the continuity of scripture I am proposing here can be most useful in this discussion of land. The fundamentals of universalism set out in the Old Testament find continued expression in the vision articulated in the New Testament. But "continuity" may not be the best word to describe the rocky, twisty road that we traverse here. The Old Testament may contain all the ingredients needed for the ultimate achievement of the Kingdom of God, but the Bible does not serve up this feast all at once. We have to spend a lot of time in the kitchen. God gives the people a land—just as he gives them kings. And it is for the people—with the help of prophets—to painfully work out what this means.

In the Old Testament narrative, God comes first to mankind by choosing one family for a role in establishing his plan for a just society. The land plays a central role in the unfolding drama of this covenantal relationship. The people are special (*kadosh*)—set apart from the other peoples—and they are given the land in tenancy as a part of this covenant. The drama continues when the people demand a king. God tells Samuel to warn the people that a king will subvert the primary goal of the covenant of establishing a just world: the king will see the land as a possession, distribute resources unfairly, destroy community and family life, and ultimately bring the wrath of God down upon the entire people. Of course this is precisely what happens—ultimately the "kingdom" falls and the people are vomited out of the land, just as specified in the Levitical and Deuteronomic warnings. But even through these vicissitudes, the exclusivist frame of the original covenant persists. Throughout, the People of Israel retain their special relationship with God, and with that the primary claim to the land. The promise itself, in its exclusivist frame—is never withdrawn. Although Israel is enjoined to treat them justly and even as equals, non-Israelites are "strangers," or "resident aliens," as the

Hebrew word *ger* is sometimes translated. All through the vicissitudes of the divided kingdom, the destruction of the northern kingdom, the destruction of Jerusalem, the exile, and the return, this primary tie of people, God, and land is maintained. A theology of landedness –place— persists. Jerusalem remains the *place* where God dwells. Even with the prophets' protestations against the abuses of King and priest, this exclusivist core persists. The return recorded in Jeremiah and the time of Ezra and Nehemiah can be seen as a restorationist event. The Temple is rebuilt—this is never in question.

Fast forward to first century Palestine: The historical frame is the Roman Empire—the ultimate expression of acquisitive greed. The Temple is still standing. Jerusalem is ruled by a client government installed by that Empire. This is the context of Jesus' ministry, which is a direct response to the evil of that arrangement, and the frame for his revolutionary concept of Kingdom of God. Liberation theologian Walter Wink writes about Jesus' statement, *My Kingdom is not of this world.* Wink points out that in the gospel of John the Greek word for "world" is *kosmos*—which translates as *order* or *system.* This world, Jesus is saying, this system of empire which seeks only to increase its own power and reach at the expense of communities, families, human health and dignity, this world order will give over to the Kingdom of God—something completely different.

It's important, therefore, to realize that in its original proclamation, the Kingdom of God was *specific*. It was proclaimed in a particular historical context. And thus it is in every historical era, whenever a particular society confronts an urgent challenge to the social justice imperative. For the writers of the Gospels, Jesus' vision of the Kingdom of God dispenses, finally, with the concept of God's indwelling in the land, of a particular location as the place where God is to be worshiped. In the Christian vision, the idea of the physical land as a clause in the covenant disappears. In Jesus' Kingdom of God, both the land and the people lose their specificity and exclusivity. Temple—gone. God dwelling in one place—over. And, significantly, Jesus' Kingdom takes the next step—it jettisons the "*Am Kadosh*" or "special people" concept. The special privilege of one family/tribe/nation separated from the rest of humanity is eclipsed.

This specific, contextual issue is at play today as never before. We (the Jewish people of today) are deeply involved in the drama of this narrative. Our commitment to political Zionism has stopped our ears to the call of the Old Testament prophets to reject the idolatry of king and Temple. It has further thickened the historical wall separating us from the challenge of that first-century Galilean visionary and prophet to take one further, giant step out of our exclusivist origins toward the embrace of a universalist, community-based egalitarian society. Instead, our investment in an ethnic-nationalist project in historic Palestine has returned us to the world of Kings and to the restorationism of Ezra and Nehemiah. Not that Christians have not succumbed to the human tendency to slip back into the comfortable framework of war, territory and conquest. Medieval depictions of the New Jerusalem gave way to Crusader depredations and military sieges of the actual city of stone and wood. Christian Zionism in its most recent "progressive" manifestation seeks to undo the spiritualization of the land and grant the deed to the property to the Jewish people in an effort to overcome the horror over the ovens of Birkenau. (And it is *this* Christian Zionism, hiding in plain sight in the mainstream, that I think is more dangerous than the dispensationalist variety of Christian Zionism, which can be dismissed as extreme or heretical). But the direction is and always has been clear: Zion is not a geographical location. Rather, is a symbol of God's steadfast love—the solidity, comfort and fixed point of the covenant—and, later, in the Christian vision, of the Kingdom: God's universal gift of peace and justice to all of humankind. Can we learn to accept this gift?

FROM TRIUMPHALISM TO COMMUNITY

At the conclusion of his own contribution to the collection, Pollefeyt reminds us of the argument of Job's comforters that Job must have sinned because God can only act justly. At the end of the story, this argument is reversed to show that Job—here seen by Pollefeyt as the Jewish people—is the innocent one, the true witness to God's justice and rightness. I urge great caution here. This is standing displacement theology on its head, saying that Jewish suffering is proof not of their treachery but of their blessedness and their loyalty to God: and so the Jews are reinstated as God's elect, with Christians as their supporters and heirs. The notion of God's elect is an archaic, triumphalist concept. Christians, in resuscitating it and reassigning the role to the Jewish people are committing an act of hubris and folly. Jews, in invoking the land promise as if it were a clause in a real estate contract, are guilty of an act of catastrophic idolatry. And, put together, what we have here is a Judeo-Christian triumphalism that, in the realization of political Zionism in today's geopolitical context, represents a greater threat to humanity than the Roman Empire ever did.

There are myths operating for both faith groups here. For Christians, it is the myth of a unity, a coherence with the Judaism of the first century—as if it were possible to undo the fateful parting of the faiths that laid the foundations for anti-Semitism. For Jews, it is the myth of the possibility of a return to a mythical state of national unity and dominance, exemplified by the Davidic dynasty of Temple and political hegemony—as if this could somehow redeem the suffering of millennia, the burning of children. There is a profound denial of horror here for both groups, an attempt to make it all better. Christians can't undo two thousand years of persecution and the effects of Christian anti-Judaism on not only the Jews but on all of Western civilization. We Jews can't restore the Palestine of 1948 or reverse the effects of four generations of dispossession and refugee status—nor are we realistically expected to do so. But we can turn to a new future of community united against the common enemy of militarism and empire. Particularity is a scandal—an affront to our senses and our rationality, and a dangerous misunderstanding of God's nature and his will. There is no one, special way to God. All scriptures point in a single direction: the building of a community of humankind to confront the urgent issues facing humanity and the planet. We are *all* elected. We are *all* responsible for our fellow man and for honoring and respecting the physical environment.

This is what it means to be people of God and this is the meaning of the land. As the psalm proclaims: The earth is the Lord's, and everything in it, the world and all who dwell in it. We can find no more faithful and clear articulation of this theology than the Palestine Kairos document:

> We believe that our land has a universal mission. In this universality, the meaning of the promises, of the land, of the election, of the people of God open up to include all of humanity, starting from all the peoples of this land. In light of the teachings of the Holy Bible, the promise of the land has never been a political programme, but rather the prelude to complete universal salvation. It was the initiation of the fulfillment of the Kingdom of God on earth.

This is my message to Christians, as a Jew who is experiencing, all too vividly, the dangers of particularity: beware of slipping into a newly minted Christian triumphalism under the cover of reconciliation with the Jewish people. The challenge to people of all faiths is to take the lesson from the current nationalist project of the Jewish people: God grants specialness to no one people. The result, in Walter Wink's terms, is to become victims of the myth of redemptive violence.

CONCLUSION: WHAT CAN WE DO?

The new theology of land is important because the church, at congregational and denominational levels, as well as in the seminaries and in university departments of Bible and theology, needs to be liberated theologically to answer the urgent call for Palestine. The uncomfortable truth is that for many Christians, vigilance against anti-Semitism has come to trump commitment to justice for the Palestinian people—justice that alone will bring an end to the Israel-Palestine conflict and the hope of peace for both peoples.

In contrast to the silence and timidity of much of the church, there are strong signs that the church, at local and denomination levels, is waking up to the urgency of the situation. We are witnesses to the birth and growth of a global, grassroots civil society movement to challenge the current establishment of Apartheid in the Holy Land—a movement in which the church will continue to play a critical role. Two such signs are seen in the current Palestinian Christian witness represented by the Sabeel Ecumenical Liberation Theology Center and its partner organizations internationally, and the Palestine Kairos document and the Kairos organizations being established in Southern Africa, Europe, Asia and the Americas. Unapologetically Christian, Sabeel's mission and the prophetic message of the Kairos movements document all lay claim to the ministry of Jesus in proclaiming the duty of resistance to tyranny—resistance, in the words of the Palestine Kairos document, "with love as its logic." This phrase articulates an urgent truth: that the truest expression of love toward the Jewish people is persistent, faithful opposition to the crimes that have been visited upon the Palestinian people by the State of Israel. A theology of land must be an expression of and guide for this opposition in its many forms. As expressed in the Kairos document, the theology must give support to the growing Palestinian civil society movement of nonviolent resistance to the Apartheid and colonial policies of Israel. A theology of land is expressed in support by congregations, denominations and church leaders for the Palestinian United Call for Boycott Divestment and Sanctions. It is expressed in the growing connection between civil society organizations in Israel and Palestine and in the West and the South, and, more and more, in the involvement and commitment of the churches on congregational, denominational and ecumenical levels. A theology of land becomes the reclaimed voice of a church which, in answering this prophetic call, is claiming its legacy and its faithful heart.

I see a theology of land enabling and supporting movement toward justice in the following ways:

1. Liberate and empower the church's leadership by (a) clarifying the theology and (b) mobilizing the leadership for action. Clergy must see the struggle for justice in Palestine as one of the most urgent social justice issues of our time. A vigorous, intentional effort to develop the theology should be pursued in national and international conferences involving seminaries and universities. Prominent theologians, clergy and lay leaders should be involved, in close coordination with peace activists from the faith community and the secular realm.

2. Local action. Committees should be organized at local levels including clergy from all denominations in coordination with community leaders, activists, academics, seminarians, and their professors to educate themselves about the facts of the conflict, commit themselves to prayer, study and action, pursue ties with civil society organizations in the region and domestically, and develop plans for action at local, regional, national, and international levels. It's a big tent—action can include working to increase awareness in congregations and communities through the organization and sponsorship of educational events, involvement in the global movement for economic and cultural pressure on Israel and on companies profiting from the oppression of Palestinians, and political advocacy to influence national government policies in the region.

3. Surface and clarify the interfaith issue. As awareness of Israel's current and historic denial of Palestinian rights grows, so too does opposition on the part of powerful elements of the organized Jewish community to any criticism of Israel or any action intended to question or change America's unconditional and massive support of Israel. One focus of this opposition is the initiative by some church denominations for phased divestment from companies involved in Israel's occupation of Palestinian land. Most recently, even fiercer opposition has been leveled against those who are joining with secular and Jewish peace groups in endorsing the Palestinian call for a comprehensive economic and cultural boycott of Israel (http://

www.pacbi.org/). The acceleration in ecumenical activity on the part of Palestinians and on a global church basis for a theology of land that supports nonviolent resistance to oppression evidenced by the Palestine Kairos document and the work of the Palestine-Israel Ecumenical Forum of the World Council of Churches has also met with condemnation from Jewish advocacy groups. This is unfortunate, but it cannot be allowed to thwart the activism or distract from the doing of theology. If Christians and Jews can come together in the work of forging a theology of land that disavows particularism and privilege and shows the way to a sustainable future, so much the better. But for Christians, *this must not be seen as a project of interfaith reconciliation.* Rather, the work of theology today is about the church—ecumenically, denominationally, and locally—getting its own house in order.

The call to the church is clear—it is the same call to social justice that was heard in the United States in the middle of the last century, when the church, led by the Reverend Martin Luther King Jr., led a movement that brought an end to legally sanctioned racial discrimination. From a jail cell in Birmingham, Alabama, King penned this historic letter in 1963, at the height of the struggle. To his fellow clergy, who were counseling patience, urging him to cease his civil disobedience, King wrote in his "Letter from a Birmingham Jail":

> Yes, I love the church . . . But oh! How we have blemished and scarred that body through social neglect and the fear of being nonconformists. There was a time when the church was very powerful—in the time when the early Christians rejoiced at being deemed worthy to suffer for what they believed. In those days the church was not merely a thermometer that recorded the ideas and principles of popular opinion; it was a thermostat that transformed the mores of society. Whenever the early Christians entered a town, the people in power became disturbed and immediately sought to convict the Christians for being "disturbers of the peace" and "outside agitators." But the Christians pressed on, in the conviction that they were "a colony of heaven," called to obey God rather than man.
>
> . . . the judgment of God is upon the church as never before. If today's church does not recapture the sacrificial spirit of the early church, it will lose its authenticity, forfeit the loyalty of millions, and be dismissed as an irrelevant social club with no meaning for the twentieth century.

Reverend King's call is the same that was issued by a group of South African pastors and theologians in their 1985 "A Challenge to the Church." In this historic document, also known as the South Africa Kairos, these church leaders, many of whom had spent years in jail or in imposed exile for their resistance to the regime, proclaimed a "moment of truth not only for apartheid but also for the Church."

> It is serious, very serious. For very many Christians in South Africa this is the KAIROS, the moment of grace and opportunity, the favorable time in which God issues a challenge to decisive action. It is a dangerous time because, if this opportunity is missed, and allowed to pass by, the loss for the Church, for the Gospel and for all the people of South Africa will be immeasurable. . . A crisis is a moment of truth that shows us up for what we really are. There will be no place to hide and no way of pretending to be what we are not in fact. At this moment in South Africa the Church is about to be shown up for what it really is and no cover-up will be possible. (South Africa Kairos 1985)

These are calls that ring out clearly in our own time. Indeed, there is no place to hide. We are entering a new phase in Jewish-Christian relations. The project to disavow the anti-Jewish aspects of Christian doctrine and to build bridges of trust and understanding with the Jewish community has been and is an important effort—vigilance against anti-Semitism, like the fight against all forms of racism and discrimination, must continue. But the challenge we face today is not about repairing the past. It is, rather, about the urgent need to look forward. The task facing the faith communities today is not Christian-Jewish dialogue for its own sake, or the pursuit of interfaith reconciliation over past sins and tragedies. It is, instead, a faithful and intentional focus on bringing an end to the root cause of the Israel-Palestine conflict—the dispossession of the Palestinians and the establishment of an Apartheid structure of discrimination and ongoing displacement. In the forging of a theology that is responsive to this challenge, we confront the prophetic work that must unite us—the fact of being Christian, Jew, Muslim, American, German, South African or Israeli is not important. What matters is whether we are for triumphalism or for community, for exploiting the poor or for freeing them from poverty, for despoiling the earth or for honoring and preserving it. What matters is justice—for the sake of Israelis and Palestinians alike, and indeed for all of humanity as we seek a solution to this conflict.

References

Achtemeier, Mark P. 2009. "Jews and Gentiles in the Divine Economy." *Cross Currents* 59.2, 144–53.

Baum, Gregory. 1997. "Introduction." In *Faith and Fratricide: The Theological Roots of Anti-Semitism*, by Rosemary Ruether. Eugene, OR: Wipf and Stock.

Braverman, Mark. 2009. "Zionism and Post-Holocaust Christian Theology: A Jewish Perspective." *Journal of Holy Land Studies* 8, 31–54.

———. 2010. *Fatal Embrace: Christians, Jews, and the search for peace in the Holy Land.* Austin: Synergy.

Brueggemann, Walter. 2002. *The Land.* 2nd ed. Minneapolis: Augsberg Fortress.

———. 2010. "Foreword." In *Fatal Embrace: Christians, Jews, and the Search for Peace in the Holy Land,* by Mark Braverman, xiii–xx. Austin: Synergy.

Brown, Stephen. 2008. "Theologians Warn on 'Biblical Metaphors' in Middle East Conflict." *ENI Bulletin* (September 24) 33.

Cardin, Nina Beth. 2009. "The Place of 'Place' in Jewish Tradition." *Cross Currents* 59.2, 210–16.

Langer, Susan. 2008. "Theologies of the Land and State of Israel: The Role of the Secular in Jewish and Christian Understandings." *Studies in Christian-Jewish Relations* 3, 1–17.

Osborn, Robert T. 1990. "The Christian Blasphemy: A Non-Jewish Jesus." In *Jews and Christians: Exploring the Past, Present, and Future,* edited by James H. Charlesworth, 214. New York: Crossroad.

Pawlikowski, John T. 2009. "Land as an Issue in Christian-Jewish Dialogue." *Cross Currents* 59.2, 197–209.

Plevan, William. 2009. "Meet the New Paul, Same as the Old Paul: Michael Wychograd, Kendall Soulen, and the New Problem of Supersessionism." *Cross Currents* 59.2, 217–28.

Pollefeyt, Didier. 1997. *Jews and Christians: Rivals or Partners for the Kingdom of God?* Louvain: Peeters.

Sabra, George. 2010. "Clash of Contexts." Paper presented at the International Conference on *The People of God in Bible and Tradition.* Saint John of Damascus Institute of Theology, The University of Balamand. May 26–29, 2010.

South Africa Kairos. 1985. "Challenge to the Church: A Theological Comment on the Political Crisis in South Africa." http://kairossouthernafrica.wordpress.com/2011/05/08/thesouth-africa-kairos-document-1985/ (accessed 4 March 2014).

Van Buren, Paul M. 1984. T"he Jewish people in Christian theology: Present and future." In *The Jewish People in Christian Preaching,* edited by Darrell J. Fasching, 19–33. Lewiston, NY: Edwin Mellen.

9

Confronting the Truth: New Awakenings to the Palestinian Situation

Prof. Mary Grey

Introduction

This contribution focuses on new positive aspects to the situation now faced by the Palestinians. Despite what appeared to be political stalemate, despite the daily suffering and humiliation of people in the West Bank and Gaza, (and escalating harassment of the Israeli government) there are indications that the tide has definitely turned. Reconciliation between Hamas and Fatah will certainly bring change—and that is but one factor. I will then address challenges for spirituality, Church and theology.

There is unarguably- a new political context in the Middle East that is bringing much hope, even though the outcomes are far from clear—as we were very aware at Sabeel's conference, *Challenging Empire*, in February this year. In a recent *Guardian* article, "Europe's Israel romance is on the wane," it was pointed out that "Europeans are losing their illusions about Israel, our survey shows. Policy is out of step with the public . . ." (Abdullah 2011).

Whereas in Europe, Israel has historically enjoyed a high level of support, not least because it was perceived as a progressive democracy in a sea of Arab backwardness, at the same time, most Europeans knew very little about the Israel-Palestine conflict.

As recently as 2004, the Glasgow University Media Group found that only nine percent of British students knew that the Israelis were the illegal occupiers of Palestinian land. Astonishingly, there were actually more people (eleven percent) who believed that the Palestinians were occupying the territories.

However, according to a new poll by ICM for the Middle East Monitor, Europeans' perception of Israel has changed decisively, and their understanding of the Israel-Palestine conflict, while still giving some cause for concern, has improved significantly. The survey of 7,000 people in Germany, France, Spain, Italy, the Netherlands and Britain reveals only a small minority (10 percent) now believe their countries should support Israel rather than the Palestinians, while many more, 39 percent, think they should not.

This shift in European public opinion may owe something to an improved understanding of the conflict; 49 percent of respondents were now able to identify Israel as the occupying power. However, 22 percent still didn't know. Reasons for this persistent ignorance about issues that have been long established in international law may reflect media bias, or inadequate coverage of the conflict but could also be a result of campaigns undertaken by the Israeli public relations machinery in Europe. Whatever the cause, the shift in public opinion is clearly not mainly due to the success of a pro-Palestinian lobby but primarily a consequence of Israel's violation of international law, specifically its actions in Gaza, the 2010 attack on the humanitarian flotilla, (this was said to be illegal by 53 percent of those polled; 16 percent thought it legal), Israel's illegal settlement expansion program, the construction of the separation wall and consequent humiliation of West Bank Palestinians.

So, across Europe, we note a growing rejection of Israeli policies—(we do not here speak of the US.) While it is important to note that those polled saw fault on both sides, 31 percent considered Palestinians to be the primary victims of the conflict, while only 6 percent thought Israelis the primary victims. Thus European policy on Palestine can no longer be said to reflect the values and aspirations of the European people: there is a disturbing level of disconnect between public opinion and our governments' actions. Whereas the EU took a decision in 2003 to place Hamas on its list of terrorist organizations and preclude it from any negotiations, 45 percent of those polled said it should be included in peace talks, while only 25 percent said it should be excluded. (A recent survey by the

Institute for Jewish Policy research also found that 52 percent of British Jews support negotiating with Hamas for peace.)

It would seem that the results of this study coincide with the epic changes now engulfing the Middle East. Europe's romantic view of Israel has long been on the wane. *The Guardian* article concludes:

> [Israel's] 20th-century image as the battling underdog in a hostile neighbourhood has been shattered by its actions. European governments should bring their policies into line with universally accepted human values. Anything less will be a betrayal of the democratic standards Europe claims to uphold. (Abdullah 2011)

AWAKENINGS OF THEOLOGIANS—CHRISTIANS, JEWISH, MUSLIM

It was by being confronted with the truth of the harsh realities of life in Palestine that a volte-face or awakening consciousness that the sea of change occurred for both Christian and Jewish theologians. One of our speakers, Professor Rosemary Ruether, herself states that when writing *Faith and Fratricide*, (about anti-Semitism in Christian theology) she was unaware of conditions in the Middle East, which she had never visited, but

> came to recognize that the Jewish community was using the anti-Semitic issue to give a blank check to the state of Israel and so I needed to know something about that. So I went on a trip with Jewish feminists that was billed as ecumenical . . . in 1980, but got to see the realities a bit and then went back for an extended stay in Tantur, meanwhile reading a lot about the issue. *Once one sees what is actually happening one has to critique it.* (personal e-mail, 7 April 2010; italics added)

A similar reaction was experienced by many Christian theologians, myself included. Oxford New Testament Professor, Christopher Rowland was brought up with inherited deep-seated anti-Judaism, and the Holocaust affected him deeply: it was through a succession of personal encounters—together with the effect of Liberation Theology- that he was able to confront the actual realities. The late Michael Prior, Vincentian priest and liberation theologian, came to the situation from a combination of commitment to the Palestinian people, frequent visits to the West Bank, and a long practice of reading the Bible with a liberation exegesis.

Yet the process of freeing himself from the dominant school of biblical thinking on the Israeli right to inhabit the "promised land" was not an easy one.

But, if the challenge for Christian theologians was to confront, on the one hand, our own complicity in anti-Judaism and anti-Semitism (plus the legacy of colonialist history and the brutality of the British colonial regime in Palestine) and failure to act in the face of the oppression of the Palestinians, on the other hand, the guilt factor of the Holocaust has been kept alive as a deliberate strategy by the Zionist government.

Secondly, speaking of Jewish religious leaders, activists, prominent people—a crisis of faith and identity awaited those who were prepared to confront the truth. Mostly the awakened consciousness occurred because of being confronted by ground realities. Just to give a few examples. Mark Braverman, an American Jewish psychotherapist, now completely committed to peacemaking, and a courageous prophetic figure, writes:

> I am the grandson of a fifth-generation Palestinian Jew. My grandfather was the direct descendant of one of the great Hasidic Rabbis of Europe, a family that later settled in Jerusalem in the mid 19th century. (Friends of Sabeel North America Lecture)

Born in the United States in 1948, Braverman was raised in an amalgam of Rabbinic Judaism and political Zionism. He was taught that a miracle—born of heroism and bravery—had blessed his generation. The State of Israel was not a mere historical event—it was redemption . . . So when he visited Israel as a boy of 17 he fell in love with the young state. He was proud of the miracle of modern Israel—creating this vibrant country out of the ashes of Auschwitz. His Israeli family—religious Jews—warmly embraced him. But even as he embraced them in return, he heard the racism in the way they talked about "the Arabs" and knew then that something was fundamentally wrong with the Zionist project: yet his love for the Land stayed strong. He lived for a year on a kibbutz and ignored the implications of the pre-1948 Palestinian houses still in use, the ancient olive trees standing in silent rows at the edges of its grounds. In fact Braverman held to the Jewish narrative until he went to the West Bank. Let's hear his own words:

> Travelling in Israel and the Occupied Territories my defenses against the reality of Israel's crimes crumbled. I saw the

Separation Wall—I knew it was not for defense. I saw the damage inflicted by the checkpoints on Palestinian life and on the souls and psyches of my Jewish cousins in uniform who were placed there. I saw the settlements. I heard about the vicious acts of ideological Jewish settlers. And words like apartheid and ethnic cleansing sprang to my mind, unbidden and undeniable. And what is more, I learned that 1948, what I had learned to call The War of Liberation was the Nakba—the ethnic cleansing of ¾ of a million Palestinians from their villages, cities and farms. And I knew that what I was witnessing in the present, the whole apparatus of occupation, was a continuation of that project of colonization and ethnic cleansing. It horrified me and it broke my heart. Most important of all, I met the Palestinian people, and recognized them, no—claimed them—as my sisters and brothers. That summer, 40 years after my first encounter with the Land, I saw all that, and my relationship to Israel changed forever. (Braverman 2009)

A similar reaction is witnessed to by many Jewish thinkers and theologians, many the children of Holocaust Survivors—the most famous example being of course Marc Ellis. I will cite two more Jewish examples, for specific reasons. The awakening of Rabbi Michael Lerner, editor of the liberal Jewish journal *Tikkun*, (remember *tikkun olam* means the "healing of the world"), based in San Francisco, who had grown up in a Zionist household, visited often by David Ben Gurion and Golda Meir, among others, was dramatic. When he was 22 years old he spent an extended time in a kibbutz in Israel. Though impressed, he was stunned by the lack of social ideals that were meant to be shaping political life in Israel:

It was only when I began to ask about the origins of the kibbutz in the struggle against the Palestinian Arabs that I stumbled upon a terrible truth: the land on which I was working had been owned by Arabs who had been displaced by the Zionist enterprise. (Lerner 2003, xiv)

It was this discovery that first set him on the search for peace and to start an organization called Committee for Peace in the Middle East. He continues to experience criticism and even personal attacks for his opposition to Zionist policies. The latest incident has been an attack on his family home—three times, to date—by right-wing Zionists, because of his befriending attitude to Senator Goldstone, a South African Jewish judge who wrote the critical report on the Israeli attack on Gaza.

My next example is a woman, particularly associated with Gaza. The Jewish Harvard Research scholar Sara Roy, (now an authority on Gaza) is the child of parents who survived Buchenwald and Auschwitz. She went for research purposes to the West Bank and Gaza in 1985, and lived a summer that changed her life when she saw the humiliation of the Palestinian people and their treatment by the Israeli soldiers:

> It is perhaps in the concept of home and shelter that I find the most profound link between the Jews and Palestinians, and, perhaps, the most painful illustration of the meaning of occupation. For Jews as for Palestinians a house represent far more than a roof over ones head: it represents life itself. (Roy 2007, 21)

This statement leads logically to the last example. Jeff Halper, educator and anthropologist is an American Zionist who fell in love with Israel. One fatal day (July 1998) he witnessed the destruction of his friend Salim Shawamreh's home:

> As the bulldozer pushed through the walls of Salim's home, it pushed me through all the ideological rationalizations, the pretexts, the lies, and the bullshit that my country had erected to prevent us from seeing the truth: that oppression must accompany an attempt to deny the existence and claims of another people in order to establish an ethnically pure state for yourself. (Halper 2008, 15)

This devastating experience led him to found ICAHD, The Israeli Campaign against Housing Demolition. Along with ICAHD it is good to welcome many other Jewish initiatives for peace in Israel and beyond. For example, the growing activism of *Jewish Voices for Peace* brings hope. This is their most recent statement condemning violence:

> Any act of violence, especially one against civilians, marks a profound failure of human imagination and causes a deep and abiding trauma for all involved. In mourning the nine lives lost in Gaza and the one life lost in Jerusalem this week, we reject the pattern of condemning the deaths of Israelis while ignoring the deaths of Palestinians. We do not discriminate. *One life lost is one life too many—whether Palestinian or Israeli.* ("From Gaza to Jerusalem," 2011 [emphasis original])

No account would be complete without mention of the emergence of the Israeli "revisionist" historians—including Ilan Pappé, (now based in Exeter, UK), our speaker Professor Nur Masalha, (my colleague at

Mary's), Avi Shlaim, and Benny Morris. What these historians share is that access to the historical archives has given insight and historical testimony to the truth of the Zionist aggression, especially to the truth of events in 1948. In their different ways they have made a great contribution to altering consciousness, often at great cost to their personal lives.

Thirdly, I want to mention a shift in some Muslim thinking. A recent and promising development is the emergence of Islamic Liberation Theology. In his recent book, *Islamic Liberation Theology: Resisting the Empire*, Hamid Dabashi writes:

> What we are witnessing in much of the Muslim world today, as indeed in much of the world at large, is the rightful struggle of ordinary people for their pride of place, for social equanimity, economic justice, political participation, a legitimate and assertive place in the global redistribution of power. (Dabashi 2008, 255)

Drawing on the "founding father" of Liberation Theology, Gustavo Gutiérrez, he declares that

> "In the last instance . . . we will have an authentic theology of liberation only when the oppressed themselves can freely raise their voice and express themselves directly and creatively in society and in the heart of the People of God, when they themselves 'account for the hope,' which they bear, when they are the protagonists of their own liberation." For that to happen, that hope will have to transcend its particular (Jewish, Christian, Islamic, or any other) denominational divide and speak a metaphysics of liberation beyond the theology of one or another divisive claim on God. The particularity of that theology will have to speak a universal language, from the bosom of its particularity. (Dabashi 2008, 255)

This stance has been further elaborated in a Palestinian context. In June 2005, at the School of Oriental and African Studies in London, Dr. Saied Reza Ameli, an Iranian scholar and founder for the Institute of Islamic Studies, London, spoke of the universality of Liberation Theology. Building on the key concept that Liberation theology is an attempt to liberate people of the world from poverty and oppression, he traced its relevance for the Palestinian people in specifically Islamic categories. Its emergence is based on nostalgia for justice and nostalgia for metaphysical values.

Three elements are required. The first is return to God. This will affect our practices on the earth about ourselves and others. Selflessness is the second element. Selflessness, minimization of *personal desires* and dogmatic attachments to nationality, ethnicity, and even religion are major requirements for caring for oppressed and poor people. This means avoiding all things which can be considered as "selfishness." "Self" here is not only a person, but it can cover all "collective centralities" such as Eurocentrism, Americocentrism, and Zionism, which cause demolishing and destruction of "others" for the price of supporting the "self." Furthermore, "Selflessness" is a divine and mystical soul of all divine religions which brings God's spirit to all aspects of life. . . Here is where the Palestinian problem becomes a global issue for all human beings who care about "others," here is the position at which "all become equal to one and one becomes equal to all; here is the position at which one can observe unity within diversity and diversity within unity."

The third point—common to all liberation theologies—is the centrality of justice. Regarding Palestine, the relevance is that the "Chosen society is the oppressed society." As the Prophet Mohammad said: "Shall I let you know about the kings of the Heaven? *Every powerless deprived.*" In Islam, he continues, the future is not in the hands of those who kept the powerless deprived. He articulates:

> And We desired to show favor to those who were deprived in the land, and to make them Imams, and to make them the inheritors. (This and quotes in the preceding paragraph from Ameli, "Universality of Liberation Theology.")

This has a remarkable resonance with the Christian hope from the Sermon on the Mount that "the meek will inherit the earth." In fact, this was the text of the sermon of the opening service for the recent Sabeel Conference in Bethlehem. Speaking with his back to the infamous Separation Wall, with the Aida refugee camps on his right, Revd. Mitri Raheb, a well-known Lutheran pastor from Bethlehem, used this text to prophesy that empire after empire has fallen—"the Babylonian, Persian, Greek, Roman, Ottoman, British. . .Eventually only the meek, the indigenous people, will be left—and they will inherit the land—that has been seized from them by successive empires."

After these two sections on "new Awakenings," next I want to stress—in two parts—that it is not that suddenly Europeans/North Americans of whatever faith suddenly discovered the truth, but that this is the effect of the actions of Palestinians themselves who, because of the strength of their own resistance, (often called *sumud*—persistence, steadfastness), have been able to build up an immense international solidarity movement of thousands of people. This was stressed by Professor Mazin Qumsiyeh, at the Sabeel conference and in his book, *Popular Resistance in Palestine* (Qumsiyeh 2011). What he made abundantly clear is that this has historically been a *non-violent* resistance movement against empire. (The characteristics of this were seen in the uprising in Egypt). Secondly, it has been a movement of both women and men, even if the contribution of women has often been underplayed or even forgotten. He writes:

> How many in the west have heard of the Women's Movements of the 1920s against the British occupation and its support of colonial Zionism? (Qumsiyeh 2011, 234)

From the 1920s and 30s women took the initiative at critical times and also in the post 1967 years, when the national will was debilitated. For example, the first demonstration in spring 1968 was led by women—and dispersed by force. Similarly in 1968 over 300 women in Gaza demonstrated about the policies of occupation, expulsions and land confiscations (Qumsiyeh 2011, 117). Thirdly, his focus on non-violence is vital. (Apparently there are insufficient places for training in nonviolence in Palestinian institutions). Whereas State power is brilliant at mobilizing fear, shedding fear is vital. Hence prophetic figures like Gandhi and Martin Luther King are frequently drawn on to inspire the heart of non-violence resistance and the *sumud* of the people. This permeates every aspect of existence. Qumsiyeh writes:

> We could write volumes about resistance by simply living, eating, breathing in a land that is coveted. We resist by going to school, by cultivating what remains of our lands, by working under harsh conditions and by falling in love, getting married and having children. Resistance includes hanging onto what remains of Palestine when it has been made crystal –clear in words and deeds that we are not welcome in our lands. (Qumsiyeh 2011, 235)

Fourthly, it is a stance that calls out to the world for a response of solidarity, transformation of consciousness and action. In December 2009 Heads of the Churches in Jerusalem sent a plea to the world, "Kairos Palestine." The document pleads to the world to stand by the Palestinian people, "who have faced oppression, displacement, suffering and clear apartheid for more than six decades." It gives specific examples of the action needed. Although it emerges from Christian Churches "Kairos" covers Muslim contexts too. At another conference in Bethlehem, the Education Minister for Bethlehem schools, Dr. Barakwat Fauzi (himself a Muslim) spoke of Kairos's relevance for Muslims and for education. "It (Kairos) comes from our hearts in a country where justice is absent," he said, "from a context where every family has wounds." He called on enlightened Christian leaders around the world to oppose the misuse of the Bible. But he also called for programs around the issues of the document to be set up in all Palestinian schools.

So far reaction to the document has been muted. Only the Methodist Church in the UK has so far taken a strong stance in the Report submitted to their Conference last year (2010), a report—which did not lack controversy—signed by both Jewish and Christians groups.

> We, the undersigned, are Christians and Jews who have invested our energies and hopes in working for a just peace in Palestine/ Israel. We write to offer our wholehearted support for the "Justice for Palestine and Israel" report being submitted to this year's Methodist Conference. ("Methodist 'Justice for Palestine and Israel' Report," 2010)

Disappointingly, the working group's humane and principled conclusions have been misrepresented and attacked by those who empty powerful terms like "coexistence" and "reconciliation" of their true meaning.

Coexistence is not advanced by the bulldozer's blade as it demolishes Palestinian homes and uproots olive trees; nor is reconciliation furthered by segregation and a decades-long militarized regime of control. In opposing such injustices, the resolutions simply affirm international law.

We do nothing to advance a just peace without being realistic about the structural imbalance between Israel and the dispossessed, stateless Palestinians. In 1963, Martin Luther King wrote that the greatest "stumbling block" to freedom was the "moderate" who preferred "a negative peace" which is the absence of tension to a positive peace which is the presence of justice.

> The Methodist church has the opportunity to listen to the cry for solidarity of the Palestinian Church as expressed in the Kairos document and respond. ("Methodist 'Justice for Palestine and Israel' Report," 2010)

So far this is a lone voice crying in the wilderness. The Catholic Church, (to speak of my own allegiance) as far as I know, has only one official reaction. On the Justice and Peace website of the Westminster Diocese, this statement appears:

> The events in Egypt, Tunisia and Yemen have focused world attention yet again on the Middle East. One area which continues to suffer is Palestine, where basic human rights seem as far away as ever. This seems an opportune time for the Justice and Peace Commission to redress a regrettable silence in endorsing a poignant Christian statement which emerged from Palestine nearly 15 months ago. To date it has received very little attention from any of the Christian churches in this country.
>
> We at the Diocese of Westminster Justice and Peace Commission welcome the *Kairos* Palestine document, *A Moment of Truth*, published in December 2009 by the Christian leaders of Palestine. We invite other Christians to add their support.

This document declares "that the Israeli occupation of Palestinian land is a sin against God and humanity because it deprives the Palestinians of their basic human rights, bestowed by God," distorting "the image of God in the Israeli who has become an occupier just as it distorts this image in the Palestinian living under occupation."

> The events in Egypt, Tunisia and Yemen have focused world attention yet again on the Middle East. One area which continues to suffer is Palestine, where basic human rights seem as far away as ever. This seems an opportune time for the Justice and Peace Commission to redress a regrettable silence in endorsing a poignant Christian statement which emerged from Palestine nearly 15 months ago. To date it has received very little attention from any of the Christian churches in this country. (www. rcdow/justiceand peace)

I've quoted this in full because it is the kind of statement that we hoped to find everywhere that would inspire effective action.

So why the dead silence around the Kairos document except in these few cited cases? What has happened to the prophetic dimension of the Church? Has prophecy left the Church? Are we afraid of the Israeli government? Yet the Palestinians have overcome fear in the face of daily persecutions? (I know this should not be exaggerated or generalized). *We here do not live in the face of persecution.* Are we afraid of upsetting the Jewish community and being accused of anti- Semitism? Yet Jewish voices are speaking out, putting their lives on the line, being accused of being "Self-hating" Jews, yet standing up for justice and leading activist movements. Are we too enslaved by empire- whether the market forces of globalization, or the superior power of military might? Yet we follow a man who refused to take up arms in the face of the might of the Roman Empire. Are we so consumed with post-holocaust guilt that we are unable to speak the truth about the genocidal acts that the Zionist government now inflicts on another Semitic people?

When I was in Palestine I was reading a new biography of Dietrich Bonhoeffer and was struck by the similarity of context between resistance to Nazi Germany and the lack of resistance to injustice in Palestine by the Churches. Whereas there was all too much collusion between the established Church and the Nazi party, Dietrich Bonhoeffer and his colleagues in the Confessing Church, (and we are not very far away here from Chichester, where Bishop Bell, Bonhoeffer's supporter was active), were heroically witnessing to the authentic prophetic meaning of Church, supporting the Jewish people in the teeth of the murderous annihilation schemes, and risking their lives in the service of truth. Do we not need another Confessing Church, recalling Church to its roots in opposing all non-truth, evil and oppression? *Or a wider movement, inclusive of all faiths and in solidarity with secular movements?* Do we not need to witness to another reality that does not collude with Empire, and military aggression?

Concretely, this means many tasks. If we cannot wait for the leaders to lead, we begin with the work and commitment of ordinary people. So has it ever been for Liberation Theology. We work for the BDS campaign because this is what the Palestinian people have asked us to do. Secondly, we engage in reading the Bible differently. Still too many people in the Christian Churches are reading the Bible, on the basis of an uncritical a-historical reading of certain Old Testament texts, as if there God gave a mandate to the Zionist government to confiscate Palestinian lands. Thirdly, we engage with responsibly thinking Jewish people in this project. We attempt to work together through difficult issues like the possible meanings of "chosen-ness," "election," "superiority" . . . and the image of God behind all these notions. Fourthly, we need to challenge Christian Zionism in its fundamentalist reading of Scripture and to awaken a vision—that the Palestinians have given us —of the just sharing of the land. And finally we need to enter into the vision of non-violence as the way to a peaceful cooperation. And we only need to listen and learn from the many examples the Palestinians give us. And I will lend with one specific story.

Travelling in Palestine in March I met Daoud Nassar, the owner of "The Tent of Nations"—a 100 acre farm, on a hill top surrounded by hills whose land has been confiscated for Jewish settlements. And the Israelis want his land too. This farm is the only example of a Palestinian family which has so far been able to retain their land: Daoud's grandfather registered it in 1916 under the Ottoman Empire, re-registered it under the Jordanians, then the British—and now the struggle carries on with the Israelis. The neighboring settlers inflict damage on the water system and trees. Once they uprooted 250 olive trees. Three weeks later came an e-mail from "Jews for Justice"—in England!—who promised 250 olives trees to replace them; and they came and planted them! The farm's daily existence is under threat. There is a plan to disconnect the farm not only from the main road but even from the nearby village. Despite all this, Daoud's father held the land to be so precious that he wanted to create something on it for peace, so the Tent of Nations was born.

Daoud is a man who refuses to be bitter, to hate, to cling to anger, and finds a way to turn rejection into witness. No running water—so they have dug 11 cisterns to collect rain water. No electricity—they installed solar panels. No building permits—they turned caves into meeting places and prayer sites. No friends—so they open their lives to people of all faiths, Jews, Christians, Muslims and Hindus. Last year more than 4,000 people from around the world came to spend time here.

The determination to keep going in a spirit of non-violence was inspiring. The message of reconciliation shone from clearly: "We need to break the chains of hate—we are learning hope and planting peace." Daoud believes in small steps for change, relating to all who come to his land in the path of non-violence—treating Israeli soldiers as real people whose eyes need to be opened. The Tent of Nations is a parable of overcoming evil with good. Here we see clearly the vision of the World Social Forum—and surely this should be the inspiration for a new prophetic, Palestinian Liberation Theology?—that another reality is possible.

References

Abdullah, Daud. 2011. "Europe's Israel romance is on the wane". *The Guardian* (13 March). http://www.theguardian.com/commentisfree/2011/mar/14/europe-israel-palestine-european-disconnect-public.

Ameli, Saied Reza. 2005. "Universality of Liberation Theology." Presentation in June at the School of Oriental and African Studies, London.

Ateek, Naim S. 1989. *Justice and Only Justice: A Palestinian Theology of Liberation.* Maryknoll, New York: Orbis.

———. 2008. *A Palestinian Christian Cry for Reconciliation.* Maryknoll, New York: Orbis.

Braverman, Mark. 2009. "Justice at the Gate." Lecture at FOSNA (Friends of Sabeel, North America).

Dabashi, Hamid. 2008. *Islamic Liberation Theology: Resisting the Empire.* London: Routledge.

"From Gaza to Jerusalem: JVP Statement on the Escalation of Violence." 2011. Jewish Voice for Peace (25 March). http://jewishvoiceforpeace.org/blog/updated-from-gaza-to-jerusalem-jvp-statement-on-the-escalation-of-violence.

Halper, Jeff. 2008. *An Israeli in Palestine: Resisting Dispossession, Redeeming Israel.* London: Pluto.

Lerner, Michael. 2003. *Healing Israel/Palestine: A Path to Peace and Reconciliation.* Berkeley: Tikkun.

Justice and Peace website at http://rcdow.org.uk/diocese/justice-and-peace/.

"Methodist 'Justice for Palestine and Israel' Report." Press release, 22 June 2010. http://jfjfp.com/?p=14681.

Qumsiyeh, Mazin B. 2011. *Popular Resistance in Palestine: a History of Hope and Empowerment.* New York: Pluto.

Roy, Sara. 2007. *Failing Peace: Gaza and the Palestinian-Israeli Conflict.* London: Pluto.

10

Civil Liberation Theology in Palestine: Indigenous, Secular-Humanist, and Post-Colonial Perspectives

Professor Nur Masalha

The Hebrew Bible and Covenantial Settler-Colonialism in Palestine

IN MODERN TIMES A whole range of Western settler-colonial enterprises have used the mega-narratives of the Bible. The Book of Exodus the second and one the most important books in the Hebrew Bible, has been widely deployed as a framing narrative for European imperialism and its *mission civilisatrice*, while other biblical texts have been used to provide moral authority for colonial conquests in Africa, Asia, Australia and the Americas.

The narratives, rhetoric and prejudices of the Hebrew Bible were responsible for the creation of the myth narrative that the culture of the Philistines—who gave their name to the land of Palestine and indigenous Palestinian Arabs—and Canaanites were culturally inferior to the Hebrew tradition and "Israelite civilization'—an inferiority which justified their subjugation or even elimination. In the seventeenth and eighteenth centuries, as the European Christian "civilization" began to expand in the "wilderness" of North America, many English puritan preachers in the colonies of the New World, who also actively participated in the

Transatlantic Slave Trade, referred to the Native Americans as Canaanites, Amalekites and Philistines who should be either converted, or, if refused, annihilated. Cotton Mather (1663–1728) a prolific author, New England minister, a slave-owner and one of the most influential religious leaders in the America colonies. His books and pamphlets included *The Biblia Americana* (1693–1728); *Theopolis Americana: An Essay on the Golden Street of the Holy* City (1710); *The Christian Philosopher* (1721) *Magnalia Christi Americana* (1702); *The Negro Christianized* (1706); *Ornaments for the Daughters of Zion* (1692); is also remembered for his role in the Salem witch trials. In September 1689 he delivered a sermon in Boston, calling on that members of the armed forces in New England to consider themselves to be the new Israelites in the wilderness, out of which had erupted the civilizing law of God, confronted by new Amalek: pure "Israel" was obliged to "cast out [the "Indian savages"] as dirt in the street" and ethnic cleanse them (Niditch 1993, 3; Prior 2001, 17; also Long 2003, 180–183). Similarly, Robert Gibbs, an eighteen century American preacher, thanks the mercies of God the annihilation of the enemies of the new Israelites (that is, the Native Americans) (Bainton 1960, 112–113; Prior 2001, 17).

America support for Israel today, like British backing for Zionist colonization of Palestine previously, has effectively combined geo-political strategic interests as well as Christian (Zionist) religion and the Bible. Likewise the Zionist appeal to the land traditions of the Hebrew Bible was critical to the success of the European Zionist settler-colonial movement in Palestine. The term "Zionism" originated in Europe in the late nineteenth century. Political Zionism was, in large measure, the product of the religious and racial intolerance of the Europeans. It originated from the conditions of late nineteenth century Eastern and Central Europe, European romantic nationalist-*völkisch* ideologies and European settle-colonialism. European Zionist (Jewish) nationalism and settler-colonialism in Palestine imagined itself closely linked with the biblical Hebrew covenant and the State of Israel—established in 1948 in the name of the Hebrew Bible—was built on old biblical symbols and legends and modern Zionist nationalist myths and the Zionist claim to Palestine was based on the notion that God had promised/given the land to the Jews. In *God's Peoples: Covenant and Land in South Africa, Israel, and Ulster*, Akenson (1992) shows how the Hebrew Bible has formed the fundamental pattern of mind of the three settler- colonial societies of apartheid South Africa, Zionist Israel, and Protestant Northern Ireland and how the dominant elites of these three countries have based their cultural identity on a belief in a covenant with an all-powerful conquering God. By going back to the militant parts of the Hebrew Scriptures that defined the "promised land-chosen people" and told the people to conquer it, the religious purpose of the Bible was declared to be the same as the purpose of the secular Israeli state (1992). But does the Bible justify political Zionism, the military conquest and destruction of historic Palestine by the Israelis in 1948, and the current Israeli building of the separation/apartheid wall in occupied Palestine? The politics of reading the Bible in Israel and Zionism, a European settler-colonial movement, is a subject which is often dealt with in biblical studies in the West in abstract, with little attention to Zionism's catastrophic consequences for the indigenous inhabitants of Palestine.

While the Hebrew Bible was not the only "justification," it certainly was the most powerful one, without which political Zionism was only another conquering European colonial ideology. Read at face value, in a literalist fashion, and without recourse to doctrines of universal human rights and international law, the Hebrew Bible indeed appears to propose that the taking possession of ancient Palestine and the forcible expulsion of the indigenous population (the Canaanites) was the fulfillment of a divine mandate. From a scrutiny of the language used in the Hebrew Bible to the emergence of political Zionism from the late nineteenth-century onwards it is possible to see the way in which a secular European conquering ideology and movement mobilized the figurative language of the Jewish religion into a sacrosanct "title deed" to the land of Palestine signed by God (Prior 1997; 1999; Wetherell 2005, 69–70). Very little is said about the actual genealogy and provenance of Zionism, especially its European settler-colonial context of the late nineteenth-century from which Zionism drew its force; and almost nothing is said about what the creation of the State of Israel entailed for the indigenous inhabitants of the land (Said 1980, 57). Despite its distinct features and its nationalist ideology (exile from and "return" to the land of the Bible) political Zionism followed the general trajectory of colonialist projects in Africa, Asia and Latin America: European colonizing of another people's land while seeking to remove or subjugate the indigenous inhabitants of the land (Ruether 1998, 113).

Yahweh's Mandate to Ethnic Cleanse the Indigenous People: The Grand Narratives of the Bible and Militarism

In recent decades messianic leading rabbis in Israel have frequently referred to the Palestinians as the "Philistines" and "Amalekites of to-day" and many Zionist-Jewish zealots, including Gush Emunim rabbis and spiritual leaders, have routinely compared Palestinian Muslims and Christians to the Canaanites, Philistines, or Amalekites whose extermination or expulsion by the biblical Israelites was, according to the Bible, predestined by a divine design (Shahak and Mezvinsky 1999, 73).

The Book of Exodus and the conquest narrative of the Hebrew Bible, with its militarist land traditions, are theologically problematic and morally dubious (Prior 1998, 41–81). In the narrative of the Book of Exodus, there is an inextricable link between the imaginary liberation of the "biblical Israelites' from slavery in Egypt and the divine mandate to plunder ancient Palestine and even commit genocide; the invading Israelites are commanded to annihilate the indigenous inhabitants of "the land of Canaan" (as Palestine was then called). In the Book of Deuteronomy (often described as the focal point of the religious history and theology of the Old Testament) there is an explicit requirement to "ethnically cleanse the land" of the indigenous people of Canaan (Deuteronomy 7:1–11; see also 9:1–5, 23, 31–32; 20:11–14, 16–18; Exodus 23.27–33) (Prior 1997a, 16–33, 278–84). The militarist land traditions of the Hebrew Bible, which influenced Zionist settler-colonial in Palestine, appeared to mandate the genocide of the *indigènes* of Canaan. Of course it is possible to develop a Jewish theology of social justice, liberation and non-violent struggle with strong dependence on the Hebrew prophets—especially with reference to the counter-traditions of the Bible found in the Books of Isaiah, Amos and Ruth. Feminist approaches to religious studies, in particular, have explored counter-discourses in the Bible focusing on the tension between the dominant patriarchal and masculine discourses of the Bible and counter female voices found in the Book of Ruth—Ruth "the doubly Other"—both a Moabite women and a foreigner (Pardes 1992). But it would be no more difficult to construct a political theology of ethnic cleansing on the basis of other Hebrew Bible traditions, especially those myth narratives dealing with Israelite origins that demanded the destruction of other peoples. Clearly interpretations of Scripture whether by settler colonial movements or indigenous peoples resisting colonialism has always had theological and ideological dimensions. Inevitably post-modern feminist interpretations of the Bible can be as ideological as traditional patriarchal and masculine interpretations. But all interpretations of ancient holy texts should be subject to a moral critique in line with modern standards of ethical obligations.

Of course an important point to keep in mind is that "Biblical Israel" was a culture and faith not ethnicity and the Israelites and Canaanites were not two distinct ethnicities. At least some Canaanites worshiped Yahweh and as John L. McKenzie, a Roman Catholic biblical scholar, points out: "The influence of the Canaanites upon the biblical Israelites in religion, culture, and other human activities was incalculable" (1965, 118); ancient Hebrew, for instance, was a dialect of the Canaanite language. As biblical scholar Robert Caroll argues, so much of the religion and festivals of the Hebrew Bible belongs to Canaanite belief and practice; biblical prejudices and strong antagonism towards the Canaanites and Philistines (McDonagh 2004, 93–111) was partly a way of distancing the "new" Hebrew religion from its Canaanite antecedents (Cited in Docker 2008, 103; also Lemche 1995). Contrary to the vitriolic anti-Canaanite rhetoric of the Bible authors, the new biblical scholarship has shown that the biblical portrayal of the biblical Israelites' origins in terms of a conflict between them and the Canaanites or the Philistines is not justification for assuming that such a conflict ever took place in history, in either the twelfth century BC or any other period. Canaanites and biblical Israelites never existed as opposing peoples fighting over Palestine (Thompson 2004, 23; Lemche 1991). Biblical scholar Niels Peter Lemche comments on the invention of the ethno-racial divide between the Hebrews and Canaanites by the Bible writers during the post-exilic period:

> The "Canaanites" embraced that part of the Palestinian population which did not convert to the Jewish religion of the exiles, the reason being that it had no part in the experience of exile and living in a foreign world which had been the fate of the Judaeans who were carried off to Babylonia in 587 BCE. The Palestinian—or rather old Israelite—population was not considered to be Jews because they were not ready to acknowledge the religious innovations of the exilic community that Yahweh was the only god to be worshipped. Thus the real difference between the Canaanites and the Israelites would be a religious one and not the difference between two distinct nationals. (1991, 162, n.12)

Palestine's Multi-layered Identity and Pluralistic Settling

In the Bible the Philistines, a people who occupied the southern coast of Canaan at the beginning of the Iron Age (c. 1175 BC)—and who according to the Bible, ruled five city-states (the "Philistine Pentapolis") Gaza, Askelon, Ashdod, Ekron and Gath (Niesiolowski-Spanò 2011, 38)— were constructed as a typical ideological scapegoat (McDonagh 2004, 93–111). Biblical prejudice towards and even hatred of them survived in the derogatory meaning of the modern term: "a *philistine* is a person ignorant of, or smugly hostile to, culture" (Eban 1984, 45; Rose 2004, 17). The name "Palestine" is now associated with the Palestinian Arabs. The Palestinian Arabs are the indigenous people of historic Palestine. Their multilayered Palestinian identity is deeply rooted in the culturally diverse land of Palestine. Palestinian nationalism, however—like all other modern nationalisms—with its construction of national consciousness and identity, is a modern phenomenon (Khalidi R. 1997). The Palestinians, until the 1948 catastrophe, were predominantly peasants deeply-rooted in the land of Palestine. Preserved in medieval Arabic toponymy and geography, the term Palestine is derived from the Roman title of the province Palestina, which in turn was based on ancient Philistines. Today it is widely accepted that the Palestinians are a mixture of groups (including descendants of ancient Hebrew and Canaanite tribes) who remained in the land and converted to Christianity and Islam and were later joined by some migrants of Arab descent (Doumani 1995; Yiftachel 2006, 53; Ateek 1989, 16). Today the Palestinians are culturally and linguistically Arab and largely but not exclusively Muslim. Many Palestinians are also Christian Arabs who have historic roots in Palestine and a long heritage in the land where Christ lived. Commenting on the multilayered cultural identity and diverse heritage of the Palestinians, Palestinian sociologist Samih Farsoun (1937–2005) writes:

> Palestinians are descendants of an extensive mixing of local and regional peoples, including the Canaanites, Philistines, Hebrews, Samaritans, Hellenic Greeks, Romans, Nabatean Arabs, tribal nomadic Arabs, some Europeans from the Crusades, some Turks, and other minorities; after the Islamic conquests of the seventh century, however, they became overwhelmingly Arabs. Thus, this mixed-stock of people has developed an Arab-Islamic culture for at least fourteen centuries . . . (Farsoun 2004, 4)

Some secular Palestinian nationalists, however, have advocated deep historical roots for Palestinian nationalism—"ethnic roots' going back over the past three millennia, thus seeing in people such as the Canaanites, Jebusites, Amorites and Philistines and Phoenicians the direct forebears and linear ancestors of the modern Palestinians (Khalidi R. 1997, 149 and 253, n.13). Although the cultural heritage of the Palestinians going back over thousands of years, to the ancient, Canaanites, Phoenicians and Philistines, Palestinian nationalism, like all modern nationalism, is a distinctly modern ideology.

A Contrapuntal Reading of the Bible: Edward Said, the Exodus Paradigm and Decolonizing Methodologies

The exiled Palestinian scholar Edward W. Said (1935–2003) was the epitome of the secular-humanist scholar-critic, human rights activist and the prophetic public intellectual as moral transformer of society. Said was particularly effective in promoting the idea that "from below" civil liberation in Palestine, based on equality and freedom for all (like the liberation of apartheid South Africa) should serve as a model for Palestinian-Jewish reconciliation, and for fair-minded people everywhere. Said was often described both as "the conscience of Palestine" and as a citizen of the world. He was also described by the *New York Times* as "one of the most influential literary and cultural critics in the world" (Aruri 2004, 141). His passionate engagement as a fearless intellectual in worldly, real-life issues was a constant inspiration for many Palestinians under Israeli occupation and in exile. No one could easily fill his place on the many platforms on which he so powerfully represented the cause of Palestine and Palestinian struggle for liberation. Said's secular-humanist discourse engaged with some of the great themes of theologies of liberation: tearing down the walls between theory and practice, the act of witnessing to suffering and oppression, speaking truth to power, critique of power and inequalities and human dignity and social justice.

The focus of Said's worldly humanism and civil liberation was solidarity with the poor and oppressed. He bridged the gap between the underprivileged and the ivory tower. He took up the cause of marginalized Palestine in venues that were likely to be closed to the underprivileged—the lecture theatres, the concert stage, the high-brow journals, the principal television shows, the numerous occasions honoring him and celebrating his work worldwide (Aruri 2004, 141). Said, of course, articulated the aspirations of many indigenous and oppressed peoples, and of the disenfranchised and marginalized. But the plight of the Palestinian people, the 1948 Nakba (catastrophe), the dispossession and dislocation of the Palestinians, the exile and refugeedom, overwhelming sense of loss and cultural resistance became a main feature of his political writings. However, although this deep sense of injustice, physical and legal dislocation, and exile is unremitting in Said's writings, it is from that sense of injustice, outrage and dislocation that the empowerment and resistance of the Palestinians emerges. Over the past three decades Said, the public intellectual, played a key role in trying both to empower and to transform the international discourse on Palestine. Issues such as the dispossession of the Palestinians, memory and identity in exile, Palestinian oral history, the "right of return" of the Palestine refugees, Zionist responsibility for the ongoing Palestinian catastrophe, the authoritarianism and corruption of the Palestinian Authority (PA) and, most recently, the one-state secular-democratic, have constituted much of Said's concerns.

Prior to 1948 Palestine was overwhelmingly inhabited by Palestinian Arabs, who owned much of the land. The creation of the Israeli state entailed expulsion of the Palestinians and the turning of most Palestinians into refugees. Today there are over six million Palestinian refugees in the Middle East and nearly 70 percent of all Palestinians are refugees or internally displaced persons. In 1967 Israel occupied the West Bank and Gaza, the last two fragments of historic Palestine. One of Said's favorite themes, which he explores in *Orientalism* and *The Question of Palestine* is the relationship between power and knowledge. In terms of Palestine, the Zionist idea of a "Jewish homeland," which saw, eventually, the destruction of Palestine and establishment of Israel in 1948, was prepared for in advance by the knowledge accumulated by British biblical scholars and theologians, biblical archaeologists, colonial administrators, and experts who had been surveying the area and exploring the "Bible lands" since the mid-nineteenth century. It was this knowledge that enabled the Zionists to maintain arguments similar to those of the British imperial project. While historically the Palestine question favored the victor (Israel) and marginalized the victim, Said injected into the historiographical debate his original thoughts about issues such as representation, power relations and the production of knowledge—all very relevant issues to the writing of history and liberating methodologies.

The historical importance of biblical mega stories like Exodus for settler-colonial histories of Europeans, Americans and Israeli-Zionists was the subject of an extraordinary debate between Edward Said and Michael Walzer, an American Jewish author (Said 1986a, 289–303; 1988, 161–178; Walzer 1986, 289–303). The publication of Walzer's *Exodus and Revolution* in 1985 ignited a controversy which centered on how a religious narrative should be represented. Walzer presented an argument for the Exodus narrative as a paradigm for radical, progressive and even revolutionary politics (1985). Walzer developed Moses as a leader of a progressive national liberation movement on its way to the Promised Land and by implication on a mission to establish the ethical relationship of man to God. In a compelling critique of Walzer's book, entitled: "Michael Walzer's *Exodus and Revolution*: a Canaanite Reading," Said took upon himself the task of reading the biblical narrative with the eyes of the Canaanites (Said 1986a, 289–303). Said was impressed by Walzer's skills as a writer but not by his intellectual integrity or skills as a historian and even less as an honest interpreter of the Israel-Palestine conflict. For Said, Walzer's Exodus politics—a contemporary reading of the Hebrew Bible story—was a sophisticated obfuscation of reality, a thinly-veiled apology for the settler-colonial policies of the Israeli state and a historical repetition of the narrative of the conquest of the land of Canaan (Hart 2000, 1–6; Said 1986a, 289–303).

Like Said, the above North American native author Robert Allen Warrior, found the Exodus paradigm, with its key concept of "Yahweh the conqueror," oppressive rather than empowering and liberating. Warrior argues that the obvious characters for the native American people and other indigenous people to identify with in this story are the Canaanites—the indigenous people who already lived in the Promised Land (1995, 289)—hence the biblical injunction to exterminate the indigenous inhabitants of Canaan by the Israelites while performing their mission inspired by God. Warrior observes: "It is the Canaanite side of the story that has been overlooked by those seeking to articulate theologies of liberation'; "Especially ignored are those parts of the story that describe Yahweh's command to mercilessly annihilate the indigenous population (Warrior 1995, 279). Both Warrior and Said are aware of the fact that the biblical stories are not necessarily rooted in reality; chapter seven has shown the impossibility of the Exodus, the Sinai Revelation and the conquest of the land of Canaan; both Warrior and Said make a clear distinction between the Exodus paradigm and the actual historical events in ancient Palestine. Like Warrior, Said argues that the Exodus paradigm demonstrates that there was no Israel without the conquest of Canaan and the expulsion or inferior status of Canaanites–then as now. Said, in his resistance "Canaanite reading" of the Bible, observes:

> Walzer uses the rhetoric of contemporary liberation movement to highlights certain aspects of the Old Testament history and to mute or minimize others. The most troubling of these is of course the injunction laid on the Jews by God to exterminate their opponents, an injunction that somewhat takes away the aura of progressive national liberation which Walzer is bent upon giving the Exodus (1988, 165–66).

Engagement with the Worldly and Self-Liberation

The argument made here is that reality and experience do produce theologies, histories, cultures and memories. Theologies are the product of realities, not the other way around. Theologians believe they can influence reality, and sometimes they do, but theologies and theologians, whether in Palestine and in Latin America, are a product of reality. Moreover liberation cannot be imposed "from above': it has to come "from within" and "from below," along with indigenous traditions that are democratic and popular.

Palestinian Liberation "from within," "from without" and "from below" were central Edward Said's "battle for worldly humanism" and prophetic activism. Said's account of humanism evolved over time but his battle for worldly humanism and his insistence on secular-humanist, non-religious and none-supernatural, ways of thinking, colored much of his writings (Apter 2004, 35–53; Davis 2007, 125–135). Said's own personal experience and intellectual evolution are central to his concept of worldly humanism. For Said, worldly humanism was a continuous process of unending discovery, self-clarification and self-criticism and auto-emancipation (Davis 2007, 125–135). Driven from his homeland into exile and living much of his life in the United States, Said, more than any other public intellectual/activist, sought to overcome history and exile by creating a cosmopolitan intellectual space and by giving a theoretical and practical underpinnings to the influence of one's own experience and worldliness on understanding texts and overcoming history.

From the 1970s onwards Said began to highlight the peculiar claims of the *"redemptive"* settler-colonial Zionist project in Palestine, with its political uses of the biblical text and notions of "land redemption-redemptive occupation" and settler-colonialism as the fulfillment of biblically ordained, divine promises. The Zionist "redemptive/restorative" project, Said observed, dehumanizes the indigenous inhabitants of Palestine and vouchsafes the supremacist "chosen people" with the extremely problematic gift of redemption, elevating them into the status of divine agents, while reducing the unredeemed, displaced indigenous inhabitants of the land, the Palestinians, and putting them outside any humanist, moral and ethical concerns (Said 1986a, 289–303).

But Said was also criticized by biblical scholar Keith Whitelam, in his seminal work, *The Invention of Ancient Israel* (1996), for not devoting sufficient attention to the field of biblical studies. In 1999 Said even wrote:

> [Keith] Whitelam is quite right to criticize my own work on the modern struggle for Palestine for not paying any attention to the discourse of biblical studies. This discourse he says was really part of Orientalism, by which Europeans imagined and represented the timeless Orient as they wished to see it, not as it was, or as its natives believed. Thus biblical studies, which created an Israel that was set apart from its environment, and supposedly brought civilization and progress to the region, was reinforced by Zionist ideology and by Europe's interest in the roots of its own past. Yet, he concludes, "this discourse has excluded the vast majority of the population of the region." It is a discourse of power "which has dispossessed Palestinians of a land and a past. Whitlam's subject is ancient history and how a purposeful political movement could invent a serviceable past which became a crucial aspect of Israel's modern collective memory. When the mayor of Jerusalem a few years ago proclaimed that the city represented 3,000 years of unbroken Jewish dominance, he was mobilizing an invented story for the political purposes of a modern state still trying to dispossess native Palestinians who are now seen only as barely tolerated aliens (Said 1999a, 15).

However for Said, Zionism and its modern mobilizing myths have to be studied not in abstract, but in practice and mainly from the standpoint of its victims. The impact of Said's historical perspective—which we find not only in *The Question of Palestine* and *Orientalism* but in many of his articles—on rewriting the history of Zionism from the perspective of its victims cannot be overestimated. Said's historical perspective on the 1948 Palestinian Nakba—combined with the new historiographical picture that emerged from the archival material of recent years and

Palestinian oral history—introduced us to the catastrophe inflicted upon the Palestinians in the 1948 war. Furthermore Said was never uncritical when it came to the Palestinian leadership and its share in the Palestinian disaster. It was the failure of the Palestinian leadership to respond to the effectiveness of Zionist designs which became one of the main causes of the Palestinian refugee exodus of 1948.

Said's publications have also inspired my own work on Palestine. In 1992 I published a book called *Expulsion of the Palestinians: The Concept of "Transfer" in Zionist Political Thought, 1882–1992,* which is largely based on Hebrew archival material. This was followed by two books, *A Land Without a People* (1997) and *The Politics of Denial: Israel and the Palestinian Refugee Problem* (2003). More recently, I published two volumes, *The Bible and Zionism: Invented Traditions, Archaeology and Post-Colonialism in Palestine-Israel* (2007) and (2012) *The Palestine Nakba: Decolonising History, Narrating the Subaltern, Reclaiming Memory* (2012). In the last two decades we have had major contributions by other Palestinian authors, some of whose critical accounts have been based on the oral history of the Palestinian refugees themselves. But I think it was Said who was the first to locate the Nakba in a wider perspective. His critical strength was in juxtaposing the Palestinian catastrophe, and all its horrors, with its *denial,* not only in Israel, but also in the West. In many of his works Said exposed the Western media's attempts to sideline, if not altogether eliminate from the public domain, the tragedy of Palestine. While most people opposed the exclusion and injustices of the apartheid regime in South Africa, Said pointed out, there has been a deep reluctance among both liberal and radicals in the West to condemn Zionist "ethnic cleansing" and the exclusion of the Palestinians under Israeli apartheid policies.

In *The Question of Palestine* Said also documents the manner in which Zionism began as a European conquering ideology and a settler colonial movement seeking to colonize Palestine, not unlike that of European colonial expansion in the nineteenth century: "Zionism has appeared to be an uncompromisingly exclusionary, discriminatory, colonialist praxis' (Said 1980, 69). But the colonization of Palestine also differed from other European settler colonial projects. Said thought that a peculiar feature of Zionist colonization was the notion of a "redemptive" occupation and the fulfillment of God's promise. For Said, Zionism (in its both secular and religious versions) has reduced the inhabitants of Palestine to an aberration that had challenged the supremacist and xenophobic notions of God-given biblical status of the "Promised Land" (Said 1980, 56–114). Said, the secular humanist, had this to say:

> That Messianic, redemptive quality . . . [is] so foreign to me, so outside me, so unlike anything I have experienced (Ashcroft 1996, 13).

Reading Said's thoughts about these topics, one can immediately connect his critique with the role of progressive narrative and decolonizing historiography in the Palestine conflict. It was Said who undermined the hegemonic Zionist narrative in both the public and academic spheres. This hegemonic Zionist narrative, which has dominated the academic discourse in the West, reads as follows: At the end of the nineteenth-century "a people without land arrived in a country without people," modernized it, and "made its deserts bloom," while it had to fight for its life against inexplicable barbaric attacks by its Islamic and Arab neighbors. For Said, to write differently and more truthfully about what happened was not merely a more professional historiography, but was also a question of truth-speaking and a political act of liberation. These questions became central to Said secular-humanist decolonizing methodologies. Said was also effective in promoting the idea that the idea of civil liberation in Palestine (like the liberation of apartheid South Africa) should serve as a model for Palestinians and fair-minded people throughout the world.

Said's Battle against the Oslo Process and the Internalization of the Israeli Occupation: The Secular-Humanist Democratic Vision for Palestine-Israel

In the 1990s the Oslo process led to the creation of the Palestinian Authority which in turn sought to internalize rather than resist the occupation. This process led to the fragmentation of the Palestinian territories into areas A, B and C and the consolidation of Israeli settlements. The search for an alternative to the process of internalizing the Occupation, an alternative anchored in universal human rights and international law, which would also uphold the Palestinian "right of return" and self-determination, led Said to the one-state solution: a secular-democratic state based on post-Apartheid South Africa and on equality for every single human being in Palestine-Israel and justice. One non-sectarian democratic state based on non-discrimination with equal rights for

Palestinians, Israelis, Jews, Muslims, Christians and atheists is closer to values of liberal democracies than a mono-religious, ethnocratic state (Yiftachel 2006) created specifically for one religious group (namely the Jewish one) at the expense of the indigenous people of Palestine, whose laws uphold the superior rights of one religion- ethnicity-race, over that of another, including the Palestinian citizens of Israel, who constitute one-fifth of the total population of Israel. The one state solution became the motto of Said's struggle in his final years: a joint Palestinian-Israeli struggle. Said's rethinking of the Palestine question was an indictment of the narrow brand of ethnic (both Israeli Jewish and Palestinian Arab) nationalism that seemed either unwilling or incapable of re-examining the foundational myths and mistakes of the past.

For Said, the ongoing Zionist settler-colonialism, Israel's ethnocractic regime and "Apartheid/Separation Wall" at the heart of Palestine have all brought about the death of the two-state solution. This also meant that the architects of the Oslo accord had inadvertently set the stage for a single non-sectarian state in historic Palestine. Such a *vision* was based on Said's notion of multiple identities, which reflected his universalist, non-ethnic, non-sectarian perspective. Such an optimistic vision does not conceive secularism or the secular democratic state and faith as contradictive. In a secular democratic state, the common denominators are still equal rights, equal citizenship, religious freedom, religious plurality, and co-existence between Israeli Jews and Palestinians. Said was not politically naïve; such a *vision* can only derive from a long-term, joint Arab-Jewish struggle for equality, expressed within a single, secular democratic framework (Aruri 2004, 142). For Said, secular and liberal bi-nationalism was not only desirable but also the only realistic way for Palestine-Israel. In his last decade Said was the principal voice for a pluralist co-existence in historic Palestine. His rethinking of the Palestine question in secular humanist and universalist terms—extending far beyond the Palestine issue, to touch wide and diverse audiences—is the key to understanding his extraordinary and enduring legacy.

Said passionately believed that only by a fundamental critique of the Zionist project in "historic Palestine" and only when the Palestinians themselves managed to rediscover, rethink, reform and reconstruct their democratic secular polity, and transform it from an empty slogan into a viable programme for the present realities in Palestine-Israel, only then could the hope for real peace be rekindled. It was this commitment that drove him and allowed him to envision a different future for

Palestine-Israel, where mutual recognition will be in place and would not mean the subjugation of the Palestinian people.

Decolonizing Civil Liberation Theology "from Below": Naji Al-Ali's Handhala as a Witness/Martyr and Drawing Defiance and Resistance

Edward Said, Naji Al-Ali (1936–1987) and Palestinian national poet Mahmoud Darwish (1941–2008) were probably the three most influential Palestinian commentators and social activists. The three we victims of/witnesses to the 1948 Nakba and the three achieved a prophetic status. Like Said and Darwish, Al-Ali was driven exile in 1948, when the Zionists combined Western support and the Bible to legitimize the ethnic cleansing of the Promised Land of its indigenous inhabitants. Al-Ali was born in the Palestinian village Al-Shajarah, located between Nazareth and Lake Tiberias. His village (like Darwish's al-Birwa village) was occupied and destroyed by the Israeli army in 1948. The barefooted and uprooted Al-Ali grew up in the Lebanese refugee camp Ein Hilwa and his first drawings were on prison walls in Lebanon. Al-Ali ended up working in the Arab Gulf and educating himself, as his way forward, and he developed his distinct activist satirical art of resisting exile.

Another influential Palestinian refugee in Lebanon, the novelist Ghassan Kanafani (1936–1972) who owned *Al-Hurriya* magazine, and who was assassinated by the Israeli army in Beirut in 1972, began publishing Al-Ali's political cartoons in his magazine. Subsequently Al-Ali worked for different Arab newspapers, eventually became a well-known cartoonist, famous for creating the figurative character Handhala, which every Palestinian person knew. Imprisoned in Lebanon and frequently censored in the Arab press, Al-Ali created—from 1969 until his assassination outside the London offices of a Kuwaiti newspaper *Al-Qabas* by unction assailants in 1987 (Farsoun 2004, 111)—the now-famous Handhala cartoons. These depict the complexities and plight of Palestinian life in exile and the anguish of dispossession and statelessness. These cartoons are still relevant today and the power of the character of Handhala, the refugee child, who is present in every single cartoon, remains a potent symbol of the defiance, hope and struggle of the Palestinian people for justice, return and self-determination.

The character of Handhala was based on an indomitable eleven-year-old barefoot child whose character was inspired by real stories of barefoot Palestinian children in Lebanon's refugee camps. Al-Ali explains why he created Handhala:

> "I am Hanzala [sic] from the Ain Al-Hilwa [sic] camp [in Lebanon]. I give my word of honor that I'll remain loyal to the cause . . ." That was the promise I had made myself. The young, barefoot Hanzala was a symbol of my childhood. He was the age when I had left Palestine and, in a sense, I am till that age today. Even though all this happened 35 years ago, the details of that phase in my life are still fully present in my mind . . . The character of Hanzala was a sort of icon that protected my soul from falling whenever I felt sluggish or I was ignoring my duty. That child was like a splash of fresh water on my forehead, bringing me to attention and keeping me from error and loss. He was the arrow and the compass, pointing steadily towards Palestine. Not just Palestine in geographical terms, but Palestine in its humanitarian sense—the symbol of a just cause, whether it is located in Egypt, Vietnam or South Africa. (cited in Kopf-Newman 2011, 124–125)

Handhala is not a detached witness: his face is either obscured or deliberately turned away from viewers and his hands are clasped behind his back as a sign of rejection of hypocrisy and defiance. The character of Handhala became a powerful icon of Palestine and the symbol of Palestinian refugee struggle for justice, return and liberation. Handhala also became phenomenally popular in the Arab world, spawning a popular industry of coffee mugs and T-shirts. Appearing in more 40,000 cartoons, Handhala became the timeless conscience of Palestine. (El-Fassed, 2004)

Handhala is very important to the evolution of an engaged civil liberation theology in Palestine. In the making of this liberation theology from within, rooted in a multi-layered identity and pluralistic context of the region, Handhala occupied a unique space in Palestinian psyche, popular consciousness and collective memory. Handhala defined the liberating resistance and symbolized the sacrifices and martyrdom of ordinary people. He is a witness, in Arabic *shahid*, to decades of Palestinian dispossession, bitterness, anger, defiance and resistance. The Arabic word *Shahid* derives from the same trilateral root, *Shahadah* which in Arabic means both martyrdom as well as the act of witnessing. Handhala is a powerful symbol of Palestinian defiance and a witness to the validity and justness of the cause for which the sanctity of a human being has been continuously violated and Palestinian life is being lost on a day basis. In the course of the Palestinian national liberation struggle for over sixty decades countless brave men, women and children have lost their lives in that path and thus becoming *martyrs* for the liberation of their homeland and a *testimony* to the nobility of that cause. Handhala is also a witness to ongoing Israeli Occupation, atrocities and dehumanization coupled with Arab impotence, corruption and betrayal. The represents these martyrs/ witnesses: witness of the suffering; of the refugees; of the refusal to give up and be defeated. Handhala is a Palestinian humanist civil theology at its best, both critical and universal. It unites Palestinians of all walks of life and is a symbol of ordinary people and human dignity. His indomitable spirit of Handhala we can also find the potent symbol of the Palestinian "right of return," a sacred right, something no Palestinian can give up.

As "bearing witness" for the just cause for which countless Palestinian martyrs have lost their lives, the ordinary Handhala commands a transformative position and power. The metamorphic figure of Handhala as witness/martyr implicates the formation of a civil liberation theology in Palestine "from below"—theology which goes far beyond any denominational Christian or Muslim theology. This civil theology of liberation "from below" is crucial to the future of Palestine-Israel and any humanistic, democratic, pluralistic context. It allows us to transcend the denominational and religious variations into something universal and more important. This new civil theology of liberation is born out of people's collective memory and popular struggle over an extended course of history and therefore can give us something wider and beyond the current religious dimensions. The ordinary figurative character of Handhala as a martyr/witness is the quintessence of resistance by a people determined to overcome exile and transcend history and look for a better future.

For the leading three Palestinian witnesses/activists: Naji Al-Ali, Edward Said and Mahmoud Darwish, the struggle for decolonization and libertarian in Palestine is rooted in the multilayered identity and multifaceted setting of Palestine. This struggle occurs across multiple sites. For the three witnesses/commentators, the determination of the Palestinians to overcome history and envisage a better future is part of a universalized vision of humanity. Palestine is not just a geo-political entity, it is the symbol of, and part of the struggle for, a just cause, whether this cause is located in Asia, Africa, Australia, Europe or the Americas.

The civil theology of Al-Ali, Said and Darwish, was not monolithic. While Said insisted on a secular-humanist discourse, the humanist poetry of Mahmoud Darwish avoided the oppositional binary between the secular and religious. Darwish's poetry was inspired not only by the Palestinian condition: of dispossession and dislocation of exile but also hugely influenced by some of the great themes and figurative language of the Quran and the Bible. For Darwish, the loss of the homeland was synonymous with the loss of Eden to be redeemed by the struggle for rebirth and cultural renaissance.

Crucially, however, the civil liberation theology of Palestine went beyond the cultural scope and sites in which Palestinian Sabeel liberation theology sought to articulate as well as beyond what Dr. Na'im Ateek articulated in his 1989 book, *Justice and Only Justice*. Both Sabeel's grass-roots theology and the Kairos Palestine Document of 2009 embodied a liberation movement among Palestinian Christians. Sabeel has sought to make the Gospel of Jesus contextually relevant to Palestine-Israel and has striven to develop a Palestinian theology based on justice, peace, non-violence, liberation and reconciliation for the different ethnic and faith communities. Sabeel has also been highly critical of Christian Zionism which has been "successful in providing not only theological justification for Palestinian displacement, forced exile and continued oppression, but also is directly responsible for marshalling material resources" in support of Zionist settler-colonialism. However the none-denominational civil liberation theology of Al-Ali, Said and Darwish has sought to bring together people from multiple traditions and multiple sites and not just Palestinian Muslims and Christians—multiple sites which articulated the multiple moral voices of Palestine and anger, pain, dignity and hope within a universalized human context.

References

Akenson, Donald Harman. 1992. *God's Peoples: Covenant and Land in South Africa, Israel, and Ulster.* McGill: Queen's Studies in the History of Religion.
Apter, Emily. 2004. "Saidian Humanism." *boundary* 2.31, 35–53.
Aruri, Naseer H. 2004. "Professor Edward W. Said, Scholar-Activist." *Holy Land Studies: A Multidisciplinary Journal* 2.2 (March) 140–43.
Ateek, Naim S. 1989. *Justice and Only Justice: A Palestinian Theology of Liberation.* Maryknoll, New York: Orbis.
Ateek, Naim S., and Michael Prior, editors. 1999. *Holy Land—Hollow Jubilee: God, Justice and the Palestinians.* London: Melisende.
Bainton, Roland H. 1960. *Christian Attitudes toward War and Peace: A Historical Survey and Critical Re-evaluation.* Nashville: Abingdon.
Boff, Clodovis. 1993. "Epistemology and Method of the Theology of Liberation." In *Mysterium Liberationis*, edited by Ignacio Ellacuria and Jon Sobrino, 57–84. Maryknoll, New York: Orbis.

Davis, Lennard J. 2007. "Edward Said's Battle for Humanism." *The Minnesota Review* 68, 125–35.

Docker, John. 2008. *The Origins of Violence: Religion, History and Genocide.* London: Pluto.

Doumani, Beshara. 1995. *Rediscovering Palestine: Merchants and Peasants in Jabal Nablus, 1700–1900.* Berkeley: University of California Press.

Eban, Abba. 1984. *Heritage, Civilization and the Jews.* London: Weidenfeld and Nicolson.

Ellacuria, Ignacio, and Jon Sobrino, eds. 1993. *Mysterium Liberationis: Fundamental Concepts of Liberation Theology.* Maryknoll, New York: Orbis.

El Fassed, Arjan. 2004. "Naji al-Ali: The timeless conscience of Palestine." *The Electronic Intifada,* 22 July 2004, at: http://electronicintifada.net/content/naji-al-ali-timeless-conscience-palestine/5166.

Farsoun, Samih K. 2004. *Culture and Customs of the Palestinians.* Westport, Connecticut and London: Greenwood Press.

Haddad, Toufic. "Book review: The timeless work of Naji al-Ali." *The Electronic Intifada,* 29 October 2009, 29 October 2009, at: http://electronicintifada.net/content/book-review-timeless-work-naji-al-ali/3563.

Hart, William D. 2000. *Edward Said and the Religious Effects of Culture.* Cambridge: Cambridge University Press.

Khalidi, Rashid. 1997. *Palestinian Identity: The Construction of Modern National Consciousness.* New York: Colombia University Press.

Knopf-Newman, Marcy Jane. 2001. *The Politics of Teaching Palestine to Americans: Addressing Pedagogical Strategies.* New York: Palgrave Macmillan.

Lemche, Niels Peter. 1988 (reprinted 1995). *Ancient Israel: A New History of the Israelite Society.* Sheffield: Sheffield Academic.

———. 1991 (reprinted 1999). *The Canaanites and their Land.* Sheffield: Sheffield Academic.

———. 1993. "The Old Testament—a Hellenistic Book?" *Scandinavian Journal of the old Testament* 7, 163–93.

———. 1998. *The Israelites in History and Tradition.* Louisville: Westminster John Knox.

———. 2000. "Ideology and the History of Ancient Israel." *Scandinavian Journal of the Old Testament* 14.2: 165–93.

———. 2003. "Conservative Scholarship-Critical Scholarship: Or How Did We Get Caught by This Bogus Discussion." *The Bible and Interpretation* (September). http://www.bibleinterp.com/articles/Conservative_Scholarship.htm.

Long, Burke O. 1997. *Planting and Reaping Albright: Politics, Ideology, and Interpreting the Bible.* Pennsylvania: Penn State University Press.

———. 2003. *Imagining the Holy Land: Maps, Models and Fantasy Travels.* Bloomington and Indianapolis: India University Press.

Masalha, Nur. 1992. *Expulsion of the Palestinians: The Concept of "Transfer" Zionist Political Thought, 1882–1948 .* Washington DC: Institute for Palestine Studies.

———. 1997. *A Land Without a People.* London: Faber and Faber.

———. 2000. *Imperial Israel and the Palestinians: The Politics of Expansion.* London: Pluto.

———. 2003. *The Politics of Denial: Israel and the Palestinian Refugee Problem.* London: Pluto.

————, ed. 2005. *Catastrophe Remembered: Palestine, Israel and the Internal Refugees: Essays in Memory of Edward W. Said.* London: Zed Books.

————. 2007. *The Bible and Zionism: Invented Traditions, Archaeology and Post-Colonialism in Palestine-Israel.* London: Zed Books.

————. 2008. "Remembering the Palestinian Nakba: Commemoration, Oral History and Narratives of Memory." *Holy Land Studies: A Multidisciplinary Journal* 7.2 (November) 123–56.

————. 2012. *The Palestine Nakba: Decolonizing History, Narrating the Subaltern, Reclaiming Memory.* London: Zed.

McDonagh, John. 2004. "The Philistines as Scapegoats: Narratives and Myths in the Invention of Ancient Israel and in Modern Critical Theory." *Holy Land Studies: A Multidisciplinary Journal* 3.1 (May) 93–111.

Mckenzie, John L. 1965. *Dictionary of the Bible.* New York: Macmillan.

Merkley, Paul C. 1998. *The Politics of Christian Zionism 1891–1948.* London; Frank Cass.

Niditch, Susan. 1993. *War in the Hebrew Bible: A Study in the Ethics of Violence.* Oxford: Oxford University Press.

Pardes, Ilana. 1992. *Countertraditions in the Bible: A Feminist Approach.* Cambridge, MA: Harvard University Press.

Prior, Michael. 1995. *Jesus the Liberator: Nazareth Liberation Theology (Luke 4.16–30).* Sheffield: Sheffield Academic.

————. 1997. *The Bible and Colonialism: A Moral Critique.* Sheffield: Sheffield Academic.

————. 1997a. "Settling for God." *Middle East International* 565 (19 December) 20–21.

————. 1998. "The Moral Problem of the Land Traditions of the Bible." In *Western Scholarship and the History of Palestine,* edited by Michael Prior, 41–81. London: Melisende.

————. 1999. "The Bible and the Redeeming Idea of Colonialism." *Studies in World Christianity* 5, no.2: 129–55.

————. 1999a. "The Bible and Zionism." In *Holy Land—Hollow Jubilee: God, Justice and the Palestinians,* edited by Naim S. Ateek and Michael Prior, 69–88. London: Melisende.

————. 1999b. *Zionism and the State of Israel: A Moral Inquiry.* London: Routledge.

————, ed. 2000. *They Came and They Saw: Western Christian Experiences of the Holy Land.* London: Melisende.

————. 2000a. "Zionist Ethnic Cleansing: the Fulfillment of Biblical Prophecy?" *Epworth Review* 27: 49–60.

————. 2001. "The Right to Expel: The Bible and Ethnic Cleansing." In *Palestinian Refugees and their Right of Return,* edited by Naseer H. Aruri, 9–35. London: Pluto.

————. 2002. "Ethnic Cleansing and the Bible: A Moral Critique." *Holy Land Studies: A Multidisciplinary Journal* 1.1 (September) 44–45.

————. 2003. "A Moral Reading of the Bible in Jerusalem." In *Jerusalem in Ancient History and Tradition,* edited by Thomas L. Thompson, 16–48. London: T. & T. Clark.

————. 2004. *Speaking the Truth about Zionism and Israel.* London: Melisende.

————. 2004a. "The State of Israel and Jerusalem in the Jewish-Christian Dialogue: A Monologue in Two Voices." *Holy Land Studies: A Multidisciplinary Journal* 3.2 (May) 145–70.

Rose, John. 2004. *The Myths of Zionism*. London: Pluto.

Ruether, Rosemary Radford. 1998. "Christianity and the Future of the Israeli-Palestinian Relations." In Remembering *Deir Yassin*, edited by Daniel McGowan and Marc H. Ellis, 112–22.

Ruether, Rosemary Radford, and Herman J. Ruether. 2002. The *Wrath of Jonah: The Crisis of Religious Nationalism in the Israeli-Palestinian Conflict*. 2nd ed. Minneapolis: Fortress, 2002.

Said, Edward W. 1978. *Orientalism*. London: Routledge and Kegan Paul.

———. 1980. *The Question of Palestine*. London and Henly: Routledge and Kegan Paul.

———. 1981. *Covering Islam*. New York: Vintage.

———. 1986. *After the Last Sky*. Photographs by Jean Mohr. London: Faber and Faber.

———. 1986a. "Michael Walzer's Exodus and Revolution: A Canaanite Reading." *Arab Studies Quarterly* 8.3 (Summer) 289–303.

———. 1988. "Michael Walzer's *Exodus and Revolution*: A Canaanite Reading." In *Blaming the Victims: Spurious Scholarship and the Palestinian Question*, edited by Edward W. Said and Christopher Hitchens, 161–78. New York: Verso.

———. 1995a. *Peace and its Discontents: Gaza-Jericho 1993–1995*. New York: Vintage.

———. 1995b. The *Politics of Dispossession: The Struggle for Palestinian Self-Determination 1969–1994*. London: Vintage.

———. 1999. *Out of Place: A Memoir*. London: Granta.

———. 1999a. "Palestine: Memory, Invention and Space." In *The Landscape of Palestine*, edited by Ibrahim A. Abu-Lughod, Roger Heacock, and Khaled Nashef, 3–20. Birzeit, Palestine: Birzeit University

———. 2000. *Reflections on Exile and Other Literary and Cultural Essays*. London: Granta.

———. 2000a. Review of *Palestinians under Siege*. *London Review of Books* (14 December) 9–14.

———. 2002. "Real Change Means People Must Change: Immediate Imperative." *CounterPunch* (21 December). http://www.counterpunch.org/2002/12/21/immediate-imperatives/.

———. 2003. "A Road Map to Where?" *London Review of Books* 25.12 (19 June) 3–5.

Said, Edward W. and Christopher Hitchens, eds. 1988. *Blaming the Victims: Spurious Scholarship and the Palestinian Question*. New York: Verso.

Shahak, Israel, and Norton Mezvinsky. 1999. *Jewish Fundamentalism in Israel*. London: Pluto.

Sobrino, Jon. 1987. *Jesus in Latin America*. Maryknoll, New York: Orbis.

———. 1990. *Companions of Jesus: The Jesuit Martyrs of El Salvado*. Maryknoll, New York: Orbis.

———. 1993. *Witnesses to the Kingdom: The Martyrs of El Salvador and the Crucified Peoples*. Maryknoll, New York: Orbis.

Thompson, Thomas L. 1974. *The Historicity of the Patriarchal Narratives: The Quest for the Historical Abraham*. Berlin: Walter de Gruyter.

———. 1991. "Text, Context and Referent in Israelite Historiography." In *The Fabric of History* edited by Diana Vikander Edelman, 65–92. JSOT Press

———. 1992. *Early History of the Israelite People*. Leiden: Brill.

———. 1999. *The Bible in History: How Writer's Create a Past*. London: Jonathan Cape. (American edition, *The Mythical Past*. New York: Basic).

————. 2003. "Is the Bible Historical? The Challenge of "Minimalism" for Biblical Scholars and Historians." *Holy Land Studies: A Multidisciplinary Journal* 3.1 (May) 1–27.

————, ed. 2003a. *Jerusalem in Ancient History and Tradition.* London: T. & T. Clark.

Walzer, Michael. 1985. *Exodus and Revolution.* New York: Basic.

————. 1986. "*Exodus and Revolution*: A Canaanite Reading." *Arab Studies Quarterly* 8.3 (Summer) 289–303.

Warrior, Robert Allen. 1989. "Canaanites, Cowboys and Indians: Deliverance, Conquest, and Liberation Theology Today." *Christianity and Crisis* 49:261–65.

————. 1991. "A Native American Perspective: Canaanites, Cowboys, and Indians." In *Voices from the Margin: Interpreting the Bible in the Third World: 287–95*, edited by R. S. Sugirtharajah. London: SPCK.

Wetherell, David Fielding. 2005. "The Use and Misuse of the Religious Language: Zionism and the Palestinians." *Holy Land Studies: A Multidisciplinary Journal* 4.1 (May) 69–86.

Whitelam, Keith. 1996. *The Invention of Ancient Israel: The Silencing of Palestinian History.* London and New York: Routledge.

Yiftachel, Oren. 2006. *Ethnocracy: Land and Identity Politics in Israel/Palestine.* Philadelphia: University of Pennsylvania Press.

Index

P. 168 — owning the land

P 186 — reform of Christian attitudes